S1

D1101421

RKCALDY
RD
0
NCT LIBRARIES

Mongoose Watch

Mongoose Watch

A FAMILY OBSERVED

ANNE RASA

Foreword by Konrad Lorenz

JOHN MURRAY · LONDON

For my Mother

Those who have helped during the fifteen years of my study of the Dwarf mongoose both in Europe and in Africa are too numerous to be thanked individually. I should like to say, however, that without the continued financial support of the Deutsche Forschungsgemeinschaft this story could never have been told, and to this organisation go my special thanks.

Drawings in the text are by Wolfgang Tambour, Göttingen. The photographs are my own.

A.R.

KIRKCALDY DISTRICT LIBRARIES

628622

599.74422 | R AS

SL

© 1984 Deutsche Verlags-Anstalt GmbH, Stuttgart

This edition published 1985
by John Murray (Publishers) Ltd
50 Albemarle Street, London WIX 4BD

All rights reserved
Unauthorised duplication
contravenes applicable laws

Typeset by Inforum Ltd, Portsmouth
Printed and bound in Great Britain
by Butler & Tanner Ltd, Frome

British Library CIP Data
Rasa, Anne
    Mongoose watch : a family observed.
    1. Mongooses   2. Animal behaviour
    I. Title
    599.74'422   QL795.M6
    ISBN 0–7195–4240–5

Contents

Maps

Colour photographs between pages 144 and 145

Foreword *by Konrad Lorenz*

The more complicated an organic system is and the more subtle its adaptation to the special environment in which a species lives, the more easily is it disturbed by the unnatural conditions of captivity. The most complicated systems known to science are the societies of social vertebrates. Their structure is in some cases, particularly in the higher mammals, more dependent on tradition and less determined by purely innate behavioural programmes than those of birds. In birds, as for example in the subjects of my own investigations, the jackdaw (*Coloeus monedula*) and the Greylag goose (*Anser anser*), genetic programming – that is to say, the influence of innate behaviour – is so strong that hand-reared birds are able to form free-flying colonies which display no appreciable differences from communities that have always lived in the wild. This is also true, to a certain extent, of wild boar. A hand-reared young animal can if necessary be introduced into a herd of wild boar, whereas Katharina Heinroth's comparable experiment with Hamadryas baboons failed. She records that a young female baboon, when transferred to a natural group of Hamadryas baboons on the 'monkey hill' at Berlin Zoo, 'misbehaved' so badly that she became a persecuted outcast.

Because one never knows from the outset how many norms of social behaviour are genetically programmed and how many are established through long-standing tradition, the artificial formation of social groups of hand-reared animals in captivity provides an unreliable means of studying social behaviour, even when the natural environment is replicated as closely as possible. The study of tame, free-living animals is undoubtedly a good method, and one that I myself have employed since I was a child. In the case of higher mammals, however, where an appreciable role is played by learning and tradition, another, more demanding research strategy is called for.

Animals living in the wild can, in fact, be so habituated to human observers that they come to ignore their presence and behave quite naturally. Jane Goodall was probably the first to engage in this truly dedicated form of research. She settled down in the forest at Gombe Stream in Tanzania and began to 'accustom' the resident chimpanzees to her presence. Her self-effacing task was to feign complete indifference and refrain from even looking when a chimpanzee came on the scene. Higher animals are extremely sensitive to human facial expressions and gestures, especially when they bear so great a resemblance to their own. Jane Goodall had to devote nearly two years to this activity, which was not only tiring but extremely tedious, before she convinced the chimpanzees of her peaceful intentions. Dian Fossey had much the same experience when observing gorillas.

Ethologists are at a particular disadvantage when the subjects of their research are too complex. In forming hypotheses and theories it is always more effective to study the phenomena concerned in the simplest possible subject to exhibit them.

Among mammals there exist groups such as certain carnivores which, although they have developed extraordinarily advanced and complex social structures, must definitely be regarded on other grounds as 'lower' mammals. This is the case with the mongooses (subfamily *Herpestinae)*. Anne Rasa began studying Dwarf mongooses (*Helogale undulata rufula*) in my laboratory at the Max Planck Institute for Behavioural Physiology in Seewiesen, Bavaria. These animals proved easy to breed when kept in a well heated enclosure, but it soon turned out that, in a large social group of peacefully coexisting Dwarf mongooses, only one pair reproduced whereas every member of the community helped to tend and feed the young. This kind of social structure, which is strongly reminiscent of that found among many social insects, might perhaps have been an artefact, i.e. a consequence of maintenance in captivity. Anne Rasa resolved to conduct the necessary comparison between the behaviour of captive animals and that of conspecifics living in the wild. The present book contains the fruit of her observations. Her findings, whose importance can hardly be exaggerated, deserve comparison with the trail-blazing discoveries made by Jane Goodall.

I wrote the preceding paragraphs before I received Anne Rasa's manuscript. Although I had known her well for many years, having enjoyed a long and amicable working relationship with her at the Max Planck Institute, I was astonished by her literary skill. The vividness and manifest integrity of her writing make this book exciting reading. We share her life in the African bush, and get to know the personalities of the individual Dwarf mongooses she describes as if they were before our own eyes. Let no one object that the author resorts to anthropomorphism. As my friend, the Israeli ethologist Amotz Zahavi, has so aptly pointed out, the most naïve anthropomorphism conveys a better picture than the best cybernetic or electronic model. The simple reason is that the difference in complexity between the brain of a human being and that of any higher vertebrate is infinitely less than that between the simplest vertebrate brain and the most complex physico-electronic simulator. Besides, Anne Rasa never anthropomorphises naïvely; she does so exclusively in the field of emotional behaviour, which differs little between man and the higher vertebrates. Her book is a comprehensive masterpiece of observation, analytical thought and descriptive writing that is outstanding in its field.

How It All Began . . .

I cannot remember a time when I was *not* fascinated by and surrounded with animals.

Some of my earliest memories were of discovering the treasure-trove of the compost heap in the small garden of our house in the little South Wales mining town of Ferndale, in the Rhondda, where I was born. I would drive my mother and grandparents to distraction by eating any of the worms or slugs I found there or bringing a spider clutched in my hand to show them. The herds of wild ponies which wandered through the streets in the winter months, retrieving all sorts of goodies out of the rubbish bins, were a source of never-ending fascination and my dream was to have one of my own (I caught one once but my grandmother made me let it go). Even at that early age – I was about five – I would explore the aquatic wonders of Ferndale lake, bringing home tadpoles, leeches and minnows which were promptly returned to their original home by my mother.

The rest of my childhood progressed in much the same way, in different parts of Britain and in Cyprus, for my father was a serving officer in the RAF: with me trying to bring Nature into the house and my parents firmly relegating it to the outdoors again. At some point or other, my mother seems to have capitulated, for by the time I left home to start my studies at London University, I had managed to accumulate a menagerie of nearly two hundred animals such as mice, snakes, rabbits, guinea-pigs, dogs, cats, garden tits and warblers, box terrapins, cane toads, pygmy tree frogs and a horse. Now, in retrospect, after having raised children of my own, I have nothing but sympathy for my poor mother. Her attempts to stem the tide of new arrivals – I was regularly forbidden to add a single new creature to my menagerie – were met by me with surprised stares and 'Oh, *that* one? But it's been here for *ages!*' I just couldn't resist any lost or injured creature and my bedroom resembled an animal clinic with cages and vivaria up to the ceiling.

My mother's life must have been one long series of minor calamities: bird droppings all over the furniture; a hundred red Cornish toads in the bath; a horse stuck in the dining room; an owl landing at her feet with clicking bill every time she opened the refrigerator door; a Belgian hare which enjoyed beating up the neighbour's dog and she having to rush out and separate them; a guinea-pig regularly squeaking at the door to be let in or out; a hamster chewing up her best Axminster carpet to make a nest for its babies – not to mention the time my mouse colony chewed through its cage and over fifty mice distributed themselves all over the house! If anyone was a martyr to Science, she was.

When it was time to start my university career, it was a bitter parting from all these friends. At that time I was most interested in insects and envisaged myself as an applied entomologist, using Nature's own forces to combat pest insects through biological control.

After finishing my degree, I went to the University of Hawaii to study for my doctorate on the biological control of insect pests on sugarcane. Here, however, my career plans changed dramatically. I met a fish. I was an avid scuba-diver and snorkeller and, while cruising underwater along a reef, my faceplate was attacked by a little black finny fury which gave me no peace until I had moved out of the area of reef he claimed for his own. I remember watching him for over an hour as he hurled himself against any fish, no matter what its size, which dared to enter his territory. Curious, as usual, I asked myself: Why? And then my fate was sealed, for my thesis no longer dealt with the biological control of the sugarcane mealybug but the reasons behind the aggressiveness of Damselfish. I metamorphosed from an entomologist into a marine biologist and spent the next years studying (apart from the Damsel-fishes) hermit crabs, shrimps, butterfly fish, in fact anything I came across in my underwater forays – and aggression in a freshwater fish, the Orange Chromide, a very aggressive cichlid.

This study resulted in another big jump that shaped my future. On the other side of the world, in Germany, Konrad Lorenz of the Max Planck Institute for Behavioural Physiology had just written his famous book *On Aggression*, and his observations on the Orange Chromide were the same as mine. He got to hear of my work and invited me to continue my investigations on the innate basis of aggression at his Institute in Germany. Thanks to this invitation, I was fortunate to complete my thesis on the aggression of Damselfish under Lorenz just before he retired and went back to Vienna.

By this time I had spent over six years studying the basis of aggression in a solitary animal and the next question that cropped up was 'How does the system work in a social species?' I decided I would like to study a social mammal.

I. Eibl-Eibesfeldt, the mammalogist at the Institute, was at this time about to embark on the study of human behaviour and offered me the choice of one of the many mammals that he had in his laboratory. Not being very well up on mammals, I was nonplussed at the selection, which ranged from tree-shrews and fruit bats to agoutis and Madagascan insectivores. Then, in an enclosure at the back of the lab, I saw a familiar shape – a mongoose. Shades of Rikki-tikki-tavi and valiant fights against huge snakes flitted through my brain. *If* there was a social mammal one could study aggression on, then this must be it. I little knew at this time that, in making my choice, I had stumbled on one of the most fascinating creatures of the Animal Kingdom. Suffice it to say that, although I have been working with Dwarf mongooses now for fifteen years, I have never got round to my planned studies on aggression. I have been too busy trying to work out even more amazing aspects of their behaviour!

Nothing seemed to be known about Dwarf mongooses and it took me almost five years to unravel what was going on in the close-knit mongoose family I studied so assiduously in Germany. Slowly but surely, the most astounding pattern of mutual helping and everything *other* than aggression developed as I got to know the little creatures better. Then I was faced with yet another question: 'Is what I am seeing here in the laboratory just an artefact of captivity, or do they behave similarly in the wild?' The only way of answering this was to find out for myself, so I applied for funds to study the species in the field in Kenya. Thanks to the generosity of Mr Ray Mayers, who allowed me to study them on his ranch in the Taru desert, I made contact with my first wild mongoose group, Diana and Co., who opened up a whole new world for me – the world of the dry bushlands.

I don't regret in the least the years I spent studying the little animals in the laboratory for, without this basis, I would not have been able to understand much of what I saw in the wild. The captive group also came in useful, on more than one occasion, for questions that arose out of things I had seen in the field I could test under more controlled conditions with them. The final answer to the 'laboratory artefact question' was that there was no qualitative difference between the animals' behaviour in captivity and in the wild, just a quantitative one. In the bush, the mongooses have to spend nearly all their time searching for food, while in captivity, this is provided for them. This means that, in captivity, they can spend much more time in social behaviour and play than they can in the harsh environment of the dry bushlands. The field studies, however, revealed whole new aspects of the mongooses' behaviour which I would not have known about if I had restricted myself to laboratory studies, for they involved various animals that lived with the mongooses in the bush under situations that could not be replicated in captivity. This book is an attempt to describe a close-knit web of interactions, not only between the mongooses within the family, but also between the family and the denizens of their fascinating environment.

I know of no other mammalian society, except Man's, which has such a high degree of mutual 'caring' and division of labour – even to the point of nursing their sick or injured group members – as that of the Dwarf mongoose. Also like Man, as individuals these animals are rather weak and helpless, but together, acting as a group, there are not many enemies in their bush world that can stand against them. The social parallels between these little carnivores and ourselves are greater than between us and the majority of our closest cousins, the Great Apes. Although the Apes may look more like us physically, they have solved the problems of survival in different ways from our own. By studying the mongooses, we can get a glimmering of which factors must have shaped our own society, from its primitive origins to present times . . . and in matters of family life, we can learn from the Dwarf mongoose.

1 In Which I Meet the Family and Friends

A glimmer like polished copper in the East. The Elephant thorn trees emerge from the gloom, their bare twisted branches like some surrealist painting. Nearby a sound like someone pouring water out of a bottle – the White-browed coucal's paean to the sunrise. Slowly the sun slips over the horizon and light floods the land. A new day has begun.

Now I can see my surroundings more clearly – as far as the eye can see, gnarled trunks with their crowns of thorny branches. Beneath them a tangle of leafless bushes and fallen trees and all grey – a sun-baked, sun-bleached wilderness only broken here and there by patches of green from the sparse Boscia and Cassia trees and tufts of asparagus-like 'Wait-a-bit' thorn. Like blood-red castles the termite mounds rear their heads out of the tangle of dead vegetation which almost smothers them. This is the Taru desert at dawn.

The Taru desert – quite a change from most people's concept of a desert, with rolling sand-dunes and not a blade of grass in sight, but this is a desert none the less. No native tribes live here for there is no permanent water, only the sun-baked, dry waterholes which fill when the twice-yearly cloudbursts flood the place. If the rains fail, the whole area seems to draw in on itself and hold its breath, waiting . . . waiting until the life-giving fluid comes again. Animals that need water to survive drift away, and those that remain have no need of it – they can metabolise it from their food. Only the plants have no choice but, over the millennia, have adapted themselves so that not a drop of the precious fluid is lost. In this harsh world the struggle for survival mirrors itself in every thorned twig and every water-swollen root.

The Taru desert forms a wide strip between the East African coastal plain and the higher inland areas and has played an important part in history. It was this strip of unfriendly land that effectively stopped the slave traders and forced them to restrict their marauding to the more southern chain of hills leading to Mount Kilimanjaro. It was not until the Mombasa Railroad was built that people could travel in any comfort through this mass of tangled thorn and colonise the fertile Uplands. The Taru desert was the haunt of the huge elephant herds which wandered through on their continual migrations, feeding on the water-filled branches of the thorntrees and drinking the shallow waterholes dry.

What strikes one here is the monotony . . . everything is the same yet different: variations on a theme of thorntrees, bushes and termite mounds, a

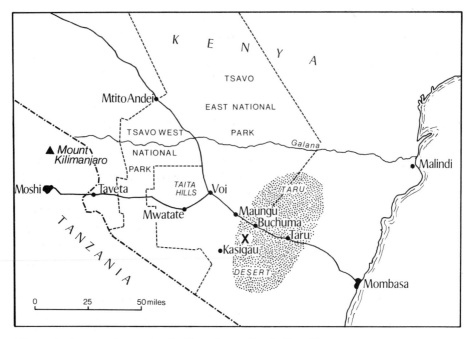

The author's research area in the Taru desert, South-East Kenya

place where it is easy to get lost, for there are no landmarks. Even the elephant-hunting tribes that sometimes used to invade the area have horror stories to tell of experienced hunters who left their camp in the morning, were unable to find their way back and died of thirst. Temperatures here can reach 120 degrees Fahrenheit in the shade (what little there is of it) and directions can easily get confused for the sun beats down almost perpendicularly at midday as the area is only a few degrees south of the equator. The thorntrees effectively block the horizon and one feels that one is in a maze where all the clues are devised to confuse.

I sit in my Landcruiser and wait like a cat in front of a mousehole, but my mousehole is all around me. Motionless, only my eyes moving, I watch the comings and goings. Dawn in the bush is my favourite time of day, the time at which the night-folk and the day-folk are abroad, the one heading home to a cool hole to sleep through the day's heat, the other waking up to start the day's hunting. A skink lizard crawls out of a hole in a termite mound to my right and spreads itself flat in the warming rays of the sun while in front of me, just visible above the sea of grey grass-stems, the bobbing ears and back of a Black-backed jackal on its way back to its lair after a morning's hunting go past, accompanied by a chorus of screeches from a mixed flock of Fischer's and Golden-breasted starlings. Their mobbing cries alert every animal in the surroundings and the Red-billed hornbill on the branch above my head cranes its neck to see what's going on.

This is the sixth day that I have spent driving aimlessly through this dead jungle hoping to catch a glimpse of the animals I have come here to find, the Dwarf mongooses, but with no success. My only reward has been the panic-stricken flight of every animal I come across, and I ponder on the concept of 'Man the Hunter'. The hours of patient waiting, bathed in sweat; the hours of driving through this wilderness, over the trunks of fallen trees and through bushes; the falling into holes where it has taken me what seemed like all day to get the car jacked up and the hole filled with stones, earth and branches so that I could move on again; and the constant fear of getting lost and trying to get my bearings by climbing onto the car roof and looking for my landmark, Mount Kasigau – all this has made me depressed. I begin to think my task is hopeless. It is hard enough to spot an antelope in this tangle of dead vegetation, let alone an animal about the size of a weasel, but I still hope against hope.

It is getting on towards seven o'clock. The birds are busily feeding, some on the berries of the leafless thorntrees and some, like the little Grey flycatcher whose post is on a branch to my right, on the insects that are starting to stir as the sun warms them. The Red-billed hornbill above my head is joined by his wife whom he greets by handing her a berry plucked from the thorntree, which she graciously accepts. Then they go into what I call their '*wok-wok* ceremony'. In unison, their rapid *wok-wok-wok* calls reach a crescendo which breaks off sharply as, together, they bow their heads and stretch their wings, still folded, backwards so that they meet behind them. Then they busy themselves in filling their crops with berries from the tree and I catch the faint odour of frankincense from the bruised tissues. Right next to the car, a Pill-roller beetle laboriously pushes a pellet of dik-dik dung up the dried stem of a plant, keeping it from falling by clasping it between its back legs. I watch, fascinated, as it cements the dung into place with earth moistened in its mandibles. In time, the egg inside will hatch and the larva devour the food its parent provided, anchored safely here above the ground so that no other dung-eater can usurp it.

The hornbills leave. I watch their undulating flight, flashes of black and white against the background. They land in a tree about thirty yards away and start preening. One of them cocks its head and peers at the termite mound beneath the tree. I try to see what it is looking at but can discern nothing. All is still except for the little flycatcher which continues its fluttering sorties against the insect world. Then another glimpse of flapping black and white amongst the trees. A pair of von der Decken's hornbills have joined the Red-bills, he with his technicolour bill and she with her black one. They also peer down at the termite mound but again I can see nothing. The four birds sit there preening and looking around almost as if they were waiting for something.

A movement in the shadows of the termite mound ahead of me, a flat, snub, arrow-like head appears and, after it, a long, scaly body blotched with browns and fawns, fat and repulsive. The puff adder slowly makes its way down the mound, walking on its ribs so that rhythmic undulations run the length of its body like waves along a breakwater. Its tongue flickers, testing the ground in front of it. Then slowly it curls itself up into a coil, flattening its body to catch as much sun as possible, basking in the pattern of light and shade at the base of the mound, almost invisible.

The hornbills continue their vigil. I become curious. What are they waiting for? The thought has barely crossed my mind when something small and brown appears as if by magic on top of the termite mound beneath the tree. Almost shaking with excitement, I grab my binoculars, hoping against hope that this time I've been lucky. Slowly I get the binoculars (powerful ones, twelve by fifty) into focus – and I can't prevent myself from smiling. There, fur bottlebrushed in the cool morning air, looking about him as he yawns and scratches, is the animal I have come so far and worked so hard to find, a young male Dwarf mongoose performing his morning toilet and surveying his surroundings for potential danger, as yet unaware of my presence. Almost immediately other brown bodies appear beside him as if spirited out of the volcano-like craters of the termite mound. I start counting and reach thirteen before the tide stops. Thirteen small, brown animals, almost rat-like in appearance but surely one of the most unusual and fascinating creatures on earth.

I try desperately to make head or tail of who is who. The process is made even more difficult as the animals continually pop into the holes in the mound and emerge somewhere else. The whole termite mound seems in uproar, individuals trotting hither and thither, up, down and inside the mound, grooming themselves and each other fleetingly before going on to the next job in hand. I start counting again. This time I make it fourteen. I still don't have the faintest idea exactly how many there are. It is well known that animal counts in the wild usually lie about a third under the number of animals actually present. This group could number anything up to twenty.

Slowly a routine seems to emerge out of the chaos. The grooming session is now slackening off and I see animals slipping off down the side of the mound to be hidden by the grass and bushes. I stand up slowly until my head pokes through the open hatch in the roof of the car and I can get a better view. The ones that have moved down the mound all seem to be defecating in a pile to the north-east of it. They are defecating entirely on a small patch of bare earth at the mound's base. Some appear to be waiting their turn, and the ones occupying the spot squat stiffly, their tails almost perpendicular and curved at the end like a question mark, giving a little shake of the body when they have finished before turning round to sniff what they have produced and then trotting on. Some move up the mound again afterwards, others head out to the edge of the red earth apron surrounding the termite mound, worn almost flat by the action of sun, wind and water. They stop at the relics of a fallen thorntree root and begin sniffing it carefully, standing on their hind-legs like little bears to reach as high as they can.

They seem to be concentrating hard on the messages that this marking post, for that is obviously what it is, is conveying to them through its odour. Then a large, greyish-coloured female trots purposefully down the mound towards the root and the animals clustered there make way for her as she pushes between them. To date, no animal has marked, being content to 'read' rather than 'write'. The female examines the post as well, grasps it with her forepaws and rubs her cheek glands across it from snout to ear, one side after the other. Then, with a quick leap, she is upside down in handstand position, grabbing the root with her hind-paws and pressing her pink-coloured anal scent gland against it, smearing its secretion down the length of the root as, with scrabbling motions of her hind-legs, she slowly moves her body down-wards. Once on the ground again, she whips round, rears up on her hind-legs and checks the mark, sniffing it carefully before repeating the process. This time, others join her, one of them a large, battle-scarred male with a yellowish ruff of hair around his neck. His face is much broader than that of the female which marked first, but I did notice the two of them grooming each other intensively on the mound earlier and realised that, since they were in the forefront of the group when it came to marking, these are more than likely the group's founders and leaders, the alpha male and female. It is always easier to follow individuals within a group when they have names and these two, which I think I can recognise again from their faces and colouring, I immediately dub 'George' and 'Diana', for no other reason than that these are the names that come to mind when I look at them. Diana is lithe and powerful, a real little huntress, while George gives the impression of being a rather staid patriarch, and somehow the name fits him.

At the tree-root, things are starting to get chaotic again. Every mongoose seems to be trying to get its mark up as high as possible simultaneously, and there is a mad jostling with bodies leaping vertically and toppling over, their owners whipping round to sniff the post to see if *some* of the scent has managed to get where it was meant to go and then repeating the process. I have difficulty suppressing a laugh, for the whole thing looks so ludicrous; animals landing on top of one another or falling backwards while those that are trying to mark with their cheek glands continually have others' anal glands pushed in their faces. George and Diana seem to have completed their ritual as they trot back

Diana is lithe and powerful, a real little huntress

towards the mound again while the three animals which have remained on the mound as the others marked, eagerly dash down it to join the fray round the tree-root. George goes to the top of the mound and sits there, alert, scanning the bush around.

With a flutter and bump, one of the Red-billed hornbills in the tree above lands right next to the termite mound. I hear the twittering alarm call: 'Danger, close' and, in a body, the markers rush for the mound, jamming the holes in their efforts to get to safety as fast as possible. Three rumps with tails and scrabbling hind-legs are wedged into one of the smaller mound entrances and only with difficulty do their owners seem able to get them inside. Then a head appears in a hole at the top of the mound and looks about in all directions. The hornbill still sits there, waiting. A body follows the head and then, almost on signal, the group is out and moving back to the marking post again. False alarm! When the other three hornbills flutter down to join the first they are more or less ignored. Only a few of the shyest group members make a half-hearted dash for the mound but stop half-way and return to the serious business of marking.

George gives the impression of being a rather staid patriarch

I spent eight years studying these animals in captivity before I had the chance of watching them in the field, and one of my special studies was the meaning of the marks which they so assiduously place on objects near their sleeping quarters. In order to find out what the marks were saying, I trained tame mongooses to distinguish odours by what I called the 'Cruft's Dogshow Method'. I gave them an object on which a scent substance had been smeared to sniff and then they had to try and match the smell from a series of dishes in which this smell was one of many. When they found the right one, they were to come back to me and receive a reward for their efforts. I was amazed not only by the fact that they learned to pick out the right odour but that they learned to do so so quickly. Once they had grasped what was wanted of them, it only needed one or two trials for them to pick out completely strange scents. In this they were even better than dogs, whose olfactory powers are well known.

By using combinations of different scents from the anal and cheek glands of different animals I found out that the two glands left very different messages. The anal gland secretion is the animal's 'signature'. It tells the reader who has marked, and at the same time acts like a clock. The slow decay of certain substances within it measures the time at which the mark was made. This time measurement is so accurate that animals can tell time differences of only a few minutes apart, a feat that really seems incredible, especially when my experiments showed that this mark still remains 'readable' after twenty days, at least in a European climate. How long it would last here, in this land of baking heat and torrential downpours, I have no idea. The cheek mark seems to complement the anal one. This is the animal's 'emotional' register. The more excited it is, the more often it rubs these glands against the object. My trained animals were able to read the amount of secretion deposited fairly accurately but the cheek mark differed from the anal one in two respects. First, it was anonymous, and secondly, it lasted only forty-eight hours. After that, my animals could no longer detect it. Since, in marking an object, both glands are always used, it is obvious that a second signature would be more or less superfluous. That the mark lasts only a short time also has its point. Other groups reading the mark several days later would be uninterested in what sort of emotional state the marker was in when he made it. It would be like reading a newspaper a week old. The news is no longer interesting, whereas *who* left the mark and *when* may convey important information, like which group is in the area and how big it is, and also whether it is known to the reader.

The marking session seems to be over. The markers return in dribs and drabs to the mound, squatting there in the sunshine, nibbling each other's fur and scratching themselves. The hornbills peer into grass tussocks and amongst the tangle of dead branches and seem to be making no move to go. Some of the youngsters – I can count three which look to be between four and five months old from their size and slender build – start a game of chase around the base of the mound, grappling with each other and rolling over and over when they make contact. Sometimes the game ends up in a 'Viennese Waltz', the players standing upright, holding each other round the shoulders with their forepaws and, with heads raised, slowly circling in time to some unheard orchestra. The whole scene seems idyllic, Diana and George sitting in the midst of their happy family who look as if they haven't a care in the world.

The male von der Decken's hornbill flies up onto the mound and the mongooses move aside to give him room. I get the impression that he's starting to get impatient but I can't work out why. Then Diana gets up and moves down the mound, giving the 'Moving out' call like a series of hollow sonar bleeps. George follows her, and with him the majority of the group and, to my astonishment, the hornbills as well. The little conclave disappears into the dry grass and all I can see are the heads of the birds which appear now and again between the grass stems. Only two of the adult males remain behind, sitting high up on the mound and scanning the surroundings. I look at them closely to see if I can discover some distinguishing marks. One of them has a patch of white hair on the underside of the neck and is immediately named 'Whitethroat', while the other has a small scar on the right side of his muzzle and I dub him 'Scar'. They watch the departing group, the sky, the trees and the bush around, but all is still.

I have difficulty in accepting what I have seen. To all intents and purposes, the birds knew that the mongooses were in that particular mound and obviously waited for them to get up. It even looked as if the male von der Decken's hornbill chivvied them along to go foraging, but what it all means I have no idea at present. I shall shortly realise that I am watching one of the most intricate cases of mammal-bird mutualism known in the Animal Kingdom.

The little cavalcade moves slowly through the bush, the hornbills flapping and flopping around in the grass. The glimmer of silver wings fluttering madly as an insect shoots out of hiding gives me the answer to what is going on. The hornbills are after grasshoppers and locusts that the mongooses are flushing for them: *that* is why they were waiting! With their silver-grey striped bodies and motionless behaviour, the insects would be almost invisible to the sharp-eyed birds in this place where nearly everything is silver-grey. The approach of the mongooses, as they bustle through the grass, poking into tussocks and holes and scrabbling about in any hiding-place where food might be found, disturbs the insects which, with their powerful hind-legs, are able to leap yards, well away from the hunting mongooses . . . but not away from the agile birds! I never saw a locust escape their rapacious bills. Although they

The hornbills bring up the rear of the mongooses' foraging cavalcade

look large and clumsy, hopping along the ground in the wake of their little flushing dogs, once an insect takes off, it is doomed. A rapid flapping of wings, an outstretched neck, and the locust ends up crosswise in the huge bill. It is touching to see how the males of the pairs present their wives with especially tasty morsels, the way in which the wife will carefully take the insect from her husband's beak with the tip of her own, throw it briefly into the air and, with gaping throat, swallow it whole. Sometimes all the husband gets as a 'thank you' is a sharp peck in return. Some of the contortions these birds get up to in pursuit of the flying insects are extraordinary. I once watched a locust fold its wings and stop dead in mid-flight, just as the hornbill was upon it. A quick stab, a mad fluttering and the bird turned a complete somersault in mid-air, coming up the other side with the locust firmly in its beak.

My first thought about all this is 'Parasites'. The hornbills are stealing the mongooses' food and, as yet, the mongooses don't seem to be getting any advantage out of the situation. But I am soon proved wrong. A shadow flies over the land. I look up and see it is cast by a Tawny eagle circling low above the trees. The effect on the foragers and the guards on the termite mound is electric. Before a warning call has issued from a mongoose's throat, the sharp-eyed birds have spotted the danger and shot upwards into the trees, hugging as close to the trunk as they can, safe under the canopy of thorny branches. At the same instant a penetrating '*Tcheee*' sounds. The guards have spotted the predator and given warning. Bodies scuttle for cover, those near enough to the termite mound dive back into it while others vanish under fallen trees and branches. Everything freezes. Only occasional *tchrrr* calls issue from hiding-places all around, the call that means 'Danger sighted, keep your heads down', a deeper note than the initial *tcheee* which means 'Dash for cover immediately'.

The circling eagle is watched by dozens of sharp eyes both in the trees and on the ground. Somehow the puff adder gets wind of something wrong and slowly crawls back into the safety of its mound again, the entrance hole of which is streaked white with its droppings. The eagle passes towards the West, still drawing lazy circles in the air. Through the binoculars I can see its down-pointed head with its strong, curved bill, eyes searching the vegetation below for some animal not on the alert.

Although the eagle has passed out of my line of vision, still nothing stirs. The tension can be cut with a knife. Then the world starts to breathe again. A hornbill flies down from the tree in which it was hiding and, immediately afterwards, the mongooses emerge to begin their foraging again. As if a switch is thrown, the bush turns from stillness to action almost immediately, the mongooses that were in the mound run down to join the others, and the foraging troop with its hornbills in tow carries on where it left off.

It was the hornbills that responded to the danger first. By shooting almost vertically upwards into the trees they warned the food-hunting mongooses that danger was at hand. The mongooses, with their noses poked into dead logs and grass tussocks, would not have seen the eagle until a split-second later . . . or maybe too late. Even the guards on the mound gave their warning calls *after* the birds were already in flight. Then there was the curious fact that not a mongoose moved until the first bird flew down to the ground again. Are the two working together? The hornbills are catching the locusts, yes, but are they in turn 'paying' for this by warning the mongooses when danger approaches and, equally, giving them the 'all clear' signal when it is past?

I try to draw a map of the area around me as far as I can see, putting in all the termite mounds visible so that I can plot the mongooses' wanderings in their search for food, to get an idea how far and how fast they travel daily. The termite mounds also get names to make it easier as I take notes. Each mound is different in shape and size. Some are built around Boscia and Cassia trees, others stand naked in the grass or only have stumps of sun-bleached wood sticking out of them, the remains of the tree around which they were built.

Here in the Taru desert, these insect castles are constructed of sand grains glued together by the saliva of many thousands of worker animals which carry their loads to the building site and tamp them into place with their mandibles. Once dry, the walls have a cement-like consistency and can only be broken down with a pickaxe. It takes several years for a complete mound to be

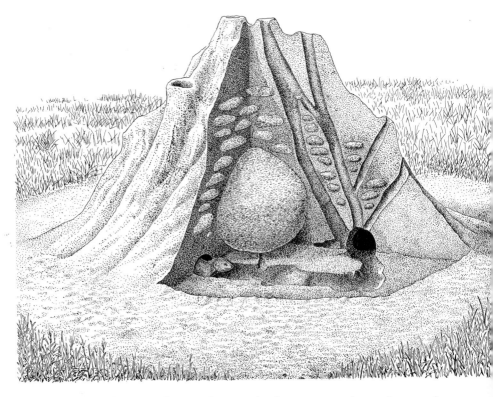

Since the termites' fungus gardens require an optimal temperature, the termite mounds are provided with ventilation shafts. Many bush animals live in them, including the Dwarf mongooses

constructed, and it grows to meet the demands of the growing termite colony within it. Some of these structures reach enormous sizes, twice the height of a man or more, and are inhabited by the insects for decades – some for up to a century. Termites of various species are found throughout tropical and subtropical climes and have been rightly termed the 'earthworms of the tropics', for it is they which, especially in the dry areas, devour the dead surface vegetation and return its nutrients to the soil once more, just as the earthworms of temperate lands do.

Most mounds in this area are built by termites of the genus *Macrotermes* and stretch up to five feet above ground level, the rest of the mound being subterranean with much the same form as an iceberg, only a fraction appearing above the surface. The termites live in galleries within the mound, these being centred around their fungus gardens to which they bring chewed wood to nourish the fungi which, in turn, provide the insects with necessary vitamins and moisture. Since this fungus needs an optimal temperature in which to do its work, the mounds are threaded with ventilation shafts to keep them cool, and it is these shafts that form the homes of so many bush-living animals, the Dwarf mongooses amongst them. Behind the walls of the mongooses' home thousands of busy insects live out their lives in darkness, scurrying along narrow subterranean tunnels which fan out from the mound itself in all directions like the rays of a spider's web from its hub.

The two guards on the mound start getting restless, and one of them trots down to vanish after the departing group. With a quick look round, the other one, Whitethroat, follows him, leaping through the grass in long bounds, his tail stuck out behind him like a poker. I look in the direction in which the group is headed and see that another animal has taken over guard duty on a mound in front of the group. At this distance I can see that it is a subadult male but little else.

The 'beep' of the contact calls which the mongooses give when they are on the move slowly fades as the group moves away. It is through these calls that the animals can stay together as they forage, for each one hunts alone and separated from the others by grass and bushes. Each voice is different, just as each human voice is different, and in this way they can tell which members of the group are nearby. The sonar-like 'beep' lies at about the two kHz level, a sound frequency ideal for penetrating vegetation and, at the volume the animals usually produce, clearly audible up to fifty yards away. The little group moves like a convoy of ships in the night, calling regularly 'Here I am', 'Here I am', in order to keep together.

The foragers continue on their way, circling round to take in every patch of dense cover, every fallen tree and every thick stand of dead grass, the birds hopping and flapping along behind them. The guard still sits on the termite mound in front keeping watch. Other birds join the group, the noisy White-crowned bush shrikes and a pair of Yellow-billed hornbills which soon get the priorities sorted out. As the latter are bigger than the other two species, a few quick pecks are enough to settle things, and from this point on the Yellow-bills march in the middle of the mongoose group while the others stay behind or on the fringe. As the group passes through a drongo territory, the drongo pair join them as well, but seem more interested in the flying insects they disturb, fluttering down from their perches above the foragers' heads to catch moths and flying beetles as the group passes. The sun glints blue-black on their feathers as they hover, forked tail spread, almost like little kestrels, before swooping down on their prey.

The minutes go by and the group of hunters has still not moved more than a hundred yards in a straight line from the mound they started from, although many times that distance if their meanderings are taken into account. I become almost mesmerised by the regular swoop and pounce of the hornbills and am only occasionally shaken out of my reverie by the squawks and shrill cries of the bush shrikes quarrelling over who should have the caught locust and who not.

Then again a vertical dash from the hornbills, a warning call from the mongooses and the world's motion freezes like a still from a movie film. I scan the sky but can see nothing. Something must be there though, as the warning *tcheees* sound loud and clear. Taking my binoculars, I scan the trees around, looking for a silhouette that doesn't 'fit', but can see nothing. Then I notice a flicker of movement in a tree towards my left. Focusing the binoculars I can just make out a curved shape that seems too regular to be a branch. Again a flicker of movement and a neck cranes, eyes peering downwards. From the curved beak I can see it is a bird of prey but its body is blocked by a branch and, in the criss-cross of light and shade within the tree, it is impossible to tell what colour it is.

The mongooses on the mound stare upwards at the intruder. At every movement it makes they dart as if to vanish to safety but stop when they see that no attack is to be launched. They obviously think it is better to keep the enemy in sight and the other members of the group informed as to its movements than to hide in the safety of the mound. Every time the bird moves, the *tcheees* are repeated. I still can't make out what it is. It is too small for an eagle and seems to be the size of a harrier. The tableau remains frozen: bird in tree, hornbills in trees, mongooses hiding or watching their enemy from the mound. Then the bird gives a half-hearted swoop at its would-be prey, skimming the mound above their heads so that they scatter in panic. I get a quick glimpse of grey wings, grey tail, white rump-patch and the bird is gone, twisting and turning through the branches while the mongooses take a nose-dive to safety. It was a Pale Chanting goshawk. A minute passes, then the hornbills give the 'all clear' and the world returns to normal.

It is almost ten o'clock. The sun beats down unmercifully from a bright blue sky dotted with white clouds. I shift position to try and keep in the shade within the car. Everything is soaked with sweat already and my body slippery with it. Beads of sweat run down my forehead and into my eyes, blurring my vision, and I am terribly thirsty. I have only one thermos of lime-juice with me to last the day, one I filled before dawn this morning from a jerrycan back at camp. Although the water must have been at least sixty-six degrees when I poured it in, it tastes cool and refreshing in this heat but I allow myself only a small sip for I know I yet have to face the real heat of the day and inside the car it will be like an oven. I watch the mongooses enviously as they still scrabble about but this time in the shade of the trees, away from the burning sun while I have to sit and bake, for to move the car at this point would mean disturbing everything and it would take hours before the animals scared away by the noise of the motor would drift back again.

As the heat increases towards midday, the bush seems to pant with it. Upwind of me a group of giraffe browse the thorny twigs, almost invisible in the criss-cross pattern of light and shade thrown by the branches. The only things I can pick out are the black tassels at the end of their tails, swishing, swishing to keep off the ubiquitous flies. Hornbills and mongooses still potter around at the base of a clump of trees. Then I see Diana move off towards a termite mound about seventy yards to my left, the juveniles following. It is a small mound at the base of a tree but full in the sun and has three matched peaks like a crown, so I dub it 'Crown' and wait to see what happens.

Diana moves up the mound and peers into the holes, one after the other. She pokes her body half into one and then retreats backwards looking behind her to where the rest of the group are still grubbing about in the grass. Then she turns and goes inside, the juveniles hard on her heels. I wait for her to emerge again but she doesn't and, one after the other, the rest of the group arrive, trot up the mound and vanish inside into its cool depths. My watch says it is shortly before eleven o'clock, the cicadas have started their shrill singing and the mongooses look as if they are having their siesta. The bush shrikes and drongos drift away and the hornbills fly into nearby Boscia trees, the only real shade around, disappearing into the dense foliage. These trees remind me of standard rose-bushes, with a long stem and neatly pruned top, almost spherical. The four-legged pruners move closer. The giraffes have still not spotted me and browse on, nibbling scraps of green here and there with their horny lips, trimming the Boscia trees as carefully as a gardener. They approach the one in which the von der Decken's hornbills are having their afternoon snooze and, as they stretch their necks to nibble, the birds fly out in a flurry of feathers. Startled, the lead giraffe throws up its head and in doing so sees me. I am fixated by eight large brown eyes with incredible lashes, then, without a sound, the four giraffes turn and melt back into the jigsaw of light and shadow from which they have come.

A head pokes out of Crown and looks about in all directions. Then it withdraws and I am left with an empty landscape. Nothing moves except the little flycatcher, still darting to and fro from his perch on the branch near my car. A hot wind starts to blow from the north, driving the clouds across the sky like ships, and I wait longingly for every patch of cloud shadow that passes and shields me from the burning eye of the sun. The car body is already too hot to touch and the real heat has not even started yet. The thorntree branches rattle like dried sticks in the wind – the only thing that makes it bearable to sit here hour after hour in the burning sun. I envy the mongooses their air-conditioned subterranean rooms.

The hours drag on and the air shimmers. Nothing moves. Even the flycatcher has given up. Above my head two vultures circle at the edge of visibility. My water supply is dwindling. Every now and again a head protrudes from Crown, looks around and withdraws again. A Rosy-patched bush shrike and his wife are singing their duet off in the trees to my right, '*Weeoo-wee, wee-oo*' over and over again, performing their stately minuet on one of the branches. Stretching himself almost on tiptoe he faces his wife, bowing deeply as he sings '*Weeoo-wee*'. She repeats the ritual a split-second later with her '*Wee-oo*', the whole sounding as if only one bird is singing, the two of them bobbing up and down like little marionettes.

The rattling in the branches gets louder. Above the tops of the trees I can see a reddish swirl in the air. A dust-devil! I quickly grab at anything moveable in the car – papers, bush-hat, books, as the little whirlwind goes past and vanishes into the trees beyond, leaving me plastered with red dust and dried vegetation. A Tawny eagle takes off from a tree not far away and flaps cumbersomely to meet the swirling air, wings beating like huge paddles. Then, straightening out, he rides the thermal, circling higher and higher in ever-widening circles until he is only a dot in the wide expanse of the sky.

Towards three o'clock, but the heat shows no sign of abating. I feel dizzy with it. When I move, pools of sweat are left on the plastic car seat and I resolve that tomorrow I am going to bring a towel to sit on. Even the cicadas are now silent and nothing moves except the patches of cloud shadow that sweep over the land. Far off in the distance I hear a Chanting goshawk call; his musical *Cheeoo-cheeoo-chip-chip-chip* rings over the death-like stillness. The minutes tick by. Then something moves in one of the Boscia trees and, with a swift glide, the von der Decken's hornbills emerge and land in the tree above Crown.

The top of the mound is now in shadow thrown by the tree's trunk, and I strain my eyes against the glare in case the mongooses have emerged again and I have missed them, but the mound is deserted. Winging through the trees, the Yellow-bills arrive and take up their station near the others. The waiting continues. At about four o'clock, one of the Yellow-bills flies down to Crown and walks across its top, peering into the dark tunnels of the ventilation shafts, his head cocked on one side. I can hear his guttural *Wok-wok-wok* call. The other hornbills sit on the branches above and peer downwards. Then, to my amazement, the mongooses emerge, yawning and stretching and putting their fur in order with quick nibbles before trotting off down the mound into the grass again, the hornbills in hot pursuit. Have I imagined it or has the hornbill woken the mongooses from their afternoon nap with a 'Come on you lot, it's time to get going!'? I begin to realise that the relationship between the hornbills and mongooses is far more intricate than I first thought.

Just as they did in the late morning, the little troop keep to the shadows, scrabbling mostly around the base of the trees. With a quick leap, hind-legs

Scar the guard fixates me, but I give no grounds to brand me as an enemy

working like little pistons to push him upwards, one of the mongooses climbs awkwardly into a thorntree, his blunt claws having difficulty in finding a purchase on the smooth bark. Finally, safe in a fork several feet above ground, he looks around. Through the binoculars I can see that it is Scar, one of the animals which held watch in the early morning. He gazes about him, then freezes. He has spotted me. His amber eyes bore like gimlets in my direction. I slowly lower my binoculars and drop my eyes, staying still as a stone. As yet he has not given the warning call that will brand me as 'enemy' and make my task of being accepted by the group almost impossible. I glance quickly in his direction, hardly moving a muscle. He is still staring fixedly at me while the rest of his family and their bird friends move slowly past the tree in which he is sitting. The war of nerves starts. Obviously he has not yet worked out what this strange metal monster sitting in the bush is and my slightest movement would give me away. The minutes tick by but he still sits there, rigid, his eyes fixed on me, and I sit there, equally rigid, eyes dropped so as not to give him the clue that he has been noticed.

The rest of the group have moved on but the animal still sits, not letting me out of his sight for a moment. A drop of sweat running down the side of my nose tickles madly but I bite my lip and don't scratch, although it takes an almost superhuman effort. I glance at the tree again. Scar is still there, still staring fixedly at me. A quarter of an hour passes and still no change. By this time, the group is almost forty yards away and swinging round to follow a line of toppled thorntrees to my right. I glance up again and, to my relief, Scar has gone – vanished as if he had never been. I breathe a sigh of relief and stretch my cramped muscles. Although under suspicion, I haven't yet been dubbed 'enemy' by the little creatures.

The hornbills hop along the branches of the fallen thorntrees, peering downwards, ready to pounce on anything that moves. The male von der Decken's takes a nosedive into the tangle and emerges with a small scorpion in his beak. I can see its tail stabbing and stabbing at the hard horn. Before he can swallow it, his wife hops over, squawks and pecks at him, at which he relinquishes his prize, offering it to her with a little bow, as if to save face. Of the mongooses, I can see nothing. Only the presence of the birds gives them away together with occasional rustlings from the dead vegetation as they scratch and scrabble their way through it.

A louder cracking draws my attention. I can see one of the mongooses at the base of a fallen tree near me wedging itself between the peeling bark and the trunk. With a snap, the bark peels away, broken off by a powerful thrust of the animal's forepaws. Something scuttles beneath the trunk, something long and metallic-looking. There is a concerted dash towards it, mongooses and hornbills jostling each other, but I can't see yet what they are after. The mongoose under the prised-off bark squeezes its body further into the split between bark and trunk and the piece of bark slowly lifts for about a foot along its length, splitting at the other end. One of the juveniles is waiting there, and other older animals flank him on both sides, waiting for the prize. The scuttling creature emerges, flushed by the animal beneath the bark which, quick as lightning, shoots backwards to catch it. Then I see what all the fuss is about. I catch a glimpse of a huge Scolopendra centipede, at least ten inches long, scrabbling like a little machine along the underside of the log. Another concerted dash from birds and mongooses and one of the juveniles emerges from the fray, the huge creature clamped fast in its jaws, its scaled body wrapped around the animal's snout. The head with its curved fangs whips back and forth and fastens itself on the mongoose's cheek but the mongoose ignores it, being far more occupied in keeping the rest of the group at bay. He bounds off, shaking his head sharply to dislodge the centipede's grip, four others and a Red-billed hornbill in close pursuit. Finally he stops only a little way from the car, head down and facing the trunk of another Commiphora tree, keeping his tormentors at bay with vicious-sounding growls and quick hipslams when they get too close. All but one, his littermates give up and return to their foraging, but the remaining one is persistent. Scanning the two quickly, I look for identifying characters. The animal with the centipede has a small nick in his right ear while his sister, the one trying to take his prize away, has a little white patch below her right eye, the remains of an old scar. I name them Moja and M'bili, the Swahili words for 'one' and 'two', reserving the name Tatu ('three') for their other sister who is smaller and more golden in colour.

Moja continues to growl, and drops the centipede which writhes in its death struggles. M'Bili makes a grab for it but is set upon by a furiously screaming Moja who dashes at her, mouth gaped, thrusting her away with his outstretched forepaws. She retreats and Moja turns to eat his prize which is still writhing in knots in the grass. With lips raised, he takes it in his incisors and shakes it vigorously, like a terrier shaking a rat, repeating this time and time again until the creature only twitches feebly. He then proceeds to eat it from one end, holding the body upright on the ground with his forefeet close together and ripping off chunks which he chews with relish. This seems to be too much for M'Bili who is hovering in the background and, with a quick pounce, she is upon him, snatching his hard-earned meal. I hear a quick scream of protest and the two of them are off, M'bili to the fore with the remains of the centipede in her mouth, Moja close on her heels. The two of them vanish in a twinkling down one of the nearby mounds from which protest shrieks issue at well-timed intervals. Moja doesn't seem to be giving up so easily. Then he emerges, a clear bite mark on one side of his neck, and trots off, resigned, to join the others. A little while later, M'bili also emerges, licking her lips with her little pink tongue.

It dawns on me that what I have seen is important. My year-long observations on my captive group have indicated that, when it comes to important priorities such as food, the juveniles have the advantage, all other members of the group except their parents letting them go first. But that was in an artificial situation in which the food source was restricted, a single bowl with mealworms in it. But here? With food all around? I can't deny the fact that all the other mongooses except Moja's littermate M'bili broke off the pursuit before it really began. Apart from this, mongooses are a matriarchy, the females higher in rank than the males of each age-group, and M'bili is a female. It was more or less her right to take the food from her brother.

It seems at this stage that the curious rank order I have observed in the laboratory, younger animals higher ranking than older ones and females higher ranking than males, was not just an artefact but the truth. If so, it would make the mongooses practically unique in the Animal Kingdom. A strange situation – a group led by a female in which the younger children have more say than the older ones. Before I can be sure, though, I need more evidence than this single observation.

The foraging group passes quite close now, heading past the car, the mongooses more or less nose to ground, poking around with their paws in every nook and cranny. They almost jump into the dead grass tussocks, tearing them apart with their strong forefeet, every now and again with success as I can see odd ones lifting their heads almost vertically, the sharp white teeth chewing and cracking away at their prey which seems, for the most part, to be beetles: which kind, I don't yet know. The hornbills keep a wary eye on me and I see I am also being watched from high in the branches of one of the fallen trees. A young male is staring hard at me and the war of nerves begins again, with me dropping my gaze and trying to remain as still as possible.

The mongooses don't seem to be able to place me in their scheme of things yet as even now there is no warning call, although the group can't be more than about ten yards away. I decide not to chance things at this stage and remain as if carved out of stone, only my eyes flickering upwards now and again to find out if the guard still has me spotted. The rest of them seem to ignore me, relying on the birds and their guard in the fallen tree to make the decision whether I am dangerous or not. The guard's attention wanders and he looks over to the left. He must have seen something as he scrabbles higher in the branches, standing on his hind-legs to get a better view.

Then comes an ear-shattering noise: '*OOM-warka, OOM-warka.*' Total panic! The guard literally falls out of the tree, the hornbills shoot off vertically and the rest of the group melts into the shadows. Even I shoot upright, the volume is incredible. I rapidly thumb through a mental list of large animals that could have produced such a cry and draw a blank. I can't see anything of the size necessary to make such a noise moving about anyway. Whatever it is, it can't be very dangerous, as the first hornbill has fluttered down to the ground again and the guard has scrabbled back to his post and is standing there on tiptoe, staring hard at something which must be just behind the fallen tree to my left. His whole attention is taken by the mysterious creature, so I turn round slowly in my seat so that I can see too. To my amazement, instead of the hulking creature I'd expected, two dainty chicken-sized birds step gracefully into view, looking this way and that and picking at things amongst the dead grass. From their shape they could only be bustards of some kind, and I hastily check through my bird book. While my head is down, peering at the captions, the incredible noise starts again and I glance up to see the two of them, heads stretched to the heavens and beaks gaped, singing – if that is what one could call it! I finally manage to identify them – White-bellied bustards, one of the ground-living birds of the dry bush country. No sooner have they finished one *OOM-marka* when they start on another, and I notice that it isn't one bird calling but two, a duet, he giving the *OOM* and she the *marka*, so synchronised that it sounds like a single voice.

By this time the mongooses are back at their never-ending foraging, having got over their fright. The bustards pass by, right through the ranks of the mongooses who don't even look up, and disappear again into the bush. I turn round . . . and it happens. '*Tchrrr*.' I've forgotten the guard but he hasn't forgotten me! Cursing my clumsiness I try to rectify things by freezing again and dropping my eyes, but he isn't going to be taken in so easily. He knows he has seen something move and I now have to pay for it, sitting still as a mouse in a half-twisted position in my seat. Out of the corner of my eye I watch him watching me. The rest of the group have gone into hiding and the birds are just sitting around. At least they haven't flown into the trees, so maybe the mongooses will not take it all too seriously as long as I don't do something stupid and make the guard warn again. The seconds pass like minutes and slowly the rest of the group emerges from hiding and continues on its way, birds in tow . . . But the guard is still very suspicious and stares unwinking in my direction. My left leg is starting to go to sleep and I have a pain in my back from sitting cramped in this uncomfortable position for so long. When I think I can't stand it any longer I start to move, slowly, slowly, an inch at a time, keeping the guard fixed out of the corner of my eye. I see him stiffen as he picks up my movement but he doesn't warn. It looks as if as long as I don't make any sudden movement, my presence will be tolerated. I resolve to be more careful in future. Finally he jumps down and follows his family and I relax, rubbing my left leg which seems full of pins and needles and trying to get the crick out of my neck.

The sun is already low in the sky, the prelude to the short African dusk. Many of the bush denizens are abroad again now that the day's heat is over. I watch two dainty little dik-dik, not much larger than a European hare, nibbling the few remaining green leaves on one of the Grewia bushes, their ears flickering back and forth to catch the slightest sound. They move jerkily, stopping and starting, listening intently at every pause and gazing about them with their huge brown eyes. The sun glints on the polished black of the little male's muzzle as, nostrils flaring, he sniffs the wind. I have the impression that almost everything here goes in daily fear of its life, and the precautions the animals take before venturing out of hiding seem to border on the extreme. I realise how difficult it must be for a small animal to survive at all in this wilderness with so many hostile conditions confronting it, and wonder why this is the reason that to date I have not seen any bird or mammal which could be termed solitary. Every single one lives either as a pair or in a group like the mongooses, starlings and White-crowned bush shrikes. The motto appears to be: 'Two pairs of eyes are better than one.'

There seems to be a gathering round the base of one of the Commiphora trees. The hornbills are feasting, and with them the mongooses, in the shade of this tree, with its distinctive shape like that of an upward-turned umbrella. Whatever they have found, it must be very small, for I can't identify anything in the beaks which are hastily tossed in the air, gaped and plunged downwards again. The crush of mongoose bodies forms a star around what looks to be a small hole in the ground. I catch a glimpse of busily munching jaws before the owner's head is thrust down into the hole again. Paws fish into its darkness and come up with something which is hastily carried to their owner's mouth. Tatu has lagged behind in the fallen trees while I can see Diana, George and, next to them, Moja and M'bili, hastily cramming the goodies from the hole into their mouths as fast as possible. Tatu's head emerges from a grass clump, she spots the others and hurries over, pushing between the clustered bodies of her older relatives which make way for her. No attempt is made to drive her off! Even though it means that the crush round the hole is worse than before. It really looks as if the juveniles are higher-ranking than the adults even under the harsh conditions here in the wild – or is it maybe because of them? Is it because without first access to food they would be doomed to die?

The first-comers seem to be replete. George and Diana move away, both round-bellied, and trot slowly towards a termite mound built round a Boscia tree to my left, one which I have already dubbed 'Dragon' because of the gnarled, bleached log with a forked end that lies across its top like a dragon with its mouth open. One by one the others leave the hole, licking their lips, and follow them. I still can't make out what they have been eating, and try to focus the binoculars better. It looks like tiny white sausages . . . I realise they must have discovered a termite pathway close to the surface and dug it open to fish out the insects as they scurried about trying to close the breach in their walls. Only one is left at the hole now, together with the Red-billed hornbills who have been forced to the fringe by the other birds and are only now permitted to cash in on the bounty. All I can see of the remaining animal is its rump, the rest of its body seems to be inside the hole. Then something happens that astonishes me. The male Red-billed hornbill doesn't seem to be satisfied with picking up the odd insects that escape the jaws of the mongoose wedged in the hole's opening. With a sharp peck, he strikes the animal in the middle of the back. The mongoose looks up and, before it seems to realise what is going on, the hornbill's long bill is in the hole, plunging up and down like a piston at full steam. With a growl, the mongoose shoulders the usurper out of the way and sticks its head into the hole again. Not to be outdone, the hornbill then takes the mongoose's ear in its beak and starts to tug. No response. Even a couple of pecks on the head only result in the mongoose swinging its body round to slam at the bird which nimbly hops out of the way. Again the hornbill tries but the mongoose isn't going to be caught out a second time. The bird takes the mongoose's ear in its beak again and strains backwards with all its might. This seems to be too much for the mongoose which, with a growl and a lunge, leaps at its feathered tormentor, mouth gaped, and chases it off. As soon as the animal relinquishes its place at the hole, the hornbill's partner is there, gobbling as fast as she can. Whipping round with a growl, the little brown body hurls itself upon her and with a squawk, she too gives way. The mongoose returns to its interrupted supper and the hornbills have to make do with the scraps until it has finished and trots off to join the others. Life here is hard for the weaker ones, even amongst friends!

On Dragon, the group seems to be preparing for the night. The shadows stretch long beneath the trees and the sky is a blaze of red in the west. After a quick read of the marking post, the group gathers in little knots on the sunward side of the mound, grooming and stretching lazily. Their day seems to have drawn to an end. Only one of the older males that looks very much like George but has a narrower head and whom I call 'Twin' is still staring at me, as if daring me to do something, but I don't oblige. Again it is Diana who makes the first move. Stretching and yawning mightily, she peers first into one hole, then another, and finally slips inside followed by Tatu. The other two youngsters, Moja and M'bili, are still playing on the apron of earth in front of the mound under George and the rest of the group's watchful eyes. One by one the animals disappear into their sleeping chamber, the game breaks up and the players vanish too. Only Twin is left in the last rays of the setting sun,

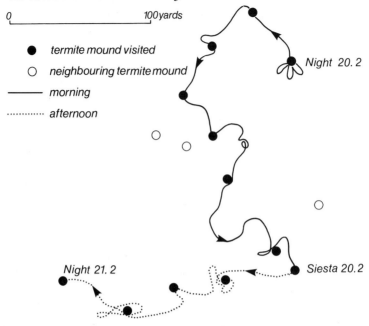

0 _____ 100 yards

● termite mound visited

○ neighbouring termite mound

——— morning

············· afternoon

Night 20.2

Siesta 20.2

Night 21.2

The mongoose group slept in a different termite mound each day. I drew a map of each day's foraging route

still watching me like a hawk, his fur bottlebrushed against the cool of the evening air. It is almost dark but he still hocks there, a shadow amongst deeper shadows, and I don't dare to move. A nightjar calls his chugging note away in the depths of the bush. The hornbills have all left, returning to their sleeping trees, and I wonder how long Twin is going to keep it up: I have no desire to drive through the bush in the pitch dark. Finally, when the last light is almost gone, he turns and disappears into the mound, and I can start the car and head back to camp, just over three miles away.

I drive carefully round the fallen trees and through the bushes praying that I won't fall into a hole at this time of night. The headlights stab the darkness and everything looks two-dimensional in their glare. I head west towards where the sun has set, hoping I won't lose my bearings in the dark, as somewhere in that direction, amongst this tangle of trees and bushes, is the only dirt road that will bring me to comparative safety. I churn along in first gear and think I must have missed the road as I seem to have been driving for ages when suddenly, there it is, like a pale river in the gloom. I stop the car and hastily get out to tie a plastic marker on a nearby bush so that I can find the place in the dark before dawn tomorrow morning.

A few minutes later I am greeted with big grins from my boys Danson and Sammy, whose job it is to guard the camp against robbers while I am off all day watching my animals. They have been getting worried since I've been out long after dark. Elated, I tell them of my success and give them instructions for the evening meal – the usual corned beef, potatoes and onions, about all that will keep out here in the heat without refrigeration. While they are preparing supper, I light the gas lamp and sit down to write up my notes for the day, drawing sketches of the animals I've been able to identify – at any rate, eight of the group now have names and I am fairly sure I will be able to recognise them again when I see them. Then I carefully redraw the map to show the route they have taken during the day's foraging, putting in approximate times of arrival at different points so that I will later be able to work out how fast they travel on an average while food-hunting and also how far their daily sorties take them.

By the time the notes are transcribed, supper is ready and we sit in the light of the kerosene lamps eating, trying to keep the buzzing beetles and moths from falling into our food and chatting about how things have been at camp and what I have seen during the day in a mixture of English and Swahili and with much checking in the dictionary. The moon is high before we are finished and the stars almost look near enough to touch. Way off in the hills a leopard calls, his rapid, sawing *krrmp-krrmp-krrmp* echoing for miles through the bush. I have my evening wash and am shocked at the brown soup-like water remaining in my plastic bowl afterwards. Tired but happy at finally finding the mongooses, and even being more or less accepted by them, I lie down to sleep. The last I hear is the churring of the nightjars and the sharp staccato yelp of a jackal before I drift off.

2 Getting to Know You

It hardly seems as though I've been asleep at all – the jackal is still barking. I open my eyes but instead of moonlight, all is dark outside. I grope for my clock and see it is nearly four-thirty – time to get up. I light the gas lamp and go through the ritual of searching my clothes before I put them on, shaking out everything, just in case. The first few days here in the desert brought some surprises on getting dressed – my total count is now two centipedes, a small snake, a very large Solifugid spider and, finally, a scorpion in my face-flannel. After knocking out my shoes and putting them on, I take the torch, scan the ground in front of the tent in case a puff adder has decided to have a snooze there, and allow myself a dribble of precious water from the jerrycan to clean my teeth and wash in. Then over to the little kitchen, a hut made of split sisal poles woven together and thatched with grass, all brought from a sisal plantation sixty miles away. I shine the torch on the kitchen floor carefully. I almost stepped on one puff adder there only two days ago and don't want a repeat performance. I still can't get over how perfectly such large animals can blend with their background to the point of almost complete invisibility, the only thing that seems to give them away being their heads whose contours they have difficulty in disguising. The bush-baby has been here again. The solitary mango which I have been so looking forward to and which was just getting ripe now lies on the floor, a big hole in its side, and the place is littered with neatly torn off pieces of green skin. I pick it up. Maybe with a wash, the rest of it will still be edible. It's the last fresh piece of fruit I have!

Time and again I am astounded at the way in which the animals here take advantage of every change man makes in the ecology in order to have his creature comforts – which also happen to be theirs! Every patch of man-made shade is almost immediately taken advantage of by something – usually snakes, lizards, spiders, scorpions, and centipedes. Within a day of our arrival and hanging a canvas waterbag in a tree where the breeze could cool it, a toad appeared from nowhere and made its home under the slow constant drip that fell from it. Just the fact that we light the keroşene lanterns at night attracts insects and with them the little gecko lizards, several of which have already made their permanent home on the walls of my tent. What they attract in turn, though, I am not so happy with. Twice now a black mamba has been to visit, streaking up the sides of the tent like lightning to catch the luckless lizards. Even our one attempt at 'civilisation', a pit lavatory, was moved into – and we moved out! Two days after having dug it with enormous trouble, dampening the rock-hard earth with water and hacking it out with pickaxes, we awoke one morning to find that a python had found the deep, moist hole and moved in to stay! Now we use the bushes like the other animals.

Sammy and Danson are still asleep. I decide not to light the campfire again to boil water as it will take too long and I am in a hurry to get back to Dragon before dawn breaks and I disturb things too much. I light the little gas stove and get things ready for tea as well as my 'hard rations' for the day – crackers and jam, things I know won't go bad or melt in the heat. When the kettle boils, I fill a thermos of tea and another one of lime-juice, collect my notebook, camera and binoculars and am off.

The car motor breaks the silence and the headlights stab the darkness. I meet the jackal and its family on the road. They shoot off into the bush at the approach of this noisy monster with its glaring eyes. Sometimes I wish I could go on foot instead of by car but two things are against such a decision. First, it is too dangerous. I am all alone and snakes abound in this hot, dry land, not to mention lions and other potentially dangerous animals, but the worst enemy is the heat and the monotonous landscape. I cannot take the risk of getting lost or hurt. Secondly, and probably more important, I have found, curiously enough, that animals are less scared of a human in a car than one on foot, especially if the car is standing still. Sometimes they will come right up to it before they catch the human scent and flee in panic. The biped silhouette of the human figure seems to all animals to be a danger more extreme than the worst hunting lion or leopard. Tiny birds react with the same panic-stricken flight as do antelope and giraffe.

I am getting near the place where I left the plastic marker the night before. Everything looks the same and I have difficulty in picking it out. My tyre tracks are just visible through the grass and I follow them faithfully, for a deviation of only a few yards at this stage might mean a difference of hundreds in a few miles and trying to find Dragon once I missed it in this tangle would be an almost hopeless task. The bushes and tree trunks pop up and disappear in the darkness like paper cutouts as I go past, following the two silvery ribbons which will bring me to my goal. A Verreaux's Eagle owl takes off from his lookout on a tree branch and glides past the car on silent wings. I hope that I have not ruined his early morning hunt. The tree trunks appear and disappear with mesmerising monotony as I twist and turn amongst them, manhandling the big car through the underbrush. I am starting to get the feeling that this is going on for ever when a familiar silhouette appears in the headlights. Dragon. I manoeuvre the car so that it is broadside on to the mound about twenty yards away, cut the motor, turn off the headlights and have breakfast – tea, crackers and jam. It is still too dark to see anything.

Dawn cannot be far off. The first birds are starting to sing. The piping and chirruping increases in volume as the sky pales in the east and more of them join the chorus. Something crashes through the underbrush behind me. I whip round but it is too dark to see anything. Out of the darkness comes a disembodied giggle. It must be one of the Striped hyenas that live in this area. I caught a glimpse of two of them at the almost dried up waterhole near the camp a few days ago, silvery shadows in the silver and black of the moonlight, almost invisible, the bristling mane running down their backs making their silhouettes practically melt into the shadowy background.

A bank of cloud obscures the sun and the light comes gradually, not with its usual burst of brilliance. All about me is a busy bustling as the bush creatures set about their task of finding breakfast. The hornbills repeat their performance of the day before and are there long before the mongooses wake up. Slowly, the cloud bank starts to disperse. The von der Decken's have flown down onto a fallen tree near the mound and are sunbathing, turning their heads on one side and fluffing their feathers so that the sun's rays can warm their skin, especially the large bare patches at the base of their throats. The Yellow-bills and Red-bills have these as well; at first I thought that they were just for decoration but they have an important function. As the heat increases, these patches swell and take on an almost purplish colour, suffused with venous blood. They seem to be acting in much the same way as an elephant's ears, a place where the breeze can cool the blood before it is carried back into the body's interior. Now, however, it is relatively cold and the patches are pale and shrivelled, almost hidden under the white neck feathers.

Finally the mongooses emerge, Twin first, as he was last the night before. He spots me immediately and freezes. The old game of complete motionlessness and dropped eyes starts. I give him no reason to warn. One by one, the others emerge and cuddle up to him, fur on end. More and more join the group on the mound, clustering together like a bunch of grapes. Some climb on top of the animals squatting there, others squeeze themselves between them. All I can distinguish is a heap of heads and rumps disturbed only when one of the ones at the bottom, almost squashed flat by the weight on top, squeezes out of its prison and clambers on top of the heap again – like a child's game of Hand Castles. Twin detaches himself from the group and comes forward onto a little buttress of the mound in order to watch me better. He looks thoroughly miserable, hunched up and all his fur on end, but his vigilance doesn't slacken for a moment. He still hasn't warned and seems content just to keep an eye on me. The rest of them are still in their heap, warming each other by the contact of bodies. I start counting again . . . fifteen including Twin. I can pick out Diana and George and the three juveniles with little trouble. Whitethroat and Scar are more difficult as the bottlebrushed hair obliterates little irregularities in the fur. A dark rump turns and is replaced by an equally dark head. A young male of about three years old, I guess, and call him Blackie, making a note of his age, sex and colour for my file. A ragged-looking female with a piece missing out of her right ear also stands out of the huddle and I call her Notch, making a little drawing of her face with its distinguishing feature. It looks as if Tatu is 'mother's darling' as she remains close to her side no matter where she goes, something that I noticed yesterday as well. She seems rather retarded in growth in comparison with Moja and M'bili, an inch or two shorter and much thinner. Two of the three-year-old subadults I can also distinguish, Rusty, a red-coloured young male, and Goldie, a yellowish female. My note-taking goes on. Now I have sketches of twelve of them. I find it curious that most of the ones I have been able to identify have been male to date. Either the group has a skewed sex ratio or the females are keeping to the background.

The sun is getting warmer and the huddle starts to break up, George leading. Rusty moves to the other side of the mound, opposite to Twin who still hasn't taken his eyes off me, and keeps watch there. Then George does something I can't make head or tail of. Grabbing a leafy branch of the Boscia tree in his forepaws he starts to demolish it with strong backward thrusts of his claws, both forelegs working together in synchrony. Back bent and tail raised, limbs stiff, he completes the process, making a loud noise in the stillness and glancing at the group as he does so. The looks he gives them seem to shrivel them where they sit and some of them drop their eyes, all with the exception of Diana who carefully nibbles one outstretched forefoot. The whole thing looks like a threat of some kind, but as yet I can't work out whom he is threatening and why. Leaving the tattered remnants of the branch behind him, George trots down to the latrine and the usual morning ritual of defecation and marking starts.

The mongooses have hardly finished defecating when a scaly head appears in one of the holes on Dragon, followed by a waddling body. It is a lizard of some kind – but a huge one, almost three feet long. With cumbersome gait, it heaves itself down the side of the mound and paces over to the mongoose group. I expect panic-stricken flight or attack but what happens? Nothing! The lizard squeezes itself between the clustered mongoose bodies and starts to feed. I can see its head bending downwards in the crush and its jaws working as it lifts it again. Two of the mongooses blocking my view move off and I can now see what it's all about. Scar is squatting there defecating and what he is producing is being carefully watched by the lizard, its head cocked on one side. Before Scar's product has hit the ground, the lizard pounces and it's gone! The thing is eating the mongooses' fresh droppings! With a shake of his body, Scar trots off, ignoring the reptile, which assiduously cleans up before waddling up the mound again. I am speechless. What is all this in aid of?

Then I remember that this is a desert and that water is at a premium. Even the bees and butterflies come to drink my sweat, not to mention hundreds of flies, and maybe the lizard is just cashing in on the moisture so conveniently supplied by the mongooses, right in front of its door, so to speak. Their droppings would probably also contain a good portion of undigested protein which the lizard could certainly use. Again a case of one helping the other. Later I have the lizard identified from photographs and it turns out to be a Tawny Plated lizard.

It spreads itself out on one of Dragon's slopes and basks, eyes blinking, in the sun. After marking, the group wanders back, even walking over the reptile which doesn't budge. The daily grooming session continues. Notch and Goldie assiduously groom George who closes his eyes and lifts his head so that they can get at the ticks fastened to his throat. Diana doesn't seem to mind and lies, spread out, in the sunlight. The rest of them nibble and scratch themselves like little dogs or ask to be groomed in turn by walking under one of the others' throats and nibbling it on the neck, upon which the favour is returned. The youngsters seem to be in a playful mood. I can hear the bird-like twitters of the 'play call' starting and Moja taps Tatu on the nose with an outstretched forepaw. This elicits a playful dart and the two bounce around like little balls, dashing up and down the mound in hot pursuit of each other and rolling over and over, arms clasped round the body of their partner.

The romp seems to be getting out of hand. The two are oblivious of all around and chase each other into the grass surrounding the mound. Diana suddenly stands up and trots after them. The rest of the group look in her direction. She dashes up to the gyrating couple and jumps between them. They stop, as if on signal, and follow her back to the mound. Diana has most definitely broken up the game – but why? Could their wild scamperings attract predators, or is it just too dangerous for them to move so far away from the mound where a predator could catch them more easily? This breaking up of games that get too intense I am to see again. Sometimes it is Diana who plays spoil-sport, at other times other older members of the group, but the situation in which it takes place is always the same: the players are too far from the mound.

In the meantime, M'Bili seems to be making a nuisance of herself. She is still giving the play call, a noise like a frantic idiot on a Morse key, and making little jumps in the air. She flings herself at Rusty but Rusty is not in the mood and moves away. Attempts to get George to join in also fail. She skips over to the lizard, picking up dead leaves in her mouth, one after the other, and flinging them away with a quick twist of her head. To my horror, she then pounces with both forefeet right on the lizard's back. I expect a wicked tail-slam from the lizard or at least a quick bite, both of which could be painful

Both youngsters and adult mongooses enjoy a wild play session

as the lizard is almost twice her length, but the lizard does nothing! It doesn't even flinch! M'Bili cheekily pats its foreleg, even taking it in her mouth and worrying it playfully. The lizard moves sluggishly to one side. Then M'Bili jumps at its head, tapping it along its snout and making playful stabs at its eyes with her snout. The lizard closes them. After a few more fruitless attempts to make her strange playmate join in, all of which are responded to with stolid impassivity, M'Bili moves on and the lizard continues its interrupted snooze.

Who would have believed that mongoose and lizard, both of them traditional enemies, would have behaved like this? A mongoose has no compunction about gobbling up smaller members of this reptilian family and I am sure that the lizard, for its part, would have no hesitation in making a snack of a young mongoose if it could catch it. But the present situation seems to be a truce, neither animal having any designs on the other except those connected with mutual friendship. A policy of 'live and let live!'

The hornbills start their chivvying again. This time it is the Yellow-bills that seem to be getting impatient, hopping round the mound and peering up at the

Neck-nibbling is the commonest form of social grooming and means friendship

mongooses, heads cocked on one side. Two black and white shapes come gliding through the trees. The Red-bills are late this morning but I have the impression that they are not so dependent on the mongooses as the other two species for I have also seen them eating a lot of fruit and berries, while the others seem to feed almost entirely on insects.

Diana gets up, stretches and yawns and heads off down the mound as she did before. It looks almost as if she is the one who decides when the group is going to move and where. The little cavalcade moves off into the grass out of sight, this meaning the end of my observations on social behaviour until the evening. While on the hunt for food, the mongooses seem to concentrate entirely on this and there is little social contact between them. I start to plot the daily route on my map, following the movements of the hornbills diving hither and thither in the grass. Without their help it would be impossible, for the little camouflaged bodies of the mongooses are completely invisible from my angle. Whitethroat looks at me and then looks past me. It seems as if the car has been more or less accepted as some sort of huge behemoth that has decided to have a snooze right in front of the mongoose's sleeping mound – not really dangerous but something one must keep an eye on, just in case!

The group is about thirty yards away now. Suddenly, off to my right, huge brown wings beat the air and a Tawny eagle struggles up into the branches of one of the thorntrees and sits there, beak gaped and crop bulging. Vertical dives from the hornbills, Whitethroat warns and the whole group dashes back to the mound as a body to sit there, sense organs strained to the utmost to find out what is going on. Another beating of wings and a second eagle takes off from almost the same spot as the first to flap awkwardly upwards, using its wings to balance its body as it tries to perch on the thin, thorny twigs. Then a third! The trio sit there like little buddhas, replete to the point of bursting. My first thought is that they have found the carcass of some animal killed by a larger predator and have polished off the remains. The mongooses remain as if riveted to the mound, seeking shelter under the twigs and branches, all eyes fixed on the three huge birds. The warning *tchrrrs* resound. One of the eagles tries to preen its wing feathers, loses its balance in the thin twigs, flaps madly to regain it and tumbles downwards, catching itself at the last moment.

Pandemonium on the termite mound! Brown bodies dash to safety and the Tawny Plated lizard shoots in too. A head emerges and looks round. Scar. The rest of them remain inside. It looks as if Scar has the job of keeping the predators under observation at present. He stiffens, flagging his head up and down in the way mongooses do when they are trying to fixate an object, but he isn't looking up at the eagles but down at an angle, into the grass. He gives a growling twitter, half-turns to go back inside, and then thinks better of it. The call means 'ground predator' but, at the moment, I can't see a thing. Rusty comes up to join him on the mound, both staring off into the grass, Rusty going into high sit to see better. Then a jackal emerges, its typical bouncy gait unmistakable. It lifts its head, sniffing the air. The eagles sit there still, completely unconcerned, but the air of tension on the termite mound is so palpable that I can almost feel it too. Rusty and Scar trot back and forth within the shelter of the branches still giving their growling twitters, but the jackal doesn't even notice them. It has obviously caught wind of what the eagles were feeding on and is coming for its share. It trots on.

High above against the blue of the sky, dots are starting to appear as if by magic. The vultures have arrived. How they manage to spot anything amongst the tangle of thorntrees I have no idea. Rows of them peel down the wind to circle above the spot, dropping lower and lower. Rusty and Scar's attention is riveted in the opposite direction and I climb slowly through the roof hatch onto the car roof to try and get a better look. The jackal has found whatever it was and is trying to pull it into the shelter of some bushes with strong backward leaps of its lithe body – but too late. Talons and neck to the fore, the first vulture lands and hops awkwardly towards the jackal and its hoped-for

White-backed vultures funnel down onto carrion

meal, snaking its bare head forward and grabbing part of the object on the ground. In the tug-of-war that ensues the carcass lifts and I can see that it is a little steenbock from its reddish colour, one of the smaller antelopes that haunt this bushy desert. There seems to be a lot of it left, though, hardly enough has been eaten for it to have been killed by one of the larger predators. Maybe the eagles, working together, killed it themselves, which they have been known to do.

The battle is starting to get one-sided now. More vultures are swooping in. This all seems to be too much for Rusty and Scar who, still growling and twittering, have retired into the safety of the mound. All the birds that have landed so far have been White-backed vultures, the commonest carrion-eater here in the dry bush. The jackal is starting to get frantic and leaps at the thieves, throwing itself into the air with snapping jaws to try and bite its tormentors. The leaps it performs are truly prodigious, at least as high as my shoulder, the huge birds flapping upwards only to land a few feet away and dive anew into the fray. The one-sided contest becomes even more one-sided as a steady stream of birds funnels down, some of them braking ineffectually and cannoning into the hopping, shambling gathering of brown feathered bodies to add to the chaos. The jackal seems to have given up and the birds have the prize, the little body being torn and tugged between them like a mess of old rags. I glance upwards as a larger shadow shoots over the car. The white wingstripes of the birds arriving now show that they are not White-backs but some other species. Three of them land almost simultaneously and I can see their clown-like faces, white with a blood-red bill. The White-headed vultures have arrived. Without a moment's hesitation they dive into the mound of shuffling brown bodies and set about them with their powerful bills. The White-backs flap backwards. Some of them even settle on the toppled thorntrees around as if they have given up, while the others form a circle around the bigger birds which delve into the pitiful remains of the carcass with gusto. Every time a White-back approaches it is driven off with a sharp stab from a blood-red bill, red now with the blood of the little steenbock as well as with its natural colour. Some of the White-backs start to flap off, soaring upwards in a passing thermal, but the Tawny eagles still sit there, gorged.

Thinking this is the end of the performance, I am just debating whether to climb down into the car again when another shadow skims above my head and a truly gigantic bird starts its glide into an almost graceful landing for a vulture. It waddles over to where the three White-heads are squabbling over the remains and they move off, dropping their prize without a word. The newcomer hisses loudly and looks around, head half-dropped, before sauntering over to collect its due. I thumb through the bird book. From the size and massive bill, this can only be a Nubian vulture and I am surprised that the White-heads, although outnumbering it three to one, just relinquish their prey as soon as it approaches without even putting up a fight. Maybe they know from previous experience that they have little chance of success against this huge rival, almost twice as big as themselves and with a beak that even a larger animal would fear. The Nubian hocks above the carcass, tearing off strips of skin with its beak and swallowing them. Practically nothing is left of the little antelope.

I climb down into the car again and settle down to wait until the mongooses have got over their fright and emerge once more. It is not until several minutes later that, crop bulging, the Nubian takes to the air, having trouble negotiating its enormous wingspan amongst the thorntree cover. Then, with a ponderous flapping of wings, it is off, skimming low over the tree-tops. Only the eagles still sit there impassively, digesting their breakfast.

The sun is getting stronger now, and the eagles are starting to pant with the heat. Then one by one they flap upwards, three strong wingbeats and a glide, repeated again and again until I see them curve into the graceful spiral that will carry them upwards almost to the fringe of human vision. Dragon remains deserted. The minutes tick by and still nothing moves.

It is nearly half an hour later before the first little head appears from a hole almost at the top of the mound and gazes about. It looks like Twin. The head disappears. A minute later, two heads are poked out, their owners peering around. This time, Scar has joined Twin. Carefully they clamber up onto the mound and survey the surrounds. Almost at the same time, the Yellow-bills glide over from the Cassia tree in which they have been hiding and sit in the branches above Dragon. The 'all clear' being given, the little troop sets off again on its interrupted hunt, again Diana in the lead, but she seems to have changed the original direction. Instead of heading at an angle towards the birds as she did early this morning, she now leads off at a bearing 180 degrees in the opposite direction, the marching route lying almost across the front of the car. The group, plus birds, move past not five yards from me with a rather determined air and almost in single file, Diana's 'moving out' call clearly audible. The whole group trot after her, 'beeping' sonorously as they go, hardly deviating right or left until they are many yards away.

Thanks to the eagles, the morning's foraging session has been cut short. The foraging is restricted to the shadows again and the little group slowly meanders towards Monkey, a mound with a broken, bleached stump on it that looks almost like a squatting vervet. Within half an hour, all have vanished inside, Twin again taking the last watch, crouched in the shade of the curved stump. I am left with the sun, the heat and the flies.

The hours drag by. The midday wind gets up and I breathe a sigh of relief as it dries the sweat on my body. The thorntree trunks in the near distance distort in the shimmering air. The bush is holding its siesta.

It must be almost three o'clock when I see a small, familiar head appear on a mound behind Monkey and look around. I seem to have made a mistake. The mongooses haven't spent the midday pause at Monkey, which I thought I'd seen them go into, but in the mound behind it. I focus the binoculars to try and identify who it is that is sitting there but the shimmering air defies my attempts. A body follows the head, a body that seems to go on and on and certainly doesn't belong to a Dwarf mongoose. Then the tail emerges as well and I see its jauntily turned-up black tassel – a Blacktip or Slender mongoose, one of the relatives of the Dwarf but almost three times its size and known as a solitary hunter of larger prey – birds, mammals and reptiles. The Blacktip looks about and spots me, its body moving from side to side like a drunk trying to keep his balance as the animal attempts to fixate me. It strikes me as strange that the Blacktips have adopted this slow side-to-side form of visual fixation while their close cousins, the Dwarfs, use a quick 'up-and-down' like a bird of prey, and I wonder what the physiology behind this difference in behaviour could be.

The Blacktip is joined by a second from within the mound which is now named 'Blacktip'. The two of them move briefly round the top of the structure before trotting off down its side. I spot them every now and again as they make their way through the fallen trees and grass, the black tips of their tails still held upright like flags, marking their route. I notice that no bird attempts to accompany them, the starlings, shrikes and drongos, in contrast, mobbing them viciously, screaming all the while, and making divebomb attacks on them. Maybe their predilection for larger prey has stamped the Blacktips as 'dangerous' for the other bush animals. I have seen Blacktips on the hunt many times, but never accompanied by birds, except in vigorous mobbing. I once saw a Golden-breasted starling taken by a Blacktip, in return for which the rest of the flock made such a noise as to alert every potential prey animal for miles around to the presence of predators in the area.

Again it is almost four o'clock before the Dwarfs put in their afternoon appearance. This time it is Whitethroat that is the first to emerge. I am practically never to see George get up first, although he is rarely more than a few seconds later than the first animal to emerge. It almost always seems to be one of the older subordinate males that takes the first look around, letting the rest of the group know whether there is any danger imminent by going out on top of the mound to test the situation. If the early guard gives no warning call or does not come shooting back into the hole from which he has emerged, this seems the signal to the others that all is clear and it is safe to come out. There is always a break, sometimes of only a few seconds, sometimes of minutes, before the guard is joined by the rest of his family.

Just as the day before, the troop sets off down the mound with little fuss and bother. Hardly any grooming, as there is in the early morning, and only a few animals defecate or sniff at something that looks as if it could be used as a marking post. Some of the mounds they spend their siesta in are thoroughly marked and others not. It is early days to say yet what the significance of this is and I need more observations.

I watch the fluttering hornbills in their eternal swoop and dive after flying insects and the White-crowned bush shrikes come chattering and scolding out of the depths of the bush to join the party. At first, their sharp cries alert the other animals and the hornbills fly up into trees but soon fly down again once the source of the noise has been identified. It looks as if every disturbance is responded to with immediate flight, whether it is dangerous or not, a policy of 'fly now and look later'. This is especially true for things that make loud noises or move on the ground. Both birds and mongooses are more discriminating when it comes to flying enemies and will distinguish between a high-flying Lanner falcon, which causes immediate flight, and a circling vulture which is noticed but, thereafter, more or less ignored. This would indicate, first, a fantastic sense of vision as, even with binoculars, I sometimes have difficulty in distinguishing between a high-flying vulture and an eagle, but the mongooses and birds never do. Secondly, it means that they must have an almost computer memory to store all the individual characteristics of their potential aerial foes, as there is a great difference between a falcon, an eagle and a goshawk in flight, but all are responded to as dangerous while vultures, secretary birds, herons and storks are ignored. I collect each little bit of information in the hope that, with time, it will crystallise into a pattern.

Something that looks like a walking-stick is protruding from a mound in the mongoose's wake. I see its end move – or is it just the shimmering in the air? I take a closer look through the binoculars and find myself staring into a pair of round, black, boot-button eyes which are staring at me. Attached to the squat, scaly face with its pointed nose is a long, finely-scaled body, grey below and green-shimmering on top, the end of which disappears into the darkness of one of the mound's openings. It is a snake of some kind, and a long one at that! The part sticking out of the mound must be three feet long or more. It seems to survey its surroundings with intelligent curiosity, turning this way and that but still remaining almost perpendicular. The mongooses are continuing on their way, backs towards the mound with the snake in. It looks as if they have not seen it, and I feel a sense of disappointment. My first chance to see how these famous snake-hunters deal with a snake and they don't even notice it! Visions of Kipling's Rikki-tikki-tavi and his fight with Nag start to fade from my imagination.

The group swings round! My excitement mounts again. Surely this time they will see it! But no, no concerted dash, no change in their behaviour at all. The group move closer, still oblivious of their traditional foe. The snake watches them then, slowly, slowly, as if someone were winding it onto a stick within the mound, the body retreats. Soon all I can see of it is the back of its head above the mound and then, finally, this disappears too. The end of a potential duel to the death. . .

The group move past the mound in which the snake is hiding, still nose to ground. I think everything is over when Rusty trots up the back of the mound, sniffs in one of the holes and gives a long, tremulous '*Tseeee*'. Like a shot, all heads are up and the first animals trot back to the mound on which Rusty is still peering into the hole. Twin and Scar are to the fore, Whitethroat and George close behind. Only after these come the younger animals and Diana. In a closed rank they rush up the mound and peer into the opening where Rusty still sits, calling his plaintive '*Tseee*' – 'Come quickly!' They cluster round the hole, peering inside, some of the bolder ones extending their bodies so that only the hind-feet grasp the hole's rim, shooting out again as if jet-propelled to land on their haunches. After investigating thoroughly, George goes down the side of the mound where Diana is waiting and starts his threat-scratching ceremony amongst a pile of dead leaves. The noise is so loud that I can hear it from the car. The rest of the mongooses seem highly excited, their tails bottlebrushed, and keep making quick darts in and out of the hole in the mound. Not one animal makes a serious attempt to enter the mound, though, and Diana hasn't even taken the trouble to go up and look for herself. After a few minutes of comings and goings, Diana sets off, away from the mound, giving the 'moving out' call, and George, who is still threat-scratching, looks almost stupidly after her. One by one, the snake-baiters leave to join the matriarch. Only Whitethroat remains at last, flagging his head up and down in the depths of the hole, then finally he too leaves, almost reluctantly, to join his departing family.

Snake-killers? It didn't look much like it. They were certainly very excited by the reptile but I never had the impression that they were out to kill it. My first thought is that maybe Dwarf mongooses don't kill snakes. My first observation of their behaviour on contacting such a reptile certainly seems to point towards such a theory, but later observations are to modify it somewhat. Mongooses don't attack snakes which are safely tucked away in termite mounds and can defend themselves, but in the open . . .

The little group move on as the evening shadows lengthen. They don't go back to Dragon as I expected but head on past it to a large mound which I've called Big. Here the usual evening session of marking, grooming and lolling around gets under way. I take this opportunity to try and identify other members of the group but can only make one certain identification, a small, greyish female who gets the name Victoria. Amongst the huddle of bodies must be two animals which have not yet caught my attention by any special distinguishing marks – both of them subadults between one and three years of age. I now have all the adults and juveniles spotted; only the subadults remain a problem. I am too far away to see anything properly at present and resolve to pay special attention to them tomorrow.

Back at camp I miss Danson's usual evening ritual. He usually comes to meet me when the car stops and we go into a rather long-winded greeting ceremony.

He: '*Habari?*' (News?).

Me: '*Mzuri*' (Good).

He: '*Salama tu*' (Many greetings to you).

Me: '*Asante*' (Thank you).

He: '*Ndio*' (Yes = Don't mention it).

This evening, though, he is nowhere to be seen. I climb out of the car and am greeted by a fusillade of chopping noises. A huge pile of dead tree-trunks lies in the middle of the camp and Danson is busily chopping them up. Surely we don't need *that* much wood for our nightly fire? Of Sammy there is no sign. Then I see him staggering out of the gloom, towing a chopped-off section of one of the thorntrees behind him, which he carefully pulls into position

Our camp was right on one of the migration routes of the huge elephant herds in the Tsavo region

amongst some others. In the gloom I can now see that we are encircled by a ring of thorny branches, almost a child's copy of the huge thorn *boma* of the Maasai – Sammy is living up to his tribal customs! I ask what is going on and Danson looks up from his wood-chopping with a smile on his face. '*Mdofu*.' (Elephants.) I can't see what all the fuss is about. A few elephants in the region couldn't possibly do us any harm.

Sammy surveys his handiwork and shakes his head. He doesn't think it's going to do much good. Then to my surprise, he, the proud Maasai warrior, afraid of nothing, insists that I turn the car round so that its nose is pointing towards the road, 'Just in case!' Anything to oblige. Supper? No one has thought of it. We sit down round the fire in the dark and share a tin of corned beef and some crackers. I start teasing the two of them about being so scared when I hear it . . . a trumpeting scream somewhere not so far away in the darkness and the sound of branches cracking like pistol shots. Sammy looks at me, eyes wide and face in a set grin, teeth flashing in the firelight. Danson starts giggling and I finally prise out of him what has been going on while I've been away.

Danson heard the elephant as dusk was falling and, knowing that Sammy comes from the Lake Magadi district, futher north where there are no elephant, decided to play a prank on him and told him that they are very clumsy creatures and have such small eyes that they are almost blind and the greatest danger is being stepped on. This was too much for Sammy who insisted on Danson collecting enough firewood for us to have the fire burning all night so that the elephants can see us, while he tried to build a wall round the camp to stop them crossing and maybe treading on him.

I try to explain to him logically that elephants can see just as well as human beings and that there is absolutely no danger of them treading on him by accident – when the cracking and trumpeting increases in volume, coming nearer and nearer. Danson looks at Sammy and Sammy at Danson and, without a word, the two of them get up, with a sheepish smile for me, and vanish into their tent, lacing the door up carefully, and I am left alone in the flickering firelight. I throw a few more logs on the fire and go into my tent to write up the day's notes. Instead of moving away, the noises come closer and I find it very difficult to concentrate on something that seems so trivial as the exact location of the mongooses at ten-fifteen this morning. The cracking and trumpeting are now reaching alarming proportions, accompanied by deep gurgling rumbles. The noise seems to be on both sides of the camp and not very far away. I grab my torch, turn the beam to 'narrow' and flash it along the lines of trees. A row of shining pink eyes is there at about crown level, eyes that disappear into the gloom as their owners turn away. Judging from the noise, I reckon that there must be at least twenty of the huge pachyderms around the camp. I call to the boys to come and build up the fire but all is silent in their little tent under the Commiphora tree. I look at my watch; almost eight o'clock. With luck, this group will have passed us within a few minutes.

At eleven o'clock I am still there, hunched over the fire. The parade of elephants has been non-stop during this time. Our camp must have been pitched right in the middle of one of their traditional pathways. The night is still filled with their trumpetings and squealings and their deep rumbles of reassurance for the more timid herd members as they go past. I have a rather fatalistic attitude to it all, though I can't help being worried in case there is an animal in the huge herd which has been wounded or still carries a poacher's poisoned arrow in its body and has a right to fear and hate man. I feel extremely vulnerable, crouching next to my dwindling fire. If an elephant decides to attack, there would be little I could do about it.

In general, elephants are very peaceful animals. When they do decide to attack, though, they are awe-inspiring. What now comes into my mind is an encounter I had once with a female leading a small calf. She had obviously got separated from her herd and was very nervous indeed. I was parked close under some trees just after dawn when I heard her approaching, crashing through the bush, alternately squealing and rumbling and shaking her head from side to side. She was only about twenty yards away and I hoped she would pass by, leaving me in peace, but then she saw the car. With a trumpet she wheeled to face me. There was no chance of my getting away as she blocked the only route I could take. Then followed one of the most frightening five minutes of my life. She charged the car, ripping off tree branches and uprooting bushes as she came, throwing them at it, wheeling away once more only to repeat the performance over and over again. The car was covered with twigs, grass, earth, anything she could get hold of. I remained still as a stone within it so as to give her no focus for her unwelcome attentions. I remember staring out of the windscreen and seeing only her feet and toenails, the rest of her being busily employed in smashing the branches of the tree above me down onto the car roof. Her trunk fastened round the front bumper and the car was heaved up and down. I don't know what would have happened if rescue hadn't come in the form of an impala buck which broke out of the bushes about twenty-five yards to my right. With a trumpet of rage, trunk outstretched and ears spread, she was after him like a flash, her baby hard on her heels, and I heard the crash of her passage through the bush dwindle into the distance. My car was left looking like a garden rubbish dump, covered with dirt, leaves and branches, a large part of which had got through the open roof hatch into the interior. I found myself trembling violently in the aftermath of this amazing performance. It was a fact, I now discovered, that one could be soaked in a cold sweat in over a hundred degrees in the shade.

Finally tiredness overcomes fear and I crawl into bed, still dressed in case I have to get up quickly during the course of this astonishing night. I lie there, listening to the cracking and elephant talk until I drift off to sleep at about one o'clock, at which time it has shown no sign of abating. I am almost surprised to find the camp and myself still in one piece the next morning. The sun is already up by the time I awake and, on hearing me stir, Danson and Sammy crawl rather shamefacedly out of their tent. We survey our surroundings. I notice a toppled tree only a few yards away from the *boma* wall, sap still oozing from its broken roots. Only about forty yards from my tent stand the sad remains of a large Boswellia thorntree, now only a shattered remnant of its former self, a chewed stump surrounded by a ring of thorny twigs. The branches are gone, eaten by one of the hungry animals in the night. I get into the car and take a drive around – and then I realise fully what the elephants have been up to. After the third puncture within an hour, I now have no spare tyres and must head back to camp to mend the punctured ones. I start to curse them. The whole ground is littered with twigs from the thorntrees, torn off and munched by the elephants as they passed. Although, when fresh, the thorns bend easily, a few hours in the sun have turned them into steel spines, each about eight inches long, which can penetrate even the heavy-duty Landcruiser tyres with ease like a needle through butter.

I try to stop before every twig I see and move it out of the way so that I can drive past, for with a puncture now I would be stuck, the tyre levers and repair outfit being far away. I move at a crawl past the waterhole and can hardly believe my eyes. Where yesterday a small puddle of water still lay in the cracked mud of the banks, today, what little is left resembles pea soup with dumplings floating in it. Totally undrinkable, no matter how filtered and boiled! Back at camp at last, I unload the punctured tyres and we set to work repairing them, none of us very expert, and it takes a long time to prise the big tyres off the rims so that we can get at the damage. The thorns stick out of the hard casing like knitting needles and we have to take the pliers to break them off. Since the day has been spoiled anyway by my getting up so late and the punctures effectively making me even more so, I decide to take this opportunity to make my fortnightly trip to Voi, about thirty miles away, to buy some fresh food, tinned supplies and the all-important petrol.

The first few miles along the dirt road are hazardous. The signs of elephant are everywhere, in the already-drying mounds of droppings, the uprooted trees which look as if they have not been strong enough to stand the elephants rubbing against them, and the ubiquitous twigs. I have been wondering what happened to the thorntrees which I have seen toppled all through this bush country, and now I realise that it is the elephants that must have been responsible for pushing them over, bringing light and space into the tangle so that other plants can grow. One could almost term them the shapers of ecosystems.

Hours later, I reach Voi, a sleepy little town nestling between the hills of the eastern Taita range. No matter what time of day it is, Voi market is always in a bustle, the women in their butterfly colours crouched under the shade of the trees selling their wares, everything from potatoes and onions to pineapples, mangoes and tomatoes. The men seem to go in European dress, sunbleached, ragged and dirty for the most part; only the women have worn the more traditional khangas since our 'civilisation' came. Their chattering sounds loud after my habitual silence of the bush. I set about filling the car and jerrycans with petrol for the coming fortnight and buying supplies. The butcher has goat-meat to offer and I buy five pounds for tonight and tomorrow. Longer than that it won't keep and tomorrow's meal must be put on the fire to cook not long after daybreak if it is not to go bad. I select only the greenest fruit, with a few ripe ones for tonight's banquet, and then set about stocking up with tins which are going to be our staple for the coming weeks. The shopping spree is quickly finished, for our wants are few and I am back on my way to camp within an hour as I want to relocate the mongooses before it gets dark.

I find out later that the elephants that have just passed through the area were the largest herd seen here for the past ten years. The warden of Tsavo East National Park did an aerial survey and estimated that there were about six hundred animals. After hearing this, I am surprised that they didn't do more damage than they did.

3 Everyday Life

As the weeks went by, life began to fall into a routine that began before sunrise with my hurried preparations for a day in the bush and ended with my falling, tired out, into bed at night. My 'hard rations' varied little, except that the type of jam I ate on my crackers changed with the selection which the shops in Voi had to offer. Even supper took on a monotony regulated by the availability of different foods. With little or no rice, flour or maize to be had, we were forced to exist on potatoes (which were relatively plentiful) and macaroni – with or without its active insect inhabitants. We soon learned that it was easier to scoop them off the surface of the boiling water than to try and pick them singly out of the dried pasta.

Through a process of trial and error, we became rather efficient at keeping perishable foods in a climate where fresh food becomes uneatable within a period of time which can only be termed amazing to inhabitants of temperate zones. Plastic bags were like gold. Within them vegetables such as carrots would last for up to five days before shrivelling into thread-like shadows of their former selves. The only problem was that the bags had to be kept open otherwise their contents would rot in the heat, and an open bag with moist contents was an invitation to all and sundry. One of the main rules in the kitchen became: 'Never put your hand where you can't see where you're putting it, and shake up all open bags before picking things out of them.' This motto saved us from many an unpleasant accident ranging from relatively harmless encounters to potentially deadly ones. I never realised before that I had such quick reflexes – fast enough to whip my hand away as soon as something moved beneath it! Our vegetable bag visitors ranged from huge Hawk moths which came to drink the sap of the slightly rotting contents to the ubiquitous Scolopendra centipedes and little brown scorpions which had failed to find their way home to their holes or crevices during the night or had simply decided that their new home was better than their old one. The toad, which seemed to find our potato box the ideal hiding-place, became quite a friend, at least of mine. With Danson and Sammy, however, it was rather different. Both considered reptiles and amphibians of any kind a mortal danger and refused to touch them. I christened the toad 'Fred' and even picked him up and held him in the palm of my hand to show them that he was completely harmless, but it did no good. 'Touch a toad, touch a snake' was all that Sammy said in reply. The little geckos which scuttled between the sisal poles of the kitchen were received with the same yells of horror as the puff

My tent was pitched under the only tree to provide big shade for miles around

adders which persistently tried to colonise the equipment store and I couldn't change this by any means at my disposal.

Washing up became a ritual in itself. As soon as the boys poured the water from the jerrycans into the *kerai*, a large, metal round-bottomed bowl, Fred would get wind of it and come hopping over to land with a little 'plunk' right among the soapsuds (which didn't seem to worry him a bit!). A shriek from whoever it was whose turn it was to wash up and the call '*Memsab, Memsab, Njoo upesi!*' (Ma'am, ma'am, come quickly!) and I would have to leave whatever I was doing and go and rescue the boys from the depredations of poor old Fred who was having a lovely wallow in his bubble-bath. One evening I thought we had lost him, as he made the mistake of taking a flying leap into a *kerai* of hot water that Sammy had just brought from the fire, but hardly had his body submerged than he was out again in a flash and little the worse for his adventure. I thought this might have taught him a lesson about leaping into *kerais* of water without waiting to find out whether it was hot or not first, but his experience didn't seem to have sunk in. The next night he was back again and the pantomime went on as usual.

One evening, while I was enjoying the last rays of the sunset, my gaze drifted to the Grewia bush next to my tent which, since it was nourished with all the dirty water used in the camp, still carried a fair number of leaves, while its brethren in the surroundings were already bare. I changed the focus of my eyes and suddenly had the strange feeling that I was being watched from within the green latticework. Looking closer, I finally picked out one leaf which didn't quite look right from the way it was lying on the branch. Then the leaf moved and two eyes swivelled in my direction, regarding me almost wisely from two truncated cones. It was a large chameleon whose colour and form were so similar to the Grewia bush's leaves that it was practically invisible. I went over to pick it up to show it to Danson and Sammy. It gaped its mouth at me, showing its bright orange throat lining, and hissed loudly, struggling in my hand. The two boys ran over to look and then froze in horror. It was all I could do to stop them heading full tilt away from the camp. All the time I held the reptile in my hand, they kept at least three yards away from me and leapt backwards, shrieking half playfully, half in fright if I approached them. Again my logical and scientific assurances that the animal was completely harmless fell on deaf ears. Chameleons were the worst creatures that one could imagine, as far as they were concerned! To hear them talk, the animal must spend its life surrounded by a cloud of the deadliest poison and was capable of putting a curse on people even from a distance. I rather wanted to keep the lizard, which was a magnificent specimen, at least six inches long, as a sort of animated flycatcher in my tent, but the boys threatened me with desertion if I did so. Reluctantly I decided to let it go.

It took me a while to work out why the boys were so scared of the chameleon as they didn't want to talk about it and always changed the subject when I asked. Finally it turned out that their fear was based on an old hate which, in turn, was based on an old fairy story – I never found out from which land it originated. The story went that when God was making the world, he sent various animals to tell the people, who were all black-skinned at that time, to come and bathe in a special pool which would make their skins fair. To Africa he sent the chameleon which was so slow in getting there that by the time the people living in Africa heard the news and hurried to the pool, the water was all gone and all that was left was a tiny dribble in which they could wet the palms of their hands and the soles of their feet. As a result, all Africans now have fair skin only in these places. Because the chameleon was tardy, the Africans were furious and since this time, enmity has existed between the chameleon and themselves.

The boys' reaction on another occasion confirmed their absolute horror of cold-blooded creatures of all kinds. One day I had been lucky enough to find a large white cabbage for sale at Voi market and brought it back to camp in triumph. For storage purposes, it was put in a woven coconut leaf basket, a *kikapu*, and hung in our bush kitchen in the shade. When, a few days later, I decided to have it for supper, I told the boys to chop and boil it and went back to my tent to carry on writing up my field notes. I'd hardly started when a scream rent the air and the usual '*Memsab! Memsab*' call brought me dashing back to the kitchen again. Danson, wide-eyed and trembling, pointed to the *kikapu* and said that an evil spirit had invaded our cabbage. Totally nonplussed by this outburst, I asked him how he knew this. 'The cabbage has grown *eyes*,' he said, backing away from the offending basket. 'Nonsense!' I answered and opened the *kikapu* – and he was right! A pair of beautiful gold-flecked orbs were visible in a crack at the top of the vegetable, the owner of these having dug itself into the cool, moist interior. It was a large treefrog whose camouflaging ability had made it almost invisible in the cabbage leaves, only its beautiful eyes giving it away. I promptly evacuated it from its pleasant home and gave instructions that the boys should carry on making dinner, after I'd washed the offending opening in the cabbage. The cabbage was totally inedible to them after it had housed such a horror, and I had to eat it all by myself. Their scruples were greater than their appetites!

Although the boys were scared stiff of cold-blooded creatures, I was amazed at the way they dealt with what, to me, were much more dangerous animals. One evening, after we had all gone to bed, the quiet of the camp was shattered by a series of bone-shaking roars. All of us were on our feet in a flash. Danson grabbed the *panga*, our big bush knife, and Sammy his *rungu* – a self-made knobkerry cut from the root of a Boscia tree. Again the roars tore the night apart. They sounded as if they were coming from inside the camp itself and the volume was terrifying. Without the least hesitation, the boys grabbed brands from the dying camp-fire and rushed to the edge of the *boma*, waving their flaming torches and yelling into the darkness. I fumbled about looking for the torch while all this was going on, trying to light the lantern with the matches which spilled out of my fingers in my haste. Finally light shone through the blackness, despite my almost spastic efforts. I was terrified but the boys didn't seem to be scared in the least. In the beams of the torch two pairs of red-gold eyes reflected back the light. I spun round, shining the torch into the gloom. Seven pairs of eyes were there, some blinking out as the light hit them, others gazing impassively at this queer creature with the 'sun' held in its hand. A pride of lions had come to visit!

The coughing and roaring went on, punctuated by the boys' piercing yells and my teeth chattering with fear. Were these the same boys that had fled in terror from a harmless chameleon? I could see tawny bodies get up and move away with the languour that only cats seem to possess, only to lie down again at a distance and continue their vigil. Sammy and Danson kept watch on the camp perimeter while I busied myself with building up the fire. The lions were making no move to attack, but were also making no move to leave and kept at about twenty yards' distance. The boys' bravery didn't extend to leaving the partial shelter of the little thorn *boma* but they certainly didn't retreat into their tent in fear as they had done on the night the elephants came to visit. A sort of truce finally developed – the lions lying watching us and we staying near the safety of the fire. I still couldn't shake off the feeling that they were more interested in us from the standpoint of plain curiosity than as a potential meal and, when midnight had come and gone with no change in the situation, the old fatalism overcame me again. 'If they're *that* hungry, then they can come and get me'! – and I went to bed, the boys following soon afterwards after having left a blazing fire more as a symbolic threat than anything. It was certainly strange, though, to lie there in the darkness listening to the huge creatures purring like cats and to know that, should they *really* be hungry, nothing stood between them and me but a thin sheet of canvas! On awaking next morning I half-expected them to be lying there still but the bush was deserted. We heard their roars far off the next night, well to the south of the camp. After satisfying their curiosity as to these strange bush-dwellers who lived in canvas caves, the lion pride had moved on.

With the mongooses, too, life had taken on a routine. They had more or less come to accept me and the car although I still had to be very careful about moving quickly. Sometimes their wanderings would take them almost out of my range of vision and, reluctantly, I would have to move, knowing that by doing so I was scaring away every bush animal for miles around and that it would take hours of patient waiting before they drifted back. To minimise the effects of this disturbance as much as possible, I always tried to move the car during the midday hours when most of the animals were asleep or safe in their hiding-places, away from the burning sun. The system worked quite well although I always had the niggling feeling 'What have you missed? What would have taken place if you *hadn't* moved?' This, however, was one of the penalties I had to pay if I was not to lose my little band with whom I now felt a bond of familiarity.

I soon learned that how far and how fast the group moved was very weather-dependent. On overcast, relatively cold days, which were few and far between at this time of the year (January to April), they hardly moved from the mound they had been sleeping in except to make short forays into the bush in its immediate surrounds. If the day promised to be a hot one, they usually left relatively early and made an early stop for their siesta, their total foraging time rarely exceeding two and a half hours in the mornings and a further two and a half hours in the evenings. It was on days when the huge cumulus clouds sailed like galleons across the sky in rapid succession that I had the most trouble, as here the group could wander for up to eight hours a day, keeping to the shade of the trees when the sun was high and taking advantage of every cloud that passed to move onwards. On such days they could travel over a mile between sun-up and sun-down.

My map of the area started to increase in size and complexity as all the mounds visited by the mongoose group were named and charted in. They never seemed to sleep in a mound more than once, heading off to a new resting place each day, quartering the ground between the two mounds thoroughly as they went. There was no sign of them retracing their steps or of having special mounds in which they spent the night. Most of the ones they visited were the castle-like *Macrotermes* mounds, which were by far the most numerous in the area, there being one per twenty square yards at least. I soon found out, however, that these were not the only mounds that the mongooses used.

It was almost midday and the group's foraging had taken them about seventy yards away from where I was parked, the usual streamer of birds in tow. Around them was empty bush, as far as I could see, and I was familiar enough with the animals' habits by this time to realise that it was about time for them to go down for their siesta. The only problem was, where? The nearest *Macrotermes* mound was at least fifteen yards off and, as far as I could make out through the binoculars, the group seemed to have called a halt under a large, leafless Grewia bush and was not moving. The accompanying birds perched in its bare branches and also made no move to carry on. Then, one by one, they flew off and I realised I'd lost the mongooses! No sign of them anywhere! I started to get very worried as the chance of finding the group again once it had vanished into the tangle of scrub was pretty remote: I might have to drive around for hours before I could relocate them. Almost against my better judgement, I decided to drive over and have a look at what had happened, for from my present vantage-point, I could see nothing at all except empty bush all around me.

Creeping along in first gear as slowly as possible, I approached the place at which I had seen the mongooses vanish. There was a blur of motion in what looked to be a heap of dead twigs and I cut the engine immediately and waited, hardly breathing, to see what would happen next. A small head appeared like magic out of the ground and stared at me, its mouth opening, and loud and clear came the one sound I had dreaded hearing – *Tchrrr*. It was Whitethroat, not at all pleased at my close proximity or the noise I had made getting there. He was joined by Scar, Blackie and a subadult male about three years old with a small white patch of hair in the middle of his forehead whom I named Fleck. All the animals seemed very excited and kept flagging their heads up and down, fixating me with their sharp little eyes. Occasionally one would turn and vanish into the ground again, only to re-emerge almost immediately. I was obviously disturbing them greatly by being so close; the front bumper of the car was only about six yards from where they kept appearing and disappearing again. I was in a quandary – should I stay and hope that they would calm down or should I risk scaring them stiff and moving the car a few yards backwards? Their agitation became even more marked and Rusty, Goldie and Twin joined the excited throng. Of Diana, George and the youngsters, there was no sign. I finally took the hint, started the motor – which resulted in panic-stricken flight into the ground – and moved backwards.

It was about three-quarters of an hour later, when I had almost given up hope of seeing anything, that the first little head emerged and stared fixedly at me. All this time I had been scanning the place where I had seen the group disappear through the binoculars but was unable to see anything that looked remotely like a mound – at least as I knew it. With the emergence of Twin, however, I now had a focus for my search and, sure enough, once my eyes had been tuned in to what to look for, I managed to distinguish several holes amongst the tangle of twigs that looked like little meteor craters on the moon, surrounded by delicate low walls. My reference book informed me that these were mounds of a different termite species called *Odontotermes* which, in contrast to *Macrotermes*, has almost its entire nest underground, only the delicate walls surrounding the ventilation shafts protruding above the surface.

As I became more familiar with the mongooses' habits, and had collected more data on their daily wanderings, a curious fact started to emerge. Although the *Odontotermes* nests were few and far between and made up a total of only six per cent of the total mounds in the area, they were very much preferred as sleeping sites during the noonday hours. The mongooses would pass by what seemed to me to be perfectly adequate, if not downright ideal, *Macrotermes* mounds only to vanish into the ground at some point further along their path – an *Odontotermes* colony. What the reason for this was, I couldn't tell. It might be that they were cooler or that their internal structure was more roomy and thus more suited to whiling away the heat of the day. This was one of the questions I intended to investigate later, when I had the proper equipment.

Another thing that struck me was that not all the *Macrotermes* mounds in the area were visited by the mongooses. Some of them were bypassed, sometimes at a distance. One of the ones which they avoided I knew was inhabited by the puff adder I had seen on the first day on which I had discovered the group. A few of the other mounds that they circled around also had tell-tale white streaks down their sides which indicated that they were being lived in, but I did not see the inhabitants. I was tempted to go and peer into them but, knowing that the beautiful red Spitting cobras with their neat black collars, as well as their more sombre relatives, the grey cobras, found termite mounds the ideal hiding-place, I had no wish to put myself in unnecessary danger.

Apart from the cobras, pythons also made their homes in the larger mounds. One day, I noticed a white-streaked termite mound that was literally swarming with flies and stepped out of the car to have a look at what could have attracted them. As I approached the mound, the stench was terrific. Something was obviously very dead inside. Taking a stick, I poked into the hole and came up with a piece of rotting dik-dik skin, and then something moved sluggishly in the depths. I retreated hastily, but was rather puzzled. As far as I could tell from the clues available, it looked as if a python had managed to capture one of the little dik-diks that abounded in the bush, had dragged it to the safety of its home mound, but was then unable to swallow its prey, maybe because it was too big.

Not only reptiles inhabited the termite mounds. Some of the larger *Macrotermes* colonies were also lived in by birds, and these mounds also were avoided by the mongooses as they set off on their daily foraging excursions. Two species of birds lived there, both belonging to the same family, the barbets. The larger and more brightly coloured of the two, the Red and Yellow barbet, seemed to select mounds that had high chimneys and their homes were easily identified by the white streaks along the sides. The birds dug their nesting tunnels into the sides of the mounds and would perch on top of them to sing their duets. Their loud *toogel-de-doogel* was an everyday sound in the bush habitat, the female leading the chorus and her mate joining in so that the whole sounded like the song of a single bird. After the rains, when they had raised their crop of young, the youngsters would also take part in this curious ceremony and sometimes up to five birds would be singing at once. This mutual song-time seems to cement the bonds between the family, and, more important, the bonds between the breeding pair for, as far as is known, barbets mate more or less for life and use the same nesting site year after year if they are not disturbed.

Every day, on completion of my daily vigil on the mongoose group, I would drive off the distance they had covered and also the distance between their last resting place and the road, reading these off from the car's tacheometer. They were then added to scale on my map which was already of quite a large size. Owing to the restricted visibility, I had difficulty orienting myself to landmarks in the surroundings and had the feeling that the mongooses were leading me further and further into the tangle of thorn and that their wanderings would never have an end. I recorded carefully every mound they marked, and made notes as to the strength of the marking that took place there. Some mounds were rushed up to, their marking posts very carefully and extensively sniffed and then thoroughly marked over by Diana and Co. Others, on the other hand, were barely noticed from a marking standpoint. They got a desultory mark but that was all. What this all meant I did not know at present, but it was curious that only the mounds the mongooses slept in were marked; those they passed by on their foraging excursions were investigated but I never saw an animal mark there. I was beginning to think that all the marking really meant was something similar to the graffiti found in public places in our own civilisation: 'Diana and Co. slept here!' but then I realised that the marks were not only concerned with sleeping places.

On a few occasions, George would wander away from the main group and head directly towards a certain bush or fallen tree, sniff it and mark over it. Usually the rest of the group would join him at this within a few minutes. Something on the branches must have attracted him and the obvious answer was that another mongoose group must have passed that way sometime before and left their scent for him to find. Marking bushes and trees looked like perimeter marking and, since I had not seen another mongoose group to date, I began to wonder whether the Dwarf mongooses really did have territories whose boundaries and main points, such as sleeping mounds, were identified as belonging to the group concerned by their odour on them. The size of the territory must be enormous, though, for I had already followed the group now over an area of nearly one square mile and there was still no sign of them returning to their starting-point. As far as I could tell at present, they were truly nomadic. How they would go about defending an area of this size against intruders was also a problem. From my relatively high perch within the car, I could rarely see more than a maximum of fifty yards in all directions and their range of vision from the ground or, at the most, from the top of a termite mound, could not have been more than that and possibly much less.

By now I had managed to identify the two more retiring members of the family, both of them subadult females, very similar in size and probably age. I reckoned them to be about two years old. One of them, Victoria, was, like her mother Diana, rather greyish in colour and had a pointed, almost weasel-like head, while the other, Vanessa, was so like Goldie, only a little smaller, that I had probably got the two of them confused on many occasions. It took them much longer to get used to my presence than it did the other group members, and they would remain in the mound until the last and try and hide themselves in the middle of the group when it rested on one of the mounds. Although the group as a whole was now more or less tolerant of my presence, they still held a certain reserve towards me and I still had to be careful how I moved so as not to scare them.

When I started to use the long 400 mm lens to photograph them, as I wanted portraits for later indentification of individuals for my files, the emergence of this huge eye on its long stalk from the car window set the group into twittering panic. It took days of me patiently holding the camera up to show them it was not dangerous before they accepted it and I could take the photographs I wanted. This was quite a feat of strength, for with the big 400 mm objective attached, the whole thing weighed about nine pounds and I could manage to hold it steady for only about five minutes before I started getting cramp in my arms. So the mongooses had to get used to it in small doses, amounting to about an hour a day over a period of about a week.

The sign of my final acceptance by the group came quite unexpectedly. I had moved to their siesta mound during the heat of the day and was keeping my usual vigil, waiting along with the hornbills for the mongooses to emerge. The hornbills had even got used to me as well and would use the roof rack of the car as a perch from which to pounce on the locusts when the mongooses passed by. The mongooses, however, tended to make a big circle around the car still and eyed it with some trepidation. This time the group set out on a course which took it about fifteen yards in front of the car's bonnet and was swinging round headed parallel to the mound on the other side of the car when the hornbills gave the alarm and a grey, white-rumped shape shot overhead to land in a tree in front of me. The mongooses were in a quandary. I stood between them and the safety of the mound and the next safe hiding place was too far away to be reached in the time left to them. As a body they dashed towards me and vanished under the wheels. From beneath my feet the warning *tchrrrs* sounded loud and clear. I peered down carefully and there were Twin and Blackie, heads flagging, staring towards their mortal enemy in the tree beyond, from behind the safety of my front wheel! They spared me a quick glance and then turned their attention to the greater danger, the Chanting goshawk which, from the way it was craning its neck and bobbing its head up and down, wasn't quite able to work out what this was all about. The tasty mongooses had found shelter under a metal monster with a human in it! I was smiling with happiness inside. It seemed as if I had now descended the scale of dangers to lie at a position below that of the goshawk and, from this point on, the relationship between the group and myself changed in nature. They no longer considered me as an enemy as long as I didn't do something stupid and frighten them and would even forage under the car. Sometimes they would come up and sniff the tyres and try to investigate the metal bottom, standing on their hind-legs and scratching at the rust and dirt with their claws. The absolute pinnacle of trust came later when Blackie, who was always a bit forward and didn't seem to be afraid of anything, came trotting over with Notch in tow and the two of them lay down in the shade near my door and started to groom each other. Notch was obviously a little nervous and kept glancing up at me, but Blackie calmed her with reassuring nibbles in the neck ruff and the two of them lay there for many minutes before finally realising that the rest of the group was already far off and went bounding after them.

As the days went past I began to get the impression that Diana always knew exactly where she was going when she set off in the morning. The group seemed to forage along certain pathways which were rarely deviated from unless some danger blocked progress. If the group were forced to return to the sleeping mound because of some disturbance, they almost invariably retraced their steps once the danger had passed. Only on a few occasions was the plan changed and the group headed in the opposite direction. One of these occasions gave me one of the most lovely memories I have.

It was early morning and the group was just getting up and performing its usual morning rituals. Far off behind me in the bush I heard Brown-throated barbets calling raucously. These tiny birds can produce a sound totally out of proportion to their size, like a cockerel's crow in the body of a blue-tit! The noise was getting louder and moving in my direction. Diana and Co. had already set off down the mound and were headed south-west, Rusty on guard in the sun-bleached stumps protruding from the mound's tip. The Fischer's and Golden-breasted starlings joined the Brown-throated barbets in their scolding and a pair of the beautiful Lilac-breasted rollers came swooping over to add their two-pennyworth as well. I craned my neck but could see nothing at present. Rusty was balancing rather precariously on tiptoe at the tip of one of the stumps, staring off behind me. The scolding increased in volume as whatever it was that was being mobbed slowly approached. There was a slight rustle behind me and I turned my head slowly to look. Out of the shrivelled bushes strode a magnificent cheetah, totally oblivious of the feathered folk chattering and screaming above him. He deigned to glance at me with his beautiful amber eyes, stalked past the car only about ten yards away from me – breathless at seeing this beautiful hunter at such close quarters – and vanished into the bushes beyond, his speckled coat throwing a cloak of invisibility around his shoulders as soon as he entered the dappled light and shade.

Rusty by this time had become almost frantic and was screaming warning at the top of his voice. The group headed back to the mound at a flat-out gallop and vanished inside, little heads poking out now and again, looking in the direction in which the big cat had gone and giving the ground predator call at the highest intensity that I had heard to date. Hardly had the first cheetah disappeared into the thorny tangle when a second followed close on his heels, turning his head to give me a quick glance and thereafter ignoring me completely, carrying on his way with a fluid, slow-measured tread that made his muscles ripple under his flecked coat, tail carried with its tip curled at a jaunty angle. I was still so awed by these magnificent creatures that I didn't even think of grabbing my camera until it was almost too late. As I turned to pick it up a third cat paced out to follow the other two. In my haste to get f-stop and shutter speed set before I tried to take a photograph, everything seemed to go wrong and, by the time I had finished, the three brothers, which was

I stare hard in the direction in which all the little heads are pointing

probably what they were as they were all males, had disappeared into the thorntrees and all that I could see were sections of bodies that merged so beautifully with their background that, had they not moved, they would have been completely invisible.

After all this excitement, it took more than an hour for Diana and Co. to calm down again and set off foraging, not south-west as originally planned, but in the opposite direction, north-east, as far away from the huge cats as possible. It was on comparison of this incident with two others that occurred later that I came to realise my original concept of all creatures that moved on the ground being enemies was erroneous and that the mongooses did differentiate between real dangers and mere disturbances, since they responded differently afterwards. The group would always flee to the safety of the mound as soon as anything stirred in the grass or bushes, but my impression was that they did so more in order to determine whether the disturbance was a real danger or not for, from the vantage-point of the mound, much was visible which would be invisible from the depths of the grass.

The two incidents that evoked different responses were in connection with herbivores – elands and zebras. On the first occasion, it was towards evening and the light was starting to reach the stage of the lovely golden glow so typical of many African sunsets. The wind in the branches had dropped and, apart from a few birds singing, all was quiet. The mongooses had been foraging for nearly half an hour, mostly in the vicinity of the mound in which they had spent their midday nap. Blackie and Fleck were on guard, then I saw Blackie start, freeze and begin the head-flagging that signalled the approach of something through the bush. His eyes were much better than mine, even with the help of the binoculars, for all I could see were dark shadows and golden light. He and Fleck started warning violently. The hornbills flew upwards and the rest of the group rushed back to the mound. I stared hard in the direction in which all the little heads were pointing and then I saw a patch of golden light move. By this time a rattling was very audible and I realised I had been staring at the creatures which were making it for the last minutes but the frame of reference I was using was completely wrong. Instead of some tiny creature skulking through the grass, I should have been looking for something the size of a cow! What was approaching was a huge herd of eland. Mothers with tiny calves by their sides stood and let their youngsters suckle while a truly enormous and majestic bull made the rounds of his ladies, sniffing their posteriors and lifting his head with its curled upper lip in the typical gesture of 'flehmen' – testing their urine to determine whether or not they were ready to mate. The whole group was upwind of me and took no notice, browsing the dried leaves from the bushes. Now I knew what to look for, I could focus my glasses to bring the animals into startling nearness. I could even see the bull's eyelashes and the tufts of hair around the base of his horns.

The herd moved slowly nearer and the mongooses remained on the mound watching them, only occasional *tchrrrs* breaking the silence. The giants of the antelope world, despite their size, moved almost soundlessly through the bush. Soon they were no more than fifteen yards from the car, the herd splitting to pass by on either side of me. The mongooses still kept up their watch but more voices were joining the *tchrrr* chorus now as the eland neared. Then the inevitable happened. The first animals came downwind of me and caught my scent. A trumpet-like snort broke the peace and then there was pandemonium. Huge bodies leapt sideways in enormous leaps that took the animals above the lower branches of some of the thorntrees and before I could look round, the place was deserted. Only the sound of snorting disappearing in the distance accompanied by the sound of twigs breaking as bodies broke through them was left of that which, only seconds before, had been an almost magical scene.

The leaping away of the eland had caused panic amongst the mongooses which had retreated into the safety of their mound, but within a few minutes they were out again and headed off towards the south-east, which was the direction from which they had fled when Blackie and Fleck had given the

Zebras stop under one of the Commiphora trees which overshadow the mound and the mongooses watch their giant visitors from a safe distance ▶

warning. It seemed obvious that, as far as Diana was concerned, about fifty eland were not as dangerous as three cheetah, for she led the group almost in their wake along the same pathway that she had been moving along before.

Zebra are some of the shyest of the bush inhabitants and I rarely managed to spot them in the thornbush, for the stallion of the herd would see me or catch wind of me long before I realised they were there. His barking warning would be followed by a thunder of hooves and then quiet – he and his mares had fled to safety away from the man-smelling metal monster. It was with some surprise, therefore, that about ten o'clock one morning, Fleck, who was on guard, gave the warning that something was approaching. The rest of the group came running up the mound and sat there, staring in the direction in which his flagging head pointed, and I did the same. My attention was drawn to something black which moved from side to side, then I could pick out several such black objects but it took me a while to realise that these were attached to tails which, in turn, were attached to zebras which were so perfectly camouflaged by their striped coats in the shadows of the bushes that I could hardly see them at all. They were upwind of me and slowly moving in my direction, heads lowered and eyes half-closed. They came within about twenty yards of the car and five of the mound on which the entire mongoose family was sitting, just staring at the approaching bush horses. The zebras stopped under one of the larger Commiphora trees which overshadowed the mound and threw more shade than could be found anywhere else around, turned and stood in pairs, head to tail like a herd of ordinary horses, and proceeded to have a snooze, whisking the flies away from the faces of their partners. I was intrigued as to what the mongooses would do. They made no move to run or even to dash to safety in the mound's interior.

Half an hour later, the situation was the same. The mongooses were sitting about, grooming each other or lying in the shade thrown by the mounds' buttresses while the zebra continued their rest. Only a few of the subadults showed any more interest in them and would sometimes go into a position I called 'high-sit', standing on tiptoe on their hind-legs to get a better look. Then the stallion woke up and led his little group of mares slowly away. As soon as the zebra started to move, the whole mongoose group was on the alert but they still made no move to safety and just watched their huge visitors. Once the striped coats had melted back into the stripes of light and shadow all around, Diana got up and set off down the mound, heading towards where the zebra had held their siesta, moving through the area and beyond it to another mound barely visible amongst the trees. It really looked as if she had planned to hold her own siesta at this particular mound and just had to wait until the zebra moved before she could lead her family where she wanted to go.

It was situations like these that made me wonder how intelligent the mongooses really were. It was clear that they could distinguish potentially dangerous bush inhabitants from non-dangerous ones although they responded to the non-dangerous ones with what amounted to a 'We'll keep an eye on them, just in case!' strategy. What was even more interesting, though, was that these observations indicated that Diana, at least, had a very good comprehension of the area in which she lived and knew all the mounds and the ways in which they could be reached and deviated little from the route she had decided on beforehand. Even I, as a human with a much greater brain capacity than the mongooses, had difficulty remembering the characteristics of various mounds and where they lay in relation to others but I never gained the impression that Diana did.

Despite their small size, mongooses are in fact highly intelligent animals. I am often greeted by surprised looks when people ask me to what group of mammals the mongooses are related, and I say – hyenas. Despite their body form, which is reminiscent of a weasel or marten, the mongooses have no relationship with the family of the Mustelids and are placed in a group called the Viverrids which also includes the civet and genet cats. Most of the mongooses are solitary or pair-living animals and only a few, such as the Dwarfs, Bandeds and the Cusimanses of West Africa, have taken to living in groups, probably as a protection against predators, especially birds of prey. It is always more difficult for a raptor to pick a single individual out of a group than to capture a solitary animal, especially when all members of the group are on the lookout for such a danger and warn their companions. In the Dwarfs' case it seemed that this protection was even augmented by outsiders – the birds, and the hornbills especially. The short, sleek body form and camouflaging brownish colour which these animals have adopted during the course of evolution make spotting them even more difficult and, in contrast to the solitary species, which are mostly nocturnal or live in habitats where the cover is so thick that birds of prey would have difficulty in attacking them, all the social mongooses are day-active and have invaded habitats which are more open, and thus more dangerous. It almost looks as if they were forced to adopt a group mode of life as a means of survival in this harsh environment.

The mongoose's intelligence cannot be disputed. Kipling was never more right than when he said of Rikki-tikki-tavi: 'It is the hardest thing in the world to frighten a mongoose, because he is eaten up from nose to tail with curiosity. The motto of all the mongoose family is "Run and find out".' My tame ones, which live in my house with me, all know their names and various commands, learning how to live with humans and what is and what is not allowed with a rapidity which rivals that of the dog. What they have in far greater measure than dogs is, however, just what Kipling remarked on . . . curiosity. Nothing is safe from them and everything that can be overturned is overturned and

In order to gain their confidence quickly, I decided to feed a group of wild mongooses to the north of my research area. It took only a few days before they begged like little dogs whenever they saw me

thoroughly investigated, their busy little paws and noses storing the information gained in their truly amazing memory. I had had an example of this the
previous year with a wild group to the north of my present study area. I had
wanted to take photographs of them and, in order to gain their confidence
quickly, had decided to feed them. It took only a few days for them to associate
the presence of a manna of fried chicken with me and that I was not dangerous
but a friend instead. They would come when I gave a particular call and would
sit in rows, like little dogs begging, for their daily bounty. After three weeks I
had to leave for Europe once more, and thought I would never see my little
friends again. The next year, almost fifteen months later, I decided to make a
quick visit to see if I could relocate them. I went to one of their favourite
mounds and called. Within a few minutes, a stream of little bodies approached
me through the grass, came right up to the car and stood on their hind-legs
begging. They had recognised my voice and knew exactly who I was, and
where was the chicken please? Luckily I had brought some with me, so they
were rewarded for their incredible behaviour.

Other observations I made on mongooses' ability to orient themselves in the
maze of termite mounds and thornbushes made me wonder whether it was

Diana alone who possessed this amazing ability to find her way. My laboratory studies had shown that the alpha female, or 'queen' of the group, was a very special animal. Not only was she the only one who was 'allowed' to have and raise youngsters but she weighed almost a third as much again as the other females in the group, tipping the scales at nearly one and a half pounds. I was once able to watch how a low-ranking female became alpha when the group's original leader had been lost. The battle of rank was fought out between her and two other eligible females but not in any way I have ever heard of in any other species of animal. Instead of outright fighting, the trio started to groom each other vigorously, salivating copiously as they did so. The lowest-ranking of the animals soon gave up and relinquished the field to the two main contestants which, from the point of view of rank and age, were more or less equal. The grooming, however, was not the usual friendly neck-nibble but very forced, and one animal would try and put her forepaws on the back of the other and nibble it between the shoulders and along the backbone until she was dislodged by the partner reciprocating this act. During the first few days, the roles of groomer and groomee changed regularly, the situation sometimes exploding into upright threat postures, both animals on their hind-legs and facing each other, mouths gaped, but then subsiding into grooming again. Slowly, as the days went by, the antagonists, who were almost permanently dripping wet from all this nibbling and saliva, fell into a routine until finally, only one of them would be on top consistently, the other crouching and letting itself be groomed and showing no attempt to reciprocate. Then suddenly, it was all over. The female which had been doing all the grooming towards the end was the acknowledged new leader of the group and the other accepted her subordinate position and I never saw any more aggression between them. Once the new 'queen' had asserted her rights, she selected one of the males to become her consort, one with which she had often been together prior to this, and the group continued as if nothing had happened.

This curious system seemed to be a means by which contests could be carried out without damage to the combatants, for Dwarf mongooses can fight viciously should the need arise. In this way, the group would still be together and no one would be expelled or even hurt. Within three weeks of gaining alpha status, the female in question increased her weight by more than fifty per cent, developed the thick neck-ruff typical of alpha females, stopped playing with the rest of the group (something in which she had previously been very active) and made all the decisions as to where and when they would move anywhere. Science is still not far enough along to explain this startling change in physiology and behaviour brought about simply by a change in social status.

I wondered whether one of the 'duties' on becoming alpha was to recall to memory the routes along which the group wandered and to lead them along these, it not being necessary for lower-ranking females to store, or rather to recall, this information. What led me to this conclusion were three occurrences in which group members became separated from the rest of the group and had great difficulty in rejoining them. On one of the occasions, I was the cause of the trouble. Diana and Co. had foraged far off one afternoon and I could barely see the birds, let alone the mongooses, so I reluctantly decided to drive over and try to relocate them before they vanished completely. I knew I would disturb things, but at this time I did not know to what extent, or the insight that my decision would bring me on some of the aspects of the mongooses' behaviour that had been a puzzle up until now.

I set the car at a crawl and followed behind the vanishing group. The birds all flew off in panic so that I could no longer pinpoint the group's last position. When I thought that I had just about reached the right place, I cut the motor and waited. After about half an hour I began to get worried as there was no sign of the mongooses or the birds returning. When I had virtually given up hope, two Red-billed hornbills flew down to a patch of bush about twenty-five yards to my left and, almost simultaneously, the Yellow-bills flew down to an almost hidden termite mound way off to my right. I then realised with horror that I must have driven right into the middle of the foraging group and half had gone one way and half the other! Through the binoculars, I could see Diana, George, two of the youngsters and three or four other animals on the termite mound. In the bushes, however, apart from fleeting glimpses of brown bodies moving, I could identify no one. The group on the mound set off in a direction behind it, the opposite one to the car and the rest of the group. A small body scrambled up into the twigs of a low acacia and looked all around, calling 'Where are you?' – a distinctive, far-carrying call sounding like a rapid *tsee-tsee-tsee-tsee- TSEE* – but there was no response from the group near the mound which seemed to be headed off, totally oblivious. Four animals sprang onto a log to my left – Notch, Whitethroat, Rusty and Victoria. It was Fleck who was in the acacia bush and soon their voices joined his in a chorus of 'Where are you?'s, but all to no avail. The little cavalcade started back the way they must have come, heading right up to the car but, since I had disturbed them so much, they no longer considered it as neutral and turned back into the safety of the bushes again. Then Notch started trying to circle me from the back, the rest of the group trotting after her in Indian file, their 'moving out' call interspersed with occasional plaintive 'Where are you?'s. The route she was taking was leading them in almost the opposite direction, away from the rest of the group, but she didn't seem to notice this. Finally, the two groups were almost a hundred yards apart and moving further and further away with every passing minute. I was furious with myself for messing things up by bursting in amongst them as I had, and worried in case I had initiated a group break-up, which was the last thing I wanted at this stage when I was just starting to get important data on inter-individual relationships within the group.

Notch with her little party in tow started to swing round in the same general direction as the rest of the group but running parallel to it about a hundred and fifty yards away by now. I could still hear faint 'Where are you?'s but Diana and Co. didn't respond to them at all and continued their lazy foraging. The same situation prevailed for the next hours, Notch and party zig-zagging through the bush, looking totally lost, and Diana and Co. slowly foraging along a line which would take them to a medieval-castle-like mound called Tintagel. Dusk was starting to fall and the two groups had still not made contact. Notch was trotting in ever-widening circles, her little band of followers close behind, sometimes approaching Diana to within about seventy yards, at other times disappearing entirely into the bush, far away to the south. Her 'Where are you?' calls were becoming less and less emphatic; sometimes only her jaws would move and no sound would emerge. I felt very sorry for her and almost wished I could point Diana and Co. out to her and say 'Look – here they are!' but, of course, that was impossible.

By about five-thirty Diana and Co. landed up on Tintagel and poor Notch was still scouring the surrounds for some sign of them. I was surprised that no one in the group had given the answering call 'Here I am!' – a loud, prolonged form of the contact call, to help the rest of the family orient themselves. Nothing, however, was forthcoming from Diana's side. As the shadows lengthened, I began to gain the impression that Notch was getting frantic. Her trot was broken by periods of long bounds and the 'Where are you?'s could be heard clearly from the car. The last swing round of the group brought them to within fifty yards of the rest of the family, now stretched out and grooming each other on Tintagel, and I saw Notch stop and stiffen. She must have heard or smelt something as she set off at a run towards the mound, the others in hot pursuit. As she ran up the washed-earth apron surrounding it, George detached himself from his grooming partners and ran down to meet her. She and the rest of them stopped dead and George trotted to a solitary bunch of dried grass and commenced threat-scratching with an intensity that was new to me. Tail curved upward in an arc, eyes down, back arched like a cat, he proceeded to demolish the grass clump, every now and again glancing over to where Notch and the others stood watching him. Then, one by one, they approached, bodies flattened to the ground and, with outstretched forepaws, patted him on the snout and head, giving the rapid, high-pitched 'greeting' or submission call, almost grovelling at his feet. Once this ritual had been completed, he stalked up the mound again towards the rest of his family, Notch and her little party following on behind. An orgy of neck-nibbles and anal grooming then broke out and the juveniles, especially, seemed very excited, running from one latecomer to another, sniffing their anal glands and giving them quick nibbles on the neck. Poor Notch looked exhausted, as did the rest of her band, all five of them flopping down wherever room could be found, lying flat like lizards basking, almost oblivious of the welcome they were receiving.

I now came to realise what George's threat-scratching must mean. I had wondered why he regularly went through this procedure every morning but couldn't work out why, as the only response it evoked under normal conditions was dropped eyes or heads turned away. After having seen the abject submission the same behaviour evoked in the lost group members I came to realise that this must be George's way of asserting his dominance and, had the latecomers not responded as they did, they would probably have been attacked. It now looked as if the early morning threat-scratching simply meant 'I am the boss' and the other group members, by not challenging his assertion, were accepting this passively. In the case of Notch and party, however, who had been absent from the group for several hours, the need for assertion had been more acute. They had to prove, I took it, that they had not left of their own accord and were willing to subjugate themselves to George's domination once more.

I wondered how Notch had managed to relocate the group. There were two possibilities. Either she had heard their contact calls and headed towards them or she had picked up their scent. At present, I had no clue as to which was nearer the truth.

On another occasion it was almost evening and I was parked between two mounds called Log and Giant, and the mongooses were foraging off to the east of them and me. From the way they were headed, it looked as if they intended to spend the night at Giant but then, suddenly, with a flurry of wings, the hornbills took off vertically and a Pale Chanting goshawk shot through the branches to land in a tree almost in the middle of the foraging group. A flurry of close-packed brown bodies bounded past me and gained the safety of Giant. The goshawk just sat there, hoping for some stragglers, but none was forthcoming. It looked as if everyone had reached safety. The goshawk brooded, crouched on a branch staring at the mongooses, which almost seemed to jeer at him from the mound for they made no move to go in but just sat there, watching him and nibbling their fur. A slight movement on his part, though, would release a volley of *tchrrrs* and the activity on the mound would cease, all eyes turning towards the enemy. After such a bout of warning, I began to have the impression that there was another little voice adding its mite to the chorus, not from the mound but from a bush behind the tree in which the bird sat. The shadows lengthened as the day drew to a close and still the

A goshawk, perched at the top of a thorntree, stares fixedly at the mongoose guard, which in turn never takes its eyes off its enemy

goshawk had not moved. It was almost dark by the time he finally took wing, swooping, as usual, low over the mound with the mongooses on, almost, I gained the impression after seeing this behaviour on many occasions, as if he *wanted* to give them a fright. They dived for cover, then, after a few minutes, emerged again. I began to count them. Two were missing, Vanessa and Moja. I waited, straining my eyes in the gloom, ears pricked for the 'Where are you?' call but there was not a sound. Then what looked like a giant mongoose appeared, trotting through the grass at a tremendous pace, and as it drew closer I saw that it was Vanessa and Moja, Vanessa in the lead and Moja following so close on her heels that they looked almost like one animal. They were headed towards me down the game trail at a rapid trot. I thought all was well and that they would soon rejoin the group, but then Vanessa must have made a mistake and missed the turning which the rest of the company had taken to reach Giant and headed on towards Log. With Moja still close behind, she dashed up the side of the mound, realised her error, for there was no one there, called briefly 'Where are you?', then dashed down again, heading off this time on another path. This led her back in a circle in front of the car, still trotting at full speed, and again she took a wrong turning and ended up on a game trail which took her well beyond her starting-point in the bush. Then she and Moja appeared again, trotting down the trail they had used the first time until they arrived at the point where the others had branched off towards Giant. Here Vanessa stopped suddenly, sniffed the grass at the side of the trail opening and, without hesitation, trotted full speed along it, Moja still looking as if he was attached to her by a short thread. Within a minute they had regained the rest of the party, George had gone through his threat-scratching ceremony, and the two of them had been welcomed with open arms by the rest of the family.

It was very obvious from this that scent laid along the trail, just by the bodies brushing against the grass as they passed, was an important clue for lost group members and enabled them to locate and rejoin their group if they happened to have become separated from it. It was only rarely, however, that the animals made mistakes, as Vanessa did on this particular evening, and usually there was no problem in finding the main group again after a brief separation. It was through such 'mistakes', though, that I was able to gain a better insight into what means of communication the animals used and how the system of pathfinding functioned.

To date, I had never observed any form of going and looking for the lost ones although I knew, from my tame animals, that mongooses would retrieve lost babies, even dashing into dangerous situations in order to save them. All I had seen here, though, was at the most, an increase in the volume of the contact calls which were equivalent to a 'Here I am'. The youngsters in

Diana's group were all about six months old by this time and well past the age of being retrieved, but one incident showed me that the mongooses could be very flexible in their behaviour from this point of view.

It had been a baking hot afternoon and the bush was almost totally deserted. Nothing moved. Then, by about three-thirty, the mongooses got up from their siesta and, with their bird friends in tow, went foraging along a line of trees, keeping to the relative cool of their shade. The familiar branch-rattling of an approaching dust-devil had me scrabbling about in the car, trying to pin down all moveable objects, then the most amazing sight greeted my eyes. Galloping through the bush at full speed and zig-zagging left and right came a little grey bush duiker and, hard on his heels, the red cone of the dust devil. It almost looked as if the swirling air was following the poor creature as its zig-zags simply had the effect of bringing it directly into the dust devil's path again! With a roar, the procession shot through the line of trees and vanished into the bush, the duiker still being chased by its strange tormentor. As they passed where the mongooses had been foraging I caught a glimpse of bodies tumbling towards the mound where they had held their siesta, tails sucked almost vertically by the swirling air. The dust devil and duiker must have passed right through their ranks.

After this tremendous disruption of their peaceful afternoon, the mongooses were very tardy in making a second appearance and it was almost an hour later before the first little head emerged to look around and see if all was clear. Then, within a short while, the rest of them trotted out and the group went off on its foraging again. My eyes were glued to them so it was some time before I noticed that, far off in the direction in which the dust devil and duiker had headed, a little figure sat forlornly on a solitary termite mound, calling plaintively, almost at the edge of my range of hearing, 'Where are you?' It was Tatu. Somehow, in the scramble, she must have been driven along in front of the dust devil and the harassed duiker and had now landed up on a mound almost a hundred yards away. Diana's plans for the afternoon seemed to have been thwarted by the dust devil incident and, instead of heading off in a relatively straight line, she led the group in a curve around the siesta mound, foraging slowly, and it looked as if she intended to spend the night there. Tatu made no move to leave her perch and I could see her mouth opening and closing, although she was all but inaudible. Finally, dusk fell and Diana led the group to the siesta mound and they started to settle in for the night.

Tatu must have spotted them as she started trotting frantically round and round the top of her mound, calling 'Where are you?' louder and louder but still making no move to run over and join the rest of the family. Diana and George increased their contact call volume and looked towards her but made no move to head in her direction either. Tatu was now calling almost continually and her agitated trotting was getting wilder and wilder, but still she made no attempt to move down the mound to join them. By this time it was nearly dark and I felt very sorry for her. Diana and Co. were still calling 'Here I am', but it looked as if Tatu just wasn't brave enough to take up their invitation. She had almost fifty yards of relatively open ground to cross before she reached safety and this was simply too much to ask of a rather weakly juvenile. When it was almost completely dark and Tatu's cries had reached the point of hoarseness and she was sitting huddled and dejected on her mound, Diana, George and Victoria suddenly got up, headed down their mound and, keeping to cover as well as they could, set off to find her. The rest of the group stayed where they were, craning their necks to watch the leaders and scanning the sky and bush to give immediate warning should danger appear. Finally the rescuers arrived on the mound and Tatu went into what looked like transports of delight. She flung herself at her mother, nibbling her all round her neck and licking her face, then turned to George who suddenly grabbed her from behind and rubbed his cheek glands along Tatu's back, not letting her go until he had finished, despite Tatu's struggles. Once this had been completed, George also got a grooming, as did Victoria, then the four of them headed back to the rest of the family.

I was very curious about George's cheek-marking of Tatu as I had never seen one animal cheek-marking another except in rather tense situations such as just before a fight was about to break out between two groups. It was difficult not to be anthropomorphic about the situation and liken it to times when my own children had been late home at night and, instead of being hugged and kissed, had got a smack on the bottom instead. It was obvious that George was very excited and maybe even angry at what had happened and that he had expressed his emotion by rubbing his cheek gland scent over his youngest daughter.

This, however, was the only time I was able to observe retrieval of a group member by other group members and it may have been a special case as Tatu was still a youngster and the smallest and weakest of Diana's last litter. Usually the lost one had to regain the group under its own steam; it was rare for the group even to stop and wait for stragglers. These observations all led me to the conclusion, though, that it was Diana that was the one who knew where to go and how to get there and it was the rest of the group's business to see that they stuck by her.

It was only after about four weeks of following the mongooses through the bush and trying to piece together, bit by bit, a map of the area they moved through, that a picture started to emerge. The penny finally dropped one afternoon after I had followed the group southwards for more than ten days, and charted over two hundred termite mounds. The mound on which the

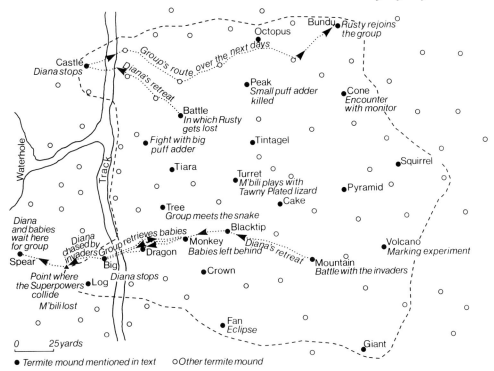

Octopus
Bundu *Rusty rejoins the group*
Castle *Diana stops*
Group's route over the next days
Diana's retreat
Peak
Small puff adder killed
Cone *Encounter with monitor*
Waterhole
Battle *In which Rusty gets lost*
Fight with big puff adder
Tintagel
Squirrel
Track
Tiara
Turret
M'bili plays with Tawny Plated lizard
Pyramid
Cake
Tree
Group meets the snake
Blacktip
Diana and babies wait here for group
Diana chased by invaders
Group retrieves babies
Monkey *Babies left behind*
Dragon
Diana's retreat
Volcano *Marking experiment*
Spear
Big
Crown
Mountain *Battle with the invaders*
Point where the Superpowers collide
Log
Diana stops
M'bili lost
Fan
Eclipse
Giant

0   25 yards

● *Termite mound mentioned in text*   ○ *Other termite mound*

Diana and Co.'s 'home range' in the Taru

group was now spending siesta looked rather familiar. The curious curved stump poking out of its top looked like a crouching Vervet monkey and then I knew – we had come full circle and were back in the region of Dragon and Monkey again! The animals were not real nomads, wandering goalless through the wide expanse of bush, but had an enormous home range, as the area in which they live is termed. Consulting my map that evening, I came to the conclusion that Diana and Co.'s home range covered an area just under two square miles, and they made the complete circuit of it in approximately four weeks. This would make my further studies on the animals much easier as I now knew roughly where they would be at certain times and how long it would take them to travel from one end of their area to the other. I tried to explain this to Sammy and Danson that evening but it was very difficult as the Swahili dictionary didn't seem to contain the right words and my vocabulary was very limited. I think by the time I'd finished they must have thought the mongooses very strange creatures indeed.

I began to relish the evenings at camp where the stars seemed only feet above my head and I could sit in the quiet and listen to the night-walkers of the bush going about their business. A little aardwolf, a relative of the hyenas, would pass by on his search for termites, the road from his den leading right past the *boma* walls, and on full-moon nights I could see him clearly, a Striped hyena in miniature, his fox-like face turning to stare at me as he trotted by. Sometimes a family of Bat-eared foxes would pass, their roly-poly puppies trotting along behind their parents whose huge ears turned this way and that continually, picking up every sound around. On occasion the Striped hyenas would start their ghostly *whooo-oops* from the bush nearby and, when the moon was full, the Pale Chanting goshawks would call and soar upwards in circles like toy aeroplanes, silhouetted against the sky. Although the business of life and death was going on all around, the impression was of a tremendous peace only broken now and again by the *hoo-hoo-hoo-hoo-HOO* of the Verreaux's Eagle owls as they hunted hares and dik-diks in the shadows.

Underfoot the less pleasant night folk made our lives hazardous and I got into the habit of changing into my thick leather bush boots when I got home to prevent accidents. The most startling of our nocturnal visitors were the huge Solifugid spiders which scuttled everywhere with the speed of mice, some of them reaching the size of mice. With their first pair of legs stuck out stiffly in front of them, they would shoot across the open spaces, running with tremendous speed up and over anything in their path, even people. On more than one occasion I leapt up from the dinner table as one of these quicksilver monsters shot up my leg, into my shorts, realised its mistake and shot down again before I could do a thing. Although reputed to be non-poisonous, I had heard too many tales from old bush hands about the nasty bites they could deliver, bites that turned black and spread until the dead skin and tissues sloughed off, leaving a flat scar. The insects our lamps attracted were also very attractive for the scorpions, who would emerge from their holes as soon as it was cool and scuttle around looking for tasty morsels which they would grab with their pincers and sting to death with the poisoned arrow they kept in their tails. Holding tight to their struggling victim – usually a large dungbeetle or locust – they would wait for its struggles to cease, then devour it piecemeal. But it was the huge Scolopendra centipedes, which moved inexorably over the ground like something from H. G. Wells' *War of the Worlds*, their heads swinging from side to side as they searched out their prey, that really gave me the shudders. Twice now I had ended up with one in my bed, woken out of my sleep by something scrabbling along my neck or arm, and it was still a wonder to me that I had not been bitten on either occasion. Compared with the splendour around me, though, the care I had to take to avoid contact with these more unpleasant bush denizens was a small price to pay. Even the boys, who had been rather nervous about accompanying me into the bush to live there alone, were coming to love it and they would often come and call me to see a passing civet cat or the green glow of a genet's eyes, perched high in one of the trees. The bush has its own magic for those who open their eyes and their hearts to it.

4 Give Us This Day . . .

Although I had watched the mongooses for weeks and seen them spend most of their time hunting for food, I still didn't know in detail what they were eating. I knew that their diet consisted mainly of insects but I didn't know what kind. This fact alone made them especially interesting, for mongooses are true carnivores, not insectivores, yet they adopted, in this desert habitat, a diet which is much more typical of the insect-eaters, which are considerably more primitive animals from an evolutionary point of view. Their teeth, as well, bore witness to their dietary habits. The huge shearing carnassials typical of carnivores have, during evolution, been modified into tricuspid choppers, ideal for crunching up insects with their hard exoskeletons but less well adapted for gnawing meat from bones. Either that, or the Dwarfs had never evolved something like a carnassial tooth in the first place.

The mongooses, as a group, probably evolved in Africa, and from there radiated out to the tropics of the Old World. Here they occupy the niche taken in the Americas and temperate regions by the Mustelids – the weasel family. The majority of the twenty or so genera are solitary, nocturnal hunters and only four of them have become social and day-active, these four all being found in Africa. There is still a great deal of controversy about the actual number of mongoose species – or even genera – alive today and even the estimates of the Dwarf mongoose (which is found throughout the African dry bushlands from Somalia in the north down to Namibia and the Transvaal) vary enormously from a single species to six species with twenty-seven subspecies. They seem to fill a position midway between the dogs and the cats, showing many characteristics of both groups both anatomically and be-haviourally. Curiously enough, their closest relatives are the hyenas and they have no relationship with the weasel family at all, even though they look so much like them. The largest of the mongooses is the African Grey or Ichneumon which is over five feet in length, while my Dwarfs represent the other extreme, measuring only eighteen inches and weighing about a pound.

While I was in Nairobi I decided to visit the Palaeontological Section of the Natural History Museum there to try and find out what the ancestors of my little creatures looked like. They showed me a whole series of skulls of a Viverrid which lived in East Africa in the Miocene era, twenty-eight to eleven million years ago. This creature bore the name *Kichechia zamanae*, a phonetic rendering of the Swahili name for the little mongoose – *Kitete* or *Kicheche*. What amazed me, however, was that I could find practically no marked differences between the skull of this ancient forebear of the mongoose race and my Dwarfs! The teeth were very similar in structure and the skull size almost identical.

I returned to my bush home with all sorts of questions running through my head. Maybe the mongooses I was watching had not changed much in dietary habits and size for millions of years? This either meant that they were very primitive members of the mongoose family, which I had difficulty in believing, knowing their high intelligence level and complicated social life, or they had reverted somewhere along the line to a way of life more typical of their ancestors, probably to fit the needs of some moment lost in the dawn of their history. It was unlikely that *Kichechia* had the numbers and variety of predators that plague *Helogale*, the scientific name of the Dwarf mongoose, and maybe, millions of years ago, the animals that were to develop into the species of *Helogale* as we know them today, began to live in family groups (the old principle of 'safety in numbers') so as to exploit the rich insect fauna of the more open bush, this more or less shaping their evolutionary development. All is speculation, though, for fossils can tell us little about the behaviour and social structure of animals that left their bones for us to find millennia later. None the less, I began to regard my little friends with new eyes, trying to imagine what they had been like millions of years before and what the impetus was that had resulted in them, and a few of their relations, abandoning the solitary hunt for larger prey and taking to hunting for insects in packs. Our knowledge of the geology and palaeontology of the world is still meagre, and this could be a question that will have to be left for future generations to answer.

Most of the prey the mongooses were catching was small and, try as I might, it was almost impossible to see exactly what it was that they were crunching up in their sharp little teeth. I therefore decided that I would have to tackle the problem another way and see if I could identify the remains of the insects in their droppings. Dwarf mongoose faeces are almost dry when they are produced, the animals being very efficient in removing almost all traces of water from them through the walls of the large intestine, an absolute necessity in this habitat where there is rarely any free water to drink and the fluid necessary to nourish body tissues must be absorbed from food. It was no problem to collect relatively fresh dropping samples and tease them apart under water and try and make some sense of the chitinous insect fragments thus revealed.

As far as I could tell using this method, their everyday fare seemed to consist mainly of beetles. I could pick out fragments of the wing-cases of many species of dungbeetle ranging from the huge scarabs to the tiny little black Aphodids which were swarming in practically every patch of dung I found.

Between these two extremes lay every size and shape of dungbeetle one could imagine. I could see the remains of the large, cylindrical yellow Rosebeetles which would come cannoning into our lamps at night as well as bits of the Giant dungbeetles (*Heliocopris*) which were huge in comparison to the largest European dungbeetle species, *Geotrupes*. Other identifiable remains indicated that the large black ground-living weevils with their cast-iron coats, so hard that I could hardly crush them between my fingers, were also made short work of by the mongooses' sharp little teeth and powerful jaws. Sections of long, pear-shaped antennal joints bore witness to the demise of several species of wood-boring beetles, and fragments of thin antennal filaments indicated that the ground-living Carabid beetle species were also relished. The most common beetle remains, however, were the Tenebrionids, to which the mealworm belongs, this beetle family being abundant in the dry bushlands.

Apart from the beetles, I also found sections of chewed legs with their fringe of wicked backward-pointing spines, which could only have belonged to grasshoppers or crickets of some sort. This meant that the hornbills and other birds were actually feeding on what could be mongoose prey but the advantages of their acting as guards for the mongooses would seem far to outweigh the loss of a few locusts. Sometimes I would find masses of the tiny head-capsules of termite workers and, amongst them, the longer-jawed soldiers, evidence that the mongooses had found a tunnel close to the surface and had filled their stomachs with the highly nutritious insect inhabitants. Parts of the hairy legs from spiders ranging in size from tiny things only a fraction of an inch in length to true giants several inches long indicated that insects were not the only prey these smallest of all the carnivore hunters captured and ate. Sometimes the remains of the sting of the little brown scorpions that inhabited the rotting logs and hid under the bark of the fallen trees which were littered through the bushland showed that, despite their poison darts, these animals were also helpless once a mongoose had spotted them. The same was true of the Scolopendra centipedes and I had even seen in detail how Moja had dealt with one of these dangerous creatures, whose bite would have a man writhing in agony for hours.

Apart from invertebrates, I sometimes found the remnants of bones, fur and feathers in the droppings. The relics of lizards were more difficult to identify as their skin seemed to be almost wholly digested and all I could hope for was the presence of claws associated with bony fragments and a few scales, which would indicate that one of these reptiles had been captured.

As the weeks went by I had opportunities to watch how the animals caught and ate the different types of prey, for not all of them were available all the year round, there tending to be mass invasions of different kinds of animals at different times of the year, depending on the rainfall and season. We noticed this especially at the camp in the evenings when the lights were lit. Sometimes we would be invaded by hundreds of moths of a certain species, this invasion lasting a few days, after which the moths seemed to disappear completely as if they had never been. The same was true of many of the beetle species which would sometimes reach a plague of such proportions that we could hardly eat our food without forking the insects out beforehand. Then, almost overnight, they would be gone. It almost looked as if many of the insect species had very short seasons during which they emerged from their larval homes, found mates, laid eggs and died again. This made trying to determine the typical diet of the mongooses very difficult as they had to be complete opportunists, cashing in on Nature's bounty and devouring whatever she dished up.

It was while watching the mongooses on their daily hunt that I came to realise what amazingly versatile organs their forepaws are. Although technically plantigrades, that is, animals that walk on the flat soles of their feet, Dwarf mongooses show a manual dexterity that would almost rival that of a primate. They are perfectly capable of using their forepaws as scoops or as hands. Once, two days after a thundershower, I noticed Goldie, who had climbed one of the Commiphora trees as guard, fishing around in the deep cleft between two of the main branches. She was lifting her paw to her mouth with the sole uppermost and licking at whatever she was holding. As far as I could see, she had nothing in her paw and, once the group had moved off far enough for me not to disturb them by getting out of the car, my curiosity got the better of me and I shinnied up the tree to have a look at what she had been hooking out of the depths of the tree crotch. It turned out to be water! This was a truly amazing discovery, rather similar to finding a dog using its paws to scoop water out of a hole. The mechanics of this action, which seems so simple for us as humans, must be extremely complicated for an animal that usually walks on all fours and has feet similar in structure to those of a dog. I noticed the same behaviour when the animals were feeding on very small insects like termites or tiny dungbeetles. Instead of picking them up in their front teeth, which would mean that they would pick up a lot of dirt with the insect, they would grasp them in their paws and carry them to their mouths in this way, tossing their heads backwards once the insect had been taken in the incisors, throwing it to the back of the mouth where it was crunched up by the sharp-cusped molars.

They rarely used their paws for larger insects, the prey being usually pinned down by one forefoot, given a quick bite in the head region and then chewed and swallowed. Prey that tended to wind itself around the animal's snout, like a centipede or lizard, was given a series of quick shakes, like a terrier shaking a rat, to immobilise it. One aspect of their hunting, however, was very different from that found in the majority of social carnivores. They never shared their

Even scorpions are helpless before the mongooses, which seem immune to their stings

prey. What one caught was one's own – if the animal in question was quick enough to remove itself and its prize from the range of vision of higher-ranking group mates.

I was watching the group going through its usual leisurely morning ritual at a mound called Octopus owing to the circle of dead branches overtopping it, the remains of the Cassia tree around which it was built. Fleck was on guard up in the tangle of dead twigs. I saw him stiffen and stare fixedly at a branch just below him and, with some difficulty, scramble down towards it whereupon he started, with frantic scratching motions, to try and pull the bark off it. Moja and M'bili, quick as ever to cash in on things, got wind that something was up and trotted underneath his perch, peering upwards. As yet, nothing was visible. Fleck was practically tying himself in knots, trying to hang onto the thin twigs with his hind-legs and, at the same time, use both forepaws to lift up the bark and scoop out whatever it was that was underneath it. He would have managed the trick if he had had another paw available but, as it was, once he had succeeded in wrenching the bark upwards, the creature it was concealing came staggering out to fall through the branches, Fleck following it as best as he could at high speed, head downwards, only to lose his balance to end up with a thump, right on his head at the top of the mound, bowling Moja and M'bili over like skittles. All I could make out were three bodies tied in knots, surrounded by a ring of curious faces. The rest of the group, as well as myself, were trying to make out what was going on! There was much furious growling and protest screaming, and finally Diana trotted over to see what was the matter. Then a head, it looked like Fleck's, emerged from the tangle of furious fur with a large wood-boring beetle held crosswise in its teeth. The mongoose glanced round, spotted Diana, made an attempt to submerge into the fray again but too late . . . a pounce and a growl and Diana was off, the beetle firmly clamped in her jaws. The three rivals disentangled themselves, looked around rather sheepishly and started to put their fur in order while Diana, lip-smacking as she chewed up their prize right in front of their eyes, just seemed to stare past them. To the high-rankers the spoils . . .

This was just one of many observations I was able to make on the lack of comradely division of spoils among the Dwarf mongooses. The state of affairs may have been associated with the fact that most of the prey the mongooses captured was so small as to be barely a mouthful for the successful hunter, and as a result there would have been no evolutionary selection for the sharing of prey, since prey that *could* be shared would make up only a small proportion of the diet. Another explanation for this apparently selfish behaviour, as compared with the high degree of cooperation found in the group from other standpoints, is that the mongooses adopted a group mode of life for different reasons from the majority of group-living carnivores. Most social carnivores are pack hunters, probably having evolved group life as a means of exploiting larger prey. A single wolf would have trouble running down and killing an elk but a whole pack of wolves could do it much more efficiently. The same is true of lions, hunting dogs and Spotted hyenas. Working together they can kill animals much larger than themselves. Built into this system is that everyone in the group gets to share the booty, dependent on age and rank. With the Dwarf mongooses, however, the situation was different. It was beginning to seem as if they had adopted a group mode of life more as a defence against enemies than as a means of killing larger prey, as they seemed to have retained their old dietary habits.

This raised the question in my mind: why didn't they then go on and develop pack hunting of larger prey? The largest prey animal I had ever seen them capture was a Multimammate rat and that was only half as big as themselves. The situation under which my first observation of rat-catching in Diana's group took place must have been unique in the annals of animal-watching, for it occurred on 16th February 1980, the day on which a total eclipse of the sun was due at eleven o'clock in the morning in the Voi area, something which was not going to be repeated for about another 360 years.

I had followed the group southward from a mound called Fan, taking occasional peeps at the sky in case anything was happening yet. The mongooses were completely oblivious of the great portents of the day and I was curious as to how they would react when the sun went out at mid-morning. I wondered whether they would think it was evening already and head for a sleeping mound or whether they would show any special behaviour patterns once the light was fading. The minutes ticked by but they continued their foraging perfectly normally, poking about in the grass, digging little holes amongst the roots to winkle out buried beetles and fishing with their paws into every nook and cranny. It was almost ten-thirty already and the light was starting to take on a bluish tinge. I glanced upward. The sun was still shining brightly in the middle of a mackerel sky. As far as I could tell, the eclipse hadn't started yet and, since I had no darkened glass with me, it was impossible to see any details with the naked eye. The mongooses continued on their way, not taking any notice of the changing light around them, the whole bush taking on an eerie bluish hue. Blackie was pottering around the edge of an earth apron surrounding the remains of a washed-out termite mound, scratching about in the dirt at the base of a dried-out shrub. His scratching became more frantic and clouds of dirt emerged between his hind-legs as he threw the rubbish from his excavations backwards out of the way. He had obviously discovered something and I was torn between watching him and watching the sky. The light faded and I could still see him, digging away, only his hindquarters and tail now protruding from the hole. By this time the moon's disc had almost covered the sun and the light was indescribable. The last rays shone on the fleecy mackerel clouds, turning them to gold, a 360-degree sunset taking place in the middle of the sky. It was so breathtakingly beautiful that I wished I had a fish-eye lens with me to take a photograph of the whole panorama. Everything was absolutely quiet – not a bird cheeped or sang and not an insect was to be heard. The silence was overwhelming. Before the last light faded I peered through the gloom to see if I could still spot Blackie and, sure enough, there he was, still grubbing away in his hole, not taking the least bit of notice of what was happening. The rest of the group were also totally unconcerned. No rushing to the safety of the nearest termite mound or acting as if this was a rather short day and it was time to go to bed already. As the last of the sun's rays were blotted out by the moon, I could see Diana, one forepaw raised, the ever-present Tatu right behind her, standing in the middle of an open patch of ground like a statue. Then all was dark.

The minutes ticked by. Absolute silence all around. I don't think I have ever felt so totally isolated in all my life. Then with a rush, the light was back. I glanced over to where I had last seen the mongooses, expecting them all to have run for the shelter of a nearby mound as the light failed and was very surprised to see that they had done no such thing. Diana was standing with Tatu exactly as I had seen her last, even to the raised forepaw. Then she simply carried on as if nothing had happened. Blackie, squatting near his hole, took a quick glance around and then delved back into it. The rest of the group were still meandering round in the grass and bushes as if total solar eclipses were an everyday part of their lives. I shivered a little as the air had gone suddenly cold with the sun's disappearance and then, with a burst, the bush life started up again, birds started cheeping and singing, and the crickets and cicadas began their sawing and shrilling once more.

Blackie had now dug down to the point that all I could see of him was his tail and a bit of his rump, earth still showering from between his hind-legs. Then he suddenly snaked forwards and, almost a split second later, came jet-propelled backwards out of the hole with a squeaking and struggling Multimammate rat (*Mastomys*) clamped by the scruff of its neck in his jaws. He released it briefly, pounced on it with both forefeet again, and then gave it a quick bite through the head. His next response was 'Away! As fast as possible!' and he went bounding off through the grass, the rat dangling from his jaws, stopping every now and again to go into high sit to see where the other members of the group were. No one had noticed that he had caught such a prize so he was unmolested. After running about twenty yards he finally drew up at the base of one of the Commiphora trees and started to eat his prey. I noticed on several occasions that mongooses had the tendency, when they had caught something big, to carry it to a place where they could defend it, either into a termite mound or, failing that, to some object where they could shield it with their bodies, preventing others from approaching head-on. I had a good view of him from my perch in the car and could see in detail how he went about dismembering the rat, which was a large adult and almost half as big as Blackie himself.

First he held its head upright between his forepaws, chewing at the snout with his sharp cheek teeth, his head turned to one side. Soon the entire head had been eaten and he started on the trunk. Still keeping the rat's body upright, he hooked his foreclaws into the skin of the neck and pulled down, at the same time taking the neck in his mouth and pulling upwards. The skin started to detach itself and turn inside out like the finger of a glove peeled off someone's hand. Blackie repeated this process several times, chewing off the exposed meat and, when he reached the entrails, carefully extracting them in his front teeth and throwing them to one side. He was so efficient that not a scrap of the precious meat was wasted, even the legs were chewed down to the paws and the base of the tail extracted from its skin covering. Finally he was finished. All that was left of the rat was a neat little rat-fur pocket with the fur inside-out and a small pile of entrails. Blackie, stomach bulging, licked his lips, nibbled the fur on his paws and then set off at a trot to catch up the others, who were now some distance away. The whole process had taken three to four minutes. After he had left, I collected the remains of his meal so as to make a drawing of them for my data files. The neatness and efficiency with which he had dealt with the rat was amazing and it was obvious that small mammals were, very early on in evolution, prey for the ancestors of the mongooses, otherwise such advanced behaviour would never have been developed. It was just too specialised to have arisen as a means of dealing with prey that was only occasionally caught, and I began to have more foundation for my theory that the Dwarf mongooses had gone back to insect-eating after being eaters of larger animals in the earliest stages of their evolutionary development.

Another interesting point of this episode was that, although Blackie had originally caught the rat by the neck, he did not use the neck bite, so typical of the majority of carnivores, to kill it, although his teeth were positioned exactly in the right place to deliver such a killing bite. First he had released his prey, then pinned it down with his forefeet, and killed it with a bite through the head. This habit was something that had puzzled me in my tame animals and I had decided to do a series of experiments to see why the head bite rather than the neck bite was used.

My tame group often got live mice as food for they could kill them far more quickly and more efficiently than I could. A pounce, a bite, and the prey was dead without a squeak. After a few struggles, in which I quite often got bitten,

A mouse is killed with a quick bite to the head: it doesn't even squeak

I managed to take freshly killed mice away from their captors and look at where exactly the killing bite had been delivered. Something very curious emerged. The Dwarf mongoose mouth seemed almost to have been made for mouse skulls, for the upper and lower pairs of the long canine teeth were very neatly closed through the mouse's eyes and ears, crushing its skull instantaneously. I began to wonder how the mongooses managed to orientate their killing bites so accurately and decided to test my hypothesis that they were using the eyes as cues on a series of models. These models consisted of sausages of mouse skin onto which model ears, or glass-topped pins to serve as eyes, could be stuck at various points. It soon turned out that ears were completely unimportant; the mongooses, in biting their pseudo-prey as I dragged it along the floor attached to a piece of string, took no notice of them at all, no matter where I moved them on the model. With the eyes, though, it was a different story. As I moved the pins along the body axis, the mongooses shifted their killing bites to follow them until the half-way mark on the fur sausage was reached. Then the eyes were ignored and they directed their bites to the front end again.

This discovery was important in two respects. First, it would be essential for an animal whose prey consisted not only of mice to have a general scheme for killing – a bite near the victim's front. Most of the prey animals the mongooses feed on have no eyes that one can recognise as such, but all of them have their main nerve centres near the front of the body so, to kill quickly, a killing pattern should develop which would paralyse these centres independently of what the prey's exterior form might be. In the case of larger prey such as mice, the use of the eyes as cues as to the whereabouts of this nerve centre, the brain, would also improve killing efficiency but the mongooses could ignore such cues if they became too erroneous, like eyes situated in the middle of the body.

The second important conclusion that emerged from these findings was probably more valuable since it helped answer the question as to why the mongooses never developed group hunting in their society. They were simply incapable of bringing down a prey animal large enough to feed the whole group! A Dwarf mongoose's mouth can only gape so wide, and the size of the prey capable of being killed is determined by the size of its skull. According to my theory, once a skull became too big for a Dwarf mongoose to crush, the mongoose would be unable to kill the animal it belonged to. I decided to test this with my tame group and gave them a large laboratory rat, almost the same size as they were themselves. They all pounced on it and tried to pin it down with their feet, which was a total failure as the rat would just whip round and nip them, being far too strong for them to hold; then they made ineffectual bites at its head, but all to no avail. The rat wriggled free and started leaping at them and biting them instead. No sign of a switch to a killing neck bite like a weasel or a cat! After a few fruitless attempts, in which they seemed to be coming off worse than the rat, my group gave up and left the creature in peace. I even tried giving them the longest neck I could think of, to try to force them into making a neck bite. I introduced a three-week-old pullet into their enclosure. The lead male was on it like a flash, a flurry of feathers, a quick bite and the chicken was dead. I shooed him away to see where he had delivered the bite. In the head again. No sign of a neck bite although in this case the neck was very much longer than the prey's head and bringing it down with a skull crush would have been far more difficult than simply breaking its neck.

All this evidence was slowly leading me to the firm conclusion that social life in the Dwarf mongoose was really an adaptation to protection against predators and had little to do with more efficient hunting although, occasionally, prey flushed by one of the group members might be caught by a neighbouring animal, this being more a question of accident than intent. The only times I ever saw them work as a group were in snake-killing, but that is another story which has little to do with food and feeding.

One of the commonest types of prey, accidentally 'shared' between members of the family and their feathered friends, I found to be grasshoppers. The majority of these were the large locusts with a wingspan of four inches or more and powerful legs capable of propelling them high into the air, on which they would glide and flutter down to a place of safety many yards away from their starting-points. Usually the mongooses had little chance of catching a flushed locust themselves, for the birds were on the insect like a flash, but sometimes the locust's leap would bring it in the vicinity of one of the other foraging group members which would attempt to pounce on it. If the first attempt failed, the fleeing insect would be pursued by its furry would-be captor who bounded after it, mouth gaped, trying to guess its trajectory and time its second pounce to coincide with the instant and position of the insect's touching the ground. If the birds did not interfere, it turned out that the mongooses were very proficient at this, keeping their eye on the insect in the air and pinning it with both forefeet as soon as it landed. It seemed a curious anachronism that they would chase it with their mouths gaped as if to bite first, but I never saw one actually catch a locust in flight in its mouth. First came the pinning, then the bite, never the other way around.

Another delicacy that the mongooses have very efficient ways of dealing with are eggs. These are, however, dietary items that are very restricted in their availability since most of the bush-inhabiting birds correlate their breeding with the rains or hide their eggs so efficiently that the mongooses never have a chance of finding them. Mongooses are notorious nest-robbers and my attention was drawn one day to the screeching and fluttering of a little Flappet lark, one of the dry bush country's smaller ground-living birds.

Whatever the lark was attacking was hidden behind a low bush, so I climbed up onto the car roof to get a better view. A brown body was crouched over something on the ground and, when I had focused my binoculars, I could see it was a mongoose with something in its forepaws. A head was turned towards me and I found myself staring into Twin's eyes as he carefully licked his chops. He dropped whatever it was he was holding, turned round and grabbed something else which he held upright in his forepaws like a child holding a beaker of milk. From its smooth shape I could tell that it was an egg and the behaviour of the frantic mother led this researcher to the not too difficult conclusion that it was a Flappet lark egg and that Twin was robbing the nest.

Once he had got the egg upright, pointed end upwards, he turned his head on one side, gave a quick crunch of his cheek teeth and the egg was capped. He then proceeded to lick out the contents, still holding the egg between his paws like a little bowl. Once the contents had been licked out, the empty shell was thrust behind him with a quick movement of one forepaw and he turned to pick up another. I had not seen a single drop spilled during the whole process.

The way in which the mongooses dealt with larger eggs, though, was quite different. One day they stumbled across a Crested francolin's nest, a ground-living bird about the size of a bantam chicken. The sitting bird must have been away somewhere, for at first I didn't realise what all the fuss was about, mongooses shouldering each other out of the way, growling horribly and the weaker ones giving penetrating protest screeches. Then George emerged rump first from the fray, walking slowly backwards with something clasped in his forelegs. He continued his rather stilted progress, occasionally glancing over one shoulder and compensating for the rather irregular movements that the object he was dragging with him was making by shifting his paws right and left on its smooth surface. It was a francolin egg, about the size of that of a bantam hen, and I could now see other lucky members of the group also moving along backwards with eggs clasped in front of them like baskets they could not quite get their arms around. The less fortunate members of the group ran from one egg-holder to another, trying to dislodge the holder's grip or hook the egg out of its arms. This was usually greeted with growls, hipslams – which sometimes had the effect of making the egg-holder lose its grip so that its tormentor had a chance of getting the prize – and sometimes gape-mouthed lunges. The three juveniles dashed hither and thither, terribly excited, but not one of them had managed to get an egg for itself.

George was now almost three yards away from the rest of the group, headed slowly backwards towards the bole of a Commiphora tree. When he was only about two feet from it, he suddenly threw the egg backwards under his body with a powerful thrust of both forefeet, leaping up into the air a split second later so that the egg shot backwards in an arc to land in a clump of grass. Growling horribly at Vanessa and Fleck who had come trotting up when they saw this, he tried again. This time the egg went wide of the trunk and landed in the dead leaves at the base of a little bush. Still growling like a furious bear, George tried again, slewing his body round so that the egg was facing towards the Commiphora tree-trunk once more. This time his efforts met with success – and I almost clapped loudly in applause. With an audible whack the egg struck the tree-trunk and came to rest at its base. George was there like a flash, licking up the tasty contents. Then I noticed Diana didn't have an egg to break and it suddenly dawned on me that she didn't really need one . . . she had an official egg-breaker already in George! Trotting over to where he was gobbling the egg as fast as he could go, she growled once at him and he turned his head away and retreated slowly while she, Tatu in tow as usual, fished in the opened shell with her forepaw, then licked it clean of its sticky covering. I could almost hear George muttering angrily to himself as he went trotting off. Poor Rusty, who had managed to get an egg for himself and open it, was right in his path, and George didn't have to do a thing! With a weak little protest scream, a quick turn of his body and a second of absolute motionlessness, Rusty relinquished his prize to his father who, still growling ominously, proceeded to demolish it.

Diana was hooking in her egg with her forefoot and Tatu was behind her, trying to squeeze past to get a bit of the delicious contents, only to be rebuffed with hipswings and growls from her mother. In contrast to George, who had licked the egg's contents directly from the ground, Diana used her paw – one could almost say in a 'ladylike' way. She didn't use it like a scoop, though, as Goldie had done when she was getting water out of the tree-crotch, but simply plunged it into the inside of the egg and licked it clean afterwards, usually starting with the upper surface. Finally she was finished and moved off to lick her whiskers and thoroughly clean her paw. This was Tatu's chance. She was on the abandoned eggshell like a flash, sticking her little snout into the open end and licking feverishly at the meagre remains her mother had left her. She pushed her head further and further into the shell and then the inevitable happened. She was stuck! Her first response was to shake her head slowly from side to side and scrabble at the shell with her forepaws but to no avail. The thing seemed stuck fast. Then she lifted her head, took a few hesitant steps forward and stopped again, waving the grotesque head covering back and forth like some antedeluvian monster. She looked so ludicrous, I almost burst out laughing. Two steps forward and one back . . . she moved almost as if in a slow-motion dance, not seeing a thing and hardly capable of putting one foot in front of the other. Then she lowered her head again, scrabbling

*A big beetle is cracked against a stone after being thrown
under the mongoose's body by its forepaws*

frantically at the smooth shell that was imprisoning it, and finally the shell came off. I expected her to trot away, looking rather bewildered, but she did nothing of the sort. After a few quick sniffs around the edge of the broken shell she did exactly as her mother had done before her, fished in it with one forepaw and licked the paw clean afterwards. I began to wonder whether she was actively copying her mother or whether her unpleasant experience with the egg had resulted in her using an alternative strategy to remove its contents. Whatever the reason behind her now using her paw instead of her tongue, she had changed her behaviour after only a single negative experience, for the last time the francolins had bred, Tatu had not even been born!

I wanted to find out how large an egg a Dwarf mongoose could recognise as being one and tackle, so when I next returned to Europe I gave my captive mongooses a choice ranging in size from a canary egg, through chicken and goose eggs, to that of an ostrich. The lead male made a beeline for the ostrich egg as soon as I let him into the enclosure and tried to throw it behind him in the typical egg-smash behaviour pattern. This, however, was a fiasco as he couldn't get his body over it. With hardly a second's hesitation, he threw himself onto his side and with an enormous thrust of his forepaws, sent the huge egg wobbling towards the nearest wall. A few repetitions of this and the egg hit the wall with an audible 'thwack!' This little experiment not only answered my question about how big an egg is recognised as being an egg but showed me how flexible the mongooses could be in their egg-breaking behaviour patterns. In contrast to the stereotyped killing head-bite used for other prey, egg-smashing behaviour patterns did not seem to be as firmly fixed genetically and could be adapted to suit the needs of the moment.

The only lizards I ever saw eaten by mongooses were geckos. These were practically invisible against the rough tree bark or in the flaking branches of the fallen thorny giants. Usually they relied on their camouflage to escape notice, freezing flat against the surface until the near approach of their predators would send them scuttling away into hiding with a snaky movement of their bodies. One day the group was foraging slowly alongside the car. As they passed by a Commiphora tree about five yards away from me, I saw something scuttle upwards to swing itself out of sight of the mongooses below, lying flat along a branch not more than a few feet from my face. Although the gecko, for that was what it was, had managed to get out of the line of vision of the mongooses below, it seemed to have forgotten or not have been aware of their feathered companions. A bright-eyed face with a long yellow bill peered through the branches from a tree opposite. The Yellow-billed hornbill which had been waiting there had spotted the flicker of movement, even though it was almost ten yards away, and came swooping over. Just as it was about to snap up the hapless lizard in its beak it became aware of me – I was too near for comfort! It braked sharply, wings beating the air, made a stab at the gecko, missed and the little lizard came tumbling out of the tree to land, wriggling, in the grass. The mongooses spotted its fall and came dashing over, but not as fast as the male von der Decken's hornbill which snapped up the prize which had almost landed at its feet. A head tossed in the air, a gaping beak, and the lizard was gone. The Yellow-bill cocked his head from above in the tree and I almost got the impression it shrugged its shoulders as if to say 'Tough luck!'

Most of the bird species that lived in the area were more or less safe from the little hunters, being too large or too agile to be caught unawares. The little cavalcade with its pennant of birds would, in any case, scare practically any other self-respecting birds that could be considered as prey well away before they reached it. I only once saw a mongoose with a bird in its mouth, one of the rusty-capped Tiny cisticolas which it had surprised on its nest inside a hollow log. It was Whitethroat that had caught the bird but I didn't see how he killed it for he emerged from the log with the dead little bunch of feathers dangling from his mouth and, despite Scar's attempts to take it off him, ran round the back of a nearby termite mound to devour his find. He was invisible from my angle so I was unable to see whether he ate it from the head downwards like a mouse or not. After the group had left, I went to look at the remains but there were surprisingly few, just a couple of the larger wingfeathers and a few tailfeathers. Everything else had been eaten!

A lot of the prey animals that the mongooses captured would have been avoided by other hunters for they were either poisonous, nasty-tasting or both. Practically all the animals of the dry bush have some special means of defending themselves and the slow-moving skulkers in holes and crevices are especially adept at this. For the mongooses, however, all poisonous and stinging creatures were just grist to the mill and they gobbled them up with relish every time they came across one.

After a particularly heavy thunderstorm during the night, the open areas in the bush had turned into seas of drying mud and I could see where the rushing water had formed miniature sandbanks along sloping stretches of the game trails as it had rushed downhill. Here and there amongst the grass tussocks were little mounds of freshly dug earth, the pellets excavated already starting to dry into a stone-like consistency as the sun hit them. The mongooses had delayed their departure from the mound until the earth had dried somewhat, but once it had reached the point where their feet no longer sank in when they walked along it, they were off. I saw Goldie stop at one of the little heaps of earth and start digging furiously. Soon she was up to her shoulders inside the hole she had dug, then she started briefly, snapped and shot out backwards, at the same time flinging what she had captured over her shoulder so that it landed on the bare patch of earth behind her. She whipped round to face her prey which was standing there at battle stations, its claws raised and its sting in an arc over its back. It was a huge black scorpion (*Pandinus*), a good six inches from head to tail-tip, one of the ones the bush people call *ingi*, and well capable of putting me in hospital in a high fever or, at the least, causing me days of pain.

The scorpion swung from side to side like a prizefighter, its claws open and tail making little stabs in the air. I expected Goldie to dash in and nip off its poisoned thorn but she did nothing of the kind. It looked as if, as far as she was concerned, the pincers were far more formidable weapons than the sting itself and with a quick lunge, she dashed at the scorpion, there was a rapid snap of her teeth, a shake, and she was out again and one of the scorpion's claws was dangling helpless from its foreleg. Another lunge and a snap and the second claw followed suit. Now, I thought, she'd go for the tail! Not a bit of it. Goldie stalked up to her defenceless prey, defenceless as far as she was concerned anyway, bit it in the head and carried it off to safety, the creature's sting pounding at her head in its death-struggles. She didn't even notice it! She carried it off to a safe corner and, in the usual manner, devoured it head first, holding it upright in her forepaws. By the time she got to the tail, she picked the whole thing up in her jaws, chewing along it to the last segment with its poison-bearing sac and recurved injection apparatus. This she let drop from the corner of her mouth, then turned to sniff it, sneezed, rubbed her nose with one paw and went trotting off after the others. I had the impression that she just didn't like the smell of the poison and this was the reason that she discarded the segment containing it rather than that it would have made her ill if she had eaten it, for I knew from my faecal samples that the little brown scorpions (*Buthus*), which are just as poisonous as their larger black brethren, if not more so, were eaten completely, sting and all.

The mongooses really had a feast that morning, for it seemed as if the thundershower of the night before had either flooded the *ingi* out of their neat oval holes with their long sloping passages and little round chambers at the ends, or had got caught outside during the rain and were unable to regain the safety of their waterlogged retreats again once the sun rose. Many were eaten. The rains had not only flushed out the scorpions but other burrowing denizens of the bush were also temporarily homeless. Huge Baboon spiders, relatives of the Bird-eating spiders of South America, not quite as large as their giant relatives but even so, a good four inches from toe-tip to toe-tip, were winkled out of their silted-up homes, dispatched with a quick bite across the thorax, and chewed with no further ado. The poison fangs on some of these giants were a good half-inch in length and they were well capable of killing a small bird or a mouse but, as far as the mongooses were concerned, they were just lambs for the slaughter.

Then I saw Vanessa fishing around with one forepaw in a grass tussock, finally hooking her prey out onto a patch of bare earth nearby where she could deal with it better. It looked like a fat black worm about eight inches long with a carmine fringe attached to one side. The creature rolled itself into a neat coil and I realised that it was one of the huge Julid millipedes, called *Songololos* or 'Mombasa Trains' which emerged from their hidy-holes once the weather was moist enough, to feed on the rotting vegetation. I knew that these creatures could exude a reddish-coloured, very bitter-tasting acid secretion from special pores in the scales above their legs and, because of this, they were left strictly alone by the majority of the bush-living insect-eaters. I wondered whether this applied to the mongooses as well and watched how Vanessa dealt with this well-protected bush denizen. First she sniffed it carefully, shook her head, sneezed, gaped her mouth wide, and then proceeded to do something I had never seen my tame group do. Like a raccoon washing mussels in the water, Vanessa started washing the millipede in the dirt. She rubbed the creature thoroughly on both sides in the drying earth, using quick little scrubbing motions of her paws, stopping every now and again to sniff it, almost as if to check whether all the nasty-tasting secretion had gone or not. After nearly a minute of furious scrubbing she seemed satisfied with the results and started to eat it from one end like a child chewing a strip of liquorice. It must still have tasted rather unpleasant, though, for she wrinkled up her nose, lifting her upper lip as far away from her prey as possible. Soon there was nothing left of the millipede and Vanessa went trotting off on the hunt again.

The thing that fascinated me most about all this was not only the variety of ways in which the mongooses dealt with different types of prey – which was interesting enough in itself when one compared them with the more special-ised carnivore killers which seem to have selected one method during the process of evolution and more or less stuck to it – but the fact that these tiny animals seemed to be almost impervious to any sort of defence that Nature had given her less attractive children, at least unattractive from the human point of view. The variety of poisons that the mongooses could withstand was truly amazing. Irrespective of whether a creature had developed neurogenic poisons (those which paralyse the nerve cells of the victim, thus causing its death to occur relatively rapidly) to defend itself or capture its prey, or haemolytic poisons (those that destroy red blood corpuscles, resulting in an oxygen-death of the body tissues, a slower process than the previous one), or even protein-digesting fluids like the Baboon spiders or extremely strong acids like the Julid millepedes, it was all the same as far as the mongooses were concerned. They seemed to be impervious to everything. Science knows nothing about the immune system of the Dwarf mongooses but it must be an amazingly versatile and efficient one, probably the most effective in the Animal Kingdom. Millions of years of evolutionary selection have turned the Dwarf mongooses, small as they are, into predators whose versatility and imperviousness to every obstacle Nature has thrown in their path in the way of defence mechanisms can be rivalled practically only by Man, the greatest predator of them all.

5 Friends and Foes

My policy of sitting motionless, as far as was possible, day after day was starting to pay off. The bush animals got used to the presence of the car and were no longer so afraid of it and I was able to make observations on their behaviour with respect to the mongooses which I should never have had the chance of recording if I had been continually on the move.

I made a practice of trying to keep at a distance of about twenty to thirty yards from the group during observations, as then there was less likelihood that I would disturb them through accidental sudden movements or noises. When the group moved away from me through the bush, I could increase my line of sight by climbing through the roof hatch and continuing my watch while squatting on the roof of the car. Only when they moved completely out of sight would I be forced to follow them, making a wide detour through the bush and parking again at a point in front of them. Such changes of position, however, I tried to restrict to the heat of the day when the mongooses had already gone down into a mound for their siesta, so as to reduce the disturbance factor as much as possible.

At first it was all very hard and I almost gave up on many occasions for my body was not used to the heat and I suffered accordingly. Twice in the first two weeks I came reeling out of the car in the evening on return to camp, nauseated, dizzy with a high fever and weak as a kitten. Heat exhaustion. A dose of quinine, a glass of salt water sipped slowly and a night spent wrapped in a wet sheet usually had me on my feet again so that I could carry on my daily visits to my animals. For the first three weeks, every scratch on my skin turned septic but my reasoning was that my body should develop a resistance to this new world of bacteria as quickly as possible, so I never put antibiotic ointments on the wounds and soon scratches meant as little to me as the scratches I would have had in other climes. They healed rapidly of their own accord. The only thing which was, and remained, a constant source of irritation was the skin rash that developed after hours and hours of having to sit in my own sweat, day after day, and no ointment or powder seemed to help in the least. My eyelids, back and buttocks started to look like raw hamburger but I had to ignore this if I was going to get on with my work. I came to the conclusion that there was a vast deal of difference between driving around in a car, when one could have a constant breeze, and sitting in it, still as a mouse, when the only breeze that was present was Nature's capricious own.

It took nearly a month before my physiology adapted to the change in climate. My skin began to look and feel like well-tanned leather despite liberal applications of moisturisers and oil but the most important thing was that the almost unquenchable thirst that had plagued me up until now gradually vanished and I was well able to exist on my single thermos of lime-juice with no ill effects.

Word must have got round about the *Mzungu daktari* (European doctor), although I was no such thing, at least not a doctor of medicine! I had, however, a well stocked medical kit and a modicum of knowledge, and soon found myself more or less pushed into this role. Very often I would return to camp in the evening and find a stranger squatting near the fire, stick and knobkerry in hand, waiting patiently for my return. The visitors were usually herdsmen, some of whom had tramped well over ten miles that day to ask for my help in curing a sick family member. Using Sammy to translate if the man spoke only a dialect of Maa, the Nilo-hamitic speech form from which the Maasai got their name, or Danson when he spoke Swahili, I usually managed to find out what symptoms the invalid had. It was often children who were ill and I went through the now standard routine . . . Was the child hot when you touched it? Did it vomit? Had it a pain somewhere? The questioning usually resulted in a picture of the disease emerging, most of the illnesses being either lung infections or intestinal ones. I would then rummage round in my medical kit, select an appropriate medicine and go into my routine of prescribing the right dosage. I knew from experience what the attitude towards *dawa* (medicine) was . . . If one pill is good, two pills are better, and taking the whole lot at once would turn you into a superman!

Since most of my visitors could not read or write, I developed a pinman drawing for the times at which the pills should be taken. In most cases it was out of the question for the patient to visit me because of distance. I would draw a rising sun and a little stick figure with a pill in its hand, a sun at midday and again the little stick figure taking a pill, completing the masterpiece with a setting sun and the little man with his pill, repeating this for the number of days the pills had to be taken. This prescription was very effective, and often the pleased parent would return to the camp several days later, a big smile on his face and a gourd of milk for us, scented with frankincense from the Commiphora berries to stop it going sour too quickly, to tell me of the complete recovery of my patient whom I had never even seen. I soon found that my neighbours had given me a nickname, as they do for most Europeans who live amongst them for any length of time. I was *Mama Kitete* (Mother of the Mongooses) for them, and the relationship between us became very cordial.

We were slowly starting to get rid of our unpleasant cold-blooded camp visitors, and Danson and Sammy were very efficient at this, wreaking wholesale slaughter amongst the snakes, scorpions and centipedes that seemed to swarm upon us during the first few weeks of our stay. I managed to prevent them from killing the more harmless animals like Fred, the little geckos and the Skarpstecker snakes which would shoot through the grass tussocks in the middle of the *boma* like little striped arrows. I was beginning to think the camp was more or less clear of the more dangerous bush inhabitants but I was mistaken.

I had retired to bed for the night and had just turned out the lamp and settled down to sleep when I heard something scratching softly against the canvas next to my head. I grabbed the torch and could just make out a bulge in the tent wall which was slowly creeping upwards, scratching softly as it went. The bulge started to snake slowly from side to side and I suddenly realised it must be the head end of a huge puff adder which, like the mamba during the day, was now trying to catch the geckos on the tent wall at night. I hit it sharply with my fist through the tent wall and heard it land with a flop on the ground outside. Ears strained to their utmost, I tried to make out what was going on. Again came the soft scraping and the snake tried once again to scale the tent wall only to be knocked back down again with a sharp thump of my fist. Then all was quiet. I thought it must have given up its attempt and gone to hunt for easier prey. Then, suddenly, all hell was let loose under my bed! I was almost thrown out of it in the process. Something almost as thick as a strong man's arm was battling around under my groundsheet. My little bedside table and lamp fell over with a crash and I shot upright, groping for one of my bush-boots in the dark. The puff adder was still chasing its prey, whatever it was, round and round underneath my camp bed, which was rocking violently as the snake was very large and powerful. I squatted on my precarious perch hammering at my unwelcome visitor with the heel of my bush-boot every time I could make out where it was from the bulge in the ground sheet. I finally managed to hit it on the head and it recoiled like a spring. Another thump and it seemed to have had enough and slithered off outside.

The pandemonium had woken Danson and Sammy who, rubbing their eyes, crawled out of their tent to see what was going on. I yelled at them '*Hatari! Nyoka makubwa!*' ('Danger, big snake!') and the two of them shot headlong into their tent again, closing the flaps with feverish fingers. Peering through the window of my tent I could see the reptile creeping off as it passed through a patch of moonlight, heading for a Grewia thicket at the edge of the *boma*. The body seemed to go on for ever, a striped and speckled fireman's hose which quickly propelled itself forwards on its rippling ribs. The creature must have been at least a yard and a half long, much larger than any puff adder I had seen to date, but I had heard reports of veritable monsters which lived in this desert country, some of which, if the storyteller was not exaggerating, reached lengths of three yards or more and were so powerfully muscled that even driving a car over them had no effect. They would just crawl on as if nothing had happened. We made a search for the snake the next morning, following its track, a broad flattened path through the dust with slightly serrated borders, which led to a tangle of dried grass and finally disappeared. After my almost sleepless night, I hoped the reptile would not make a habit of coming to visit.

One of the things that I was very interested in seeing was how the mongooses dealt with snakes. The only reference I had found about this was by one of the old East Africa explorers who had watched them attack a cobra as a group, far back in 1897. To date, however, the only snake my mongooses had come across was the one hiding in the termite mound and they had made no attempt to kill it but had just gathered round, looked at it and then moved on. It was a long time before I had the chance to see how they dealt with these reptiles, for the snakes had usually retreated to the safety of their holes before the mongooses were up and about, most of them being night hunters.

The next puff adder that I managed to spot in the bush was out in the open in broad daylight but under rather unusual circumstances. Usually their camouflage was so complete that one could hardly see them, even at close quarters, as I had twice now found out, almost-accidents which might have ended extremely painfully if not fatally for me, for the nearest hospital was thirty miles away and, since I had no refrigerator, I could not keep anti-snake-bite serum in the camp. On both occasions I had got out of the car to examine what I thought were mongoose droppings at the base of a termite mound only to recoil backwards on finding myself almost stepping on a large puff adder coiled up near what in fact were its own droppings, practically invisible in the light and shadow. On one of these occasions my foot was poised above the reptile's head and only a split-second stood between completion of my step and being bitten, the blunted, arrow-shaped head giving the snake's position away. I would be shaking inside with horror after such narrow escapes and trained myself to look carefully with every step I took through the bush.

On this particular morning I had followed the mongooses from their sleeping mound and, since their foraging had taken them almost out of sight, I decided to drive in a wide circle and position myself at a point they would pass by if they continued their wanderings in the same direction. Just as I was bringing the car to a halt, I saw something black and white fluttering madly near the base of a bush, only a few yards away. At first I couldn't make out what it was, but once I had got the binoculars trained on it, I saw to my amazement that it was a female von der Decken's hornbill which was leaping up and down, flapping its wings furiously. I had never seen hornbills behave like this before and, while I was puzzling out what it could mean, the bird slewed round and

*A huge puff adder, its fangs firmly bitten into its victim, a female von der Decken's hornbill . . .
After two minutes the bird was dead*

there, attached to her breast like a horrible, arm-like extension of herself, was
the head and neck of a huge puff adder, its fangs firmly bitten into its victim.
The hornbill's struggles got weaker and weaker and finally she expired, beak
gaping and wings outspread. The whole thing had hardly taken two minutes!

The snake tried to pull its prey into the shelter of the bush it was hiding in
with a rapid recoil of its body but the bird was too big to pull through the
branches. I watched, fascinated but horrified, as it released its hold, grabbed
the hornbill by the head and proceeded to swallow it, its jaws working from
side to side as it dislocated their hinges to increase its gape. Slowly, the snake's
body seemed to flow over and around the bird, only to come to a halt at its
shoulder girdle. It couldn't get the bird, wings and all, into its mouth! It lay
motionless, the bird's body hanging from its jaws like a bundle of feathers, and

then slowly worked its way backwards again, disgorging its prey which was now soaked with saliva at the head end. The snake slowly moved to one side then, with lightning speed, the head shot forwards and grabbed the bird from the side. Again the curious, almost hand-puppet motion of the jaws to dislocate them, and the snake tried again, first swallowing one wing and then ending up at the rump again, on which it could go no further. Again a retreat and this time it tried from the back, got almost the entire body of the bird into its mouth, but once more got stuck at the point where the bird's wings joined its body. It lay for almost an hour in this position before 'realising' that the situation was hopeless and withdrawing from its prey, working its jaws from side to side to get their joints back to where they belonged. Then it just lay there, next to the now saliva-smeared hornbill corpse. It flickered its tongue over its cumbersome prey a few times but did not bite it again. Finally it crawled off through the bushes, vanishing from sight almost instantaneously. I felt so sorry for the hornbill, for she had been killed for nothing, but I knew that her body would not remain lying there long. Some scavenger would soon snap it up, and if not, the carrion beetles and fly maggots would soon make short work of her remains.

I had misjudged the mongooses and, while I had been watching the snake, they had gone off almost at right angles in the opposite direction to where I was parked, so the chances of their meeting up with the puff adder were very slim. I was soon to get my chance of watching how they dealt with these reptiles, though.

The day promised to be a hot one and the group was away and foraging by seven o'clock. They had hardly gone fifteen yards from the mound when I saw Whitethroat flagging his head up and down, staring at the silvered grass and fallen leaves at the base of a Grewia bush. '*Tseeeeee*', 'Come quickly!' – the penetrating call resounded through the bush. All heads were up and, as a body, the group trotted towards him, closing ranks as they went until they looked like a little army on the move. I peered through the light and shade at the base of the bush but could see nothing. Then suddenly, what I had taken to be a pile of dead leaves started to writhe and pull itself together into a heap, rising upwards with a hissing sound like a locomotive letting off steam, to form a coil which waved back and forth. It was hard to make out anything in detail, the shadows were so deep, but I managed to identify what this shield-like object jerking from side to side was. The puff adder must have realised that it was in danger and was protecting its most vulnerable part, its neck, by recurving it, head downwards, in a coil of its upper body – the whole thing looking like a question mark whose curved section had been elongated and folded in on itself again, the head of the snake in the middle. By this time the mongooses had surrounded the reptile and were making little open-mouthed darts towards it. The snake must have been at least a yard long and as thick as my arm and I wondered how they would tackle it.

The puff adder kept to its shield-like stance, still hissing loudly and whipping round when one of its little tormentors nipped it in the back, striking with lightning speed at the little brown bodies which jumped in and out of the fray like rubber balls. Then George and Diana, after investigating, detached themselves from the group and went to stand together about a yard away from the rest of the family. George started to cheek-mark the ground and a little

After the guard's 'Come quickly' call, the mongooses surround the puff adder and threaten it. Finally it attempts to flee and the mongoose group blocks its retreat

tussock of grass in front of him, then going into the most furious threat-scratching routine I had seen to date. Fragments of grass went flying backwards and he kept glancing at the snake, working himself up into a frenzy. Diana stood impassively by, just watching what was going on. Then she suddenly trotted into the chaos around the bush and I saw her cut Tatu out of the throng as neatly and efficiently as a sheepdog cutting a particular ewe out of a herd of sheep. It looked almost as if she was actively preventing Tatu from taking part in the snake-baiting, for every time the little mongoose made an attempt to join the rest of the family around the Grewia bush, Diana ran after her and blocked her progress with her body, literally pushing her away.

George was still threat-scratching, marking and making little dashes towards the group round the snake, stopping half-way and going back to his threat-scratching again. The group around the snake in the bush was still harassing it, dashing in as soon as its head was turned away from them, nipping it and bounding back again before the snake could whip round and strike at them. Twin, Scar and Whitethroat seemed to be the main attackers, almost equally spaced from one another and keeping the snake more than occupied between them. The females and younger animals filled in the gaps and got their nips in as well, as soon as an opportunity was presented. The snake was lunging continually, mouth gaped so that the upper and lower jaws were almost in a straight line and hissing furiously but, quick as it was, it was no match for the mongooses who shot out of range before it had completed its strike. It was obviously trying to break away from them, for on several occasions it flung its body out almost to full stretch but recoiled again almost as quickly when one of its furry tormentors at the back bit it in the tail. Every now and again, George would dash in, give it a nip and then go back to his threat-scratching again.

Finally, the snake made a super-reptilian effort and tore itself away from the surrounding mongooses, hurrying over the ground as fast as its ribs would carry it. The entire pack trotted after it, tweaking it in the tail, on which it would whip round, stab at them with its open jaws and then dash off again. One by one its tormentors gave up the chase until, at the end, only Whitethroat, Scar and Twin were chivvying it onwards. It seemed to be frantically looking for somewhere to hide as it was sticking its snout into any hole or crevice it could find, but none seemed big enough and the mongooses gave it no peace. They were on it and biting its tail as soon as its motion faltered. Finally, it reached a fallen tree and vanished underneath it. The three mongooses clambered over the trunk, peering downwards, trotted alongside it, flagging their heads and peering into the shadows beneath. At last they seemed satisfied that the reptile was gone for good and came bounding back to the rest of the group. Then followed an orgy of neck-nibbles and anal marking of one another, vaguely reminiscent of a football team's back-slapping and hugging after a goal has been scored.

Again I had the impression that they had no intention of killing the snake. It looked to me as if they just didn't want it around and after driving it to distraction, were quite content to see it off the premises, chasing it as far away as they could. The puff adder in question, however, was a very large and powerful specimen, a yard of steel-spring coiled muscle and a handful for a man to hold down, let alone a tiny little mongoose that only weighed about a pound. They would have had difficulty in just getting their jaws around its neck, which was almost as thick as my wrist, even if the snake had given them a chance to do this.

What I found especially curious about the whole battle was that George and Diana, after having had a look to see what it was all about, had left the snake-baiting to their older children and had even stopped little Tatu from taking part. I was not sure whether George's violent threat-scratching had been for himself, to work himself up to attacking point, or whether it was just an expression of his emotional state. Diana, on the other hand, seemed to act as if snake-baiting just left her cold and, once she had got Tatu out of the way and to relative safety, she more or less ignored the whole thing, sitting watching the others get on with the job. I could hardly wait to see how they would deal with a smaller snake if they should come across one.

My wish was finally granted one afternoon as the group was passing by a rather isolated termite mound I had called Peak. This time it was Goldie who gave the *tseee* call and again the whole troop came running over like a pack of hounds in full cry. Goldie was darting at something in the grass next to the mound's earth apron. I climbed on top of the car to get a better view and, by the time I was positioned, the rest of the group had surrounded whatever it was that was hiding there. Through the binoculars I could see something coiling back and forth. Another puff adder, but a much smaller one than the first, barely two feet long. It looked as if it had been having a bask in the sun when Goldie stumbled across it. Again the darting in and out of furry brown bodies started and the snake made ineffectual efforts to regain the safety of the mound, slowly but surely working its way up the slope until it was finally on bare ground and beautifully positioned so that I could see everything that was going on.

Again George and Diana went off to one side but this time Diana made no attempt to cut Tatu out of the fray. I could hardly see the snake because of the cluster of bodies round it and I could only count its strikes from the balls of fur which would go leaping backwards at some point along the perimeter of the circle. The mongooses were jostling each other trying to get a nip at their enemy. I saw Rusty dash in, nip, the snake strike towards him as he deftly jumped out of the way – but then as he sprang backward he collided with Twin and I was shocked to hear the snake's jaws connect with an audible whack. Rusty gave a quavering little *tseep* and was back into the fight as if nothing had happened. Remembering how quickly the female hornbill had succumbed to the puff adder's blood-destroying poison, I expected Rusty to weaken slowly and at least show *some* symptoms of having been bitten, but nothing happened; he was still in there with his brethren, snake-baiting with gusto!

George had now totally demolished the grass tussock he had been threat-scratching at full speed, then he turned and in two bounds he was in the midst of his family. What then happened took place so fast I only managed to record visually isolated scenes as if it had all taken place in stroboscopic light. George's extended body, jaws gaping: George on his haunches, the snake's neck in his mouth: George flinging his head backwards, shaking it from side to side like a terrier, the snake whipping and writhing in the air, its jaws wide open: George leaping sideways and flinging the snake away from him to land in a tangled, writhing ball outside the circle of intently staring faces. . . then it was all over. George, Snake-killer Extraordinary, had despatched the reptile.

The group trotted towards the reptile in a body, tapping and hooking at it with their claws, the more timid ones, especially the juveniles, dashing in to give the still writhing body a quick nip before shooting backwards again. George just sat there watching, and Diana came over and gave him a quick nibble in the neck-ruff before joining the rest of her family who were still investigating the reptile. Gradually, the reflexive muscular action of the snake's corpse ceased and the mongooses teased the still-twitching ball apart with their paws. Focusing my binoculars as well as I could, I tried to make out exactly where George had placed his killing bite. According to what I had seen of prey-killing, it should have been in the head but it wasn't. It was in the neck about two inches behind the head. Either the mongooses didn't consider snakes as prey or they used a different killing technique on these reptiles from the one used on lizards. Knowing how lightning-swiftly a puff adder could shoot its head back and forth, though, and that George would have had no time to pin the creature down with his feet and position his bite correctly, I was amazed that he was able to bite so accurately in the first place. Once the snake was well and truly dead, George walked over to it, sniffed its open mouth carefully, sneezed, rubbed his nose with his paw and then strolled off. I expected the group to fight over who was going to eat the snake first but not one of them made an attempt to take even a bite. Now I was more or less certain that puff adders, at least, were not prey but enemies to be killed and not eaten.

The little group moved onwards, leaving the reptile spreadeagled on the slope of the mound, the three juveniles not without reluctance as they kept dashing back to it, giving it a nip and scratching it with their claws. Finally, they left as well and I was just debating whether or not to get out of the car to retrieve the body so that I could make an accurate drawing of the positioning of the killing bite when there was a flurry of wings and a thud. A juvenile Bateleur eagle, still in his brown baby plumage, came plummeting out of the sky to grab my valuable zoological specimen and, with a few huge wingbeats, vanish back to where he came from.

This positioning of the killing bite was still bothering me. Had George actually missed? Was his bite really aimed at the head? When I got back to Europe I decided to try a little experiment with my tame group and put a life-like rubber snake in their enclosure. They responded to it as if it were alive. The killing bite was not through the head but about three inches *behind* it. I continued to puzzle about this until, one day, it dawned on me why it was important *not* to bite a snake in the head. A grass snake had escaped from its box in the laboratory and had hidden itself behind the leg of my desk. All I could reach was its head, which I grabbed between my fingers. Before I knew what was happening, the snake's body was coiled round my arm like a huge bracelet. When I shifted my grip to the neck, however, it hung more or less limp, just twisting to and fro in my hand. It appeared as if the head was the fulcrum for the coiling action and, if this were the case, an animal which bit a snake in the head would very likely be enmeshed in its coils, even if it managed to kill the creature, for the reflex nervous activity would keep the body moving for some time after death. I could only marvel at the evolutionary processes that had resulted in the mongooses changing their killing tactics to fit their prey so beautifully.

As the days went by, I kept a sharp eye on Rusty to see whether he showed any after-effects of his bite but, apart from a puffiness around his eyes, he looked perfectly normal. His appetite was as good as ever and he didn't really give the impression of being ill although he was not quite as active as usual. Within three days, however, he was his old self again. A bite that would have caused me severe pain, if not killed me if it had been near a vital part of my body, was more or less shrugged off by the mongoose. There was not even a sign of necrosis to indicate a death of the tissues around the wound even though, for a human, a puff adder bite could easily result in gangrene and require amputation of the affected limb if the anti-snake-bite serum was not administered quickly enough. The mongooses seemed to be indestructible!

The only snake I ever saw eaten was a little Centipede-eater, a slender little creature with a dark red body and black collar round its neck, almost like a Spitting cobra in miniature, only about eight inches long. Strangely enough, although it was quite an easy kill for a single mongoose, the whole ceremony of snake-baiting had to be gone through before Whitethroat finally dashed in to give the killing bite. As soon as he dropped the little reptile, which had coiled itself up into a ball, Diana came charging into the group, growling horribly, and picked it up in her mouth, trotting with it, writhing in knots, to a small bush at the base of a mound. Here she dropped it, teased it apart with her forepaws and, once she had disentangled the head from the rest of the body, proceeded to eat it head-first very much like a millipede.

To date, all the snakes I had seen killed were animals which had to bite their enemies in order to poison them. When the chance came for me to obtain the body of a freshly-killed Spitting cobra, I therefore decided to try and find out what the mongooses would do to one of these reptiles which can spit its venom with a great deal of accuracy over a distance of five yards or more, reputedly aiming for its victim's eyes. The Spitting cobra was a magnificent specimen, over a yard in length and as thick as the handle of a broom. I got out to the mongoose's sleeping mound earlier than usual to set the stage for my outdoor experiment. I placed the cobra near to the mound, coiling it carefully to make it look as life-like as possible, then sat down in the car to wait. What I was mainly interested in was to see whether the mongooses could recognise this as an adversary that could harm them at a distance and would keep away from it. The light came slowly. Scar crawled out of an opening in the top of the mound and squatted, fur bottlebrushed, on the mound's top as the morning was still cool. He glanced about, turning his head this way and that and every time he looked in the direction of the snake I thought 'This is it!' but no, he didn't even seem to notice it. One by one the other members of the group emerged and sat with him. The minutes ticked by and I began to think that wild mongooses couldn't be so easily taken in as tame ones. Did they know the snake was dead already and were just ignoring it? Then George started the move down to the toilet and I realised that, inadvertently, I had put the snake right next to this in the dark. He was squatting there, looking around, when suddenly his eye fell on the red coils in the grass. Poor fellow, I had the impression he really didn't know what to do, whether to continue squatting until he had finished his business or to call the others or to run towards the snake or back up the mound.

Finally, still squatting, he let out an almost explosive *tseee* and all heads were craned in his direction. Then the rest of the group saw the cobra as well and came hesitantly down the mound towards it, heads flagging. George by this time had rushed to the marking post and was marking there with an almost frantic air, rubbing his cheek glands along the ground and over the branches of a small shrub, now and then breaking off to go into a violent bout of

George's eye falls on the red coils of a Spitting cobra. He then begins to rub his cheek glands frantically along the ground

threat-scratching. The rest of the group were dashing between the snake and the marking post in great excitement, almost as if they didn't know whether to mark or surround the snake first. At least there was no keeping of a safe distance between the snake and themselves. The older group members surrounded the reptile in the usual way, only the juveniles kept dashing back and forth between snake-baiting and marking and doing neither in the long run. George was working himself up into a frenzy of threat-scratching again and the snake-baiters were dashing in to give the motionless corpse a quick nip. They were responding to it exactly as if it were a normal snake species and not one which could blind them if it could spray its venom into their eyes! Just as things were coming to a head and I expected any moment to see the dash towards the snake and the killing bite, again there was a rush of air, something hit the ground right in the middle of the circle of brown bodies which exploded in all directions like the sparks of a Catherine-wheel, the whole bush resounding with explosive *tcheees* as the mongooses dashed for cover. I was left staring at a huge Bateleur, beak gaped, large dark eyes fixed on the cobra which it held in one claw. I was awed to see this most beautiful of all the African birds of prey at such close quarters. The red skin of its head, crowned with a lax, floppy crest of blue-black feathers, stood out sharply against the silver grey of the background. Then it noticed me watching it from the car and, after a few hops, the snake still clutched tight in one bright red talon, it took to the air, soaring off beyond my range of vision once its heavy wingbeats had lifted it above the tops of the thorntrees.

Not only had the mongooses given no sign of trying to keep a safe distance between themselves and the Spitting cobra but they had responded to the dead snake as if it had been alive. This set me asking myself whether they were so intelligent after all. If they could see that the snake was dead, why did they bother to attack it as if it were alive? Then I realised that not all snakes are active creatures. Some lie motionless in wait for their prey and many species can play possum quite effectively, rolling on their sides and opening their mouths, lying quite limp and death-like to fool their attackers. It would be maladaptive for a mongoose to be taken in by such behaviour and much more effective for all snakes to be attacked, whether they moved or not. In this way, the mongooses could be sure that their enemies were dead or chased away. Why they *were* considered enemies, I was still not sure.

I had wondered why particular mounds were avoided by the little hunters and, just before the rains broke, I had my answer. Poking out of a mound I'd called Cone because of its peculiar shape, rather like a volcano with a large crater on top, hidden almost in the leafy remnants of the tree around which it had been built, was something that looked, at first glance, like a light blue snake dancing in the foliage, appearing and disappearing with a rhythmic regularity. The flickering movement had attracted my attention but I was incapable of making out what this object was, as it was too dark to distinguish in the shadows beneath the leaves. The mongoose group was foraging near Cone when a grey streak shot through the heavens and the mongooses scattered. Whitethroat and Victoria landed up on Cone while the others were hidden under logs and bushes, the Chanting goshawk which had been the cause of the disturbance perching in a tree almost in the centre of the group. I heard a furious spitting from Cone and saw Whitethroat and Victoria darting at something in the shadows, fur on end, making noises like angry cats. Then a huge patch of shadow turned and, once I knew what I was looking at, the answer to the blue snake was obvious. It was an enormous monitor lizard and it was only its flickering tongue that had caught my attention in the beginning. These largest of the land-living reptiles can reach terrific sizes, easily six feet or more. The one I was looking at and which Whitethroat and Victoria were attacking must have been a grandfather (or grandmother) judging from the size of its head and shoulders, which was all that I could see of it, the rear of its body being inside the mound. The mongooses were bounding in and out, spitting in the enormous reptile's face and making leaps at its eyes while the huge lizard turned its head slowly back and forth, trying to avoid its tormentors. Then it jerkily disappeared backwards into the mound again, and Victoria and Whitethroat peered down the crater to make sure it was gone before turning and mobbing the goshawk in the tree.

Even when the monitors had emerged from their termite mounds, which they often did shortly before the rains started, waddling awkwardly through the bush, their thick legs hardly supporting their cumbersome bodies, the mongooses showed no fear of them and would charge them as a body, flinging themselves at their heads, spitting and growling. Either the monitor would just walk faster to get out of their way or, if the group had positioned themselves in front of it, the huge lizard would just bend its head downwards and close its eyes while the mongooses leapt to and fro, nipping it on the scaly snout and aiming particularly for the eyes. I saw a monitor try to defend itself with a vicious swipe of its huge tail only once. The mongooses were worrying at one of its hindlegs when suddenly there was a blur of motion, a snapping of twigs and a cloud of dust. Little brown bodies leapt almost vertically into the air or scattered only to regroup and charge again. The motion of the lizard's tail had been so swift that I could hardly believe that this normally sluggish animal could move so quickly. Then it was off, crashing through the grass and bushes, the mongooses scampering along behind, giving it a tweak in the tail or flanks to hurry it on its way.

They used the same tactics against other large bush predators that they would meet on their daily outings. Early one morning I noticed that they and a

The Blacktip had frozen and was staring fixedly at Vanessa

Black-backed jackal were on a collision course along one of the game trails. The mongooses didn't seem to notice the jackal approaching until the last minute, then they all dashed to hide under a Grewia bush by the side of the path. As it drew level with them, the jackal paused to sniff at the bush and there was a volley of spits and growls in answer. It started, pricked its ears, and then began to circle the bush, peering inside. The spits and growls became more violent and I saw one of the mongooses, who looked like Whitethroat, come shooting out, nip the jackal in the leg and shoot back in again. The jackal yelped and sprang backwards but, within an instant, was back at the bush, peering and sniffing more intensively than before. Again a volley of spits and the leaves moved agitatedly with the little bodies leaping about inside. The jackal almost shot backwards on its haunches but, curious, approached again, ears pricked. Again came the spits and growls and this time the jackal seemed to give up. After a last sniff, it turned and trotted on its way.

The only other terrestrial enemy that I saw the mongooses attack was their cousin, the Blacktip or Slender mongoose, which was relatively common in the dry bushland in which they lived. The Blacktip was also a daytime hunter and sometimes the hunts of the two species took them along the same paths. The Dwarfs' responses towards this rival twice their size varied with the strength of their numbers. On one occasion, Vanessa was foraging alone at the edge of one of the narrow game trails which criss-crossed through the grass of the bush. I noticed something moving in the tangle of dried grass which had grown through the branches of a fallen Commiphora tree almost directly in front of her. It looked like a little black blob and only with difficulty could I distinguish the sleek, shiny shape that the blob belonged to; the Blacktip blended in so perfectly with the silvery grass stems that it was almost invisible. Vanessa didn't seem to have noticed it, lifted her head from the grass tussock in which she had been digging and started trotting towards the Blacktip which had now frozen and was staring fixedly at her. The Blacktip made a dart forwards, Vanessa saw her danger and fled full-tilt, tail bottlebrushed, towards the rest of the group, the Blacktip in hot pursuit. As soon as it realised that the others were just in front of it, the roles were reversed and it was the Blacktip that turned tail and ran, disappearing like quicksilver into the grass.

Another Blacktip the group happened to come across was not so fortunate. The Dwarfs had surprised it while it was still in one of the termite mounds, charging in as a body on one side, the Blacktip shooting out of the other, right into the arms of the rest of the group which were waiting outside. They all seemed to pounce on the creature simultaneously, growling horribly. I heard the Blacktip scream once and then it was off. It looked a little strange to me but I couldn't work out why at first. Then I realised that the appendage to which it owed its name was missing! Scar was running off with it in his mouth into the depths of the termite mound. He had bitten the Blacktip's tail in half! I regularly saw the same Blacktip in the following weeks, the loss of its tail having little effect on it, although it made my recognition of the animal more difficult.

After watching how the mongooses dealt with different ground-living enemies, I began to think that the little animals were afraid of practically nothing that went on four legs as long as they could meet it as a group. Their defensive behaviour, as I had seen, was effective enough to deal with all the other smaller predators that lived in their bush world. How they would react to larger predators, such as lions or leopards, however, I did not know for I never saw them meet. Their response to the cheetah had been flight to the termite mound and safety, but the cheetahs had shown little interest in them as prey and they had not been caught out in the open. I had once been told by a friend that the relatives of the Dwarf mongooses, the Banded mongooses which lived more frequently out on the plains than in the thick bush and were larger than the Dwarfs, were capable of driving off lions, something that did not surprise me in the least. He had once watched three young male lions approach a group of Banded mongooses, which fled to shelter in a bush. The lions went after them and, just as I had seen in the case of the Dwarfs and the jackal, were greeted with a flurry of spits, growls and darting attacks until the lions just gave up and went on their way without having managed to kill a single one of the Bandeds' group members.

The only predators that the mongooses showed real fear of were the birds of prey. There is a great deal of difference between an enemy that walks on the ground and can be driven off by a group effort and one that suddenly appears in the sky, swoops down and takes a single individual without the rest of the group being able to do anything about it. Birds of prey were an ever-present danger in the bush habitat, the number of species occurring there being far in excess of those in more temperate climes and ranging in size from the huge Martial eagle with a wingspan of many feet to the little Pygmy falcon, not much bigger than a sparrow. Not all of these predators were real dangers to the adult mongooses, most being too small and weak to tackle a full-grown animal, but even the Pale Chanting goshawks were well able to handle a juvenile mongoose and raptors smaller than they, the younger babies. When they were on the move, the mongoose group was in continual danger of being attacked by some raptor or other.

The most common eagle species which were a danger to the mongooses, as small mammals formed a part of their diet, were the Tawny and Steppe eagles, Wahlberg's eagle, the Brown Snake eagle, and the Augur buzzard. Other eagle species were either more specialised feeders, or their appearance was so rare that they posed no continual threat. Of the smaller raptors, the Pale Chanting goshawk was by far the most dangerous enemy, not only because it was so common in the area (at some times of the year, especially during its spring migration between December and March, the population reached a level of ten birds per square mile) but because it did not swoop in from above like the eagles, but shot through the branches of the thorntrees with terrific speed. I rarely saw its swooping arrival until it was already quite near to the car, but the hornbills and mongooses always spotted it at a point far enough away for them to get under cover before it could dive on one of them.

After watching dozens of attacks from both eagles and goshawks, I came to the conclusion that they used two strategies. Some birds would come swooping in and, once they realised that it was too late, they had been spotted, they would fly off again fairly quickly, the goshawks almost always divebombing the little knot of mongooses clustered on top of the termite mound before they left. I could never make out what this behaviour meant as it was not a serious attack and the bird's swoop always took it several inches above the heads of the mobbing mongooses.

A Tawny eagle attempts to join its companion in the branches of one of the thorntrees

The other strategy was a 'wait and see' one. The bird, instead of flying away, would just remain sitting in a nearby tree, sometimes for hours on end, literally freezing the action. There seemed to be a method in this madness, though, after I had watched this strategy often enough. One afternoon, Diana and Co. had just got up from their siesta and were either already starting to forage or were sitting on the mound, giving themselves a quick groom before going down to join the others in the grass. The hornbills were already there, trotting in the wake of their little flushing dogs, and I thought everything was going on as usual. Suddenly there was panic, the hornbills did their usual vertical dive into the trees and the mongooses came shooting back to the mound to crouch on top of it in a huddle. I heard a ponderous beating of wings and a huge Tawny eagle suddenly landed in the twigs of a thorntree not fifty yards away, beating the air madly to get its balance. It must have come swooping low over the treetops, for I did not see it in the air above me beforehand and the birds and mongooses had given no hint of its presence. The drongo pair which lived in the area the mongooses were now moving through started to attack this enemy which was many times their size, diving from above to hit it in the back. The occasional feather that floated to earth showed clearly that this was no sham attack. Each time the little black birds dived, the eagle would duck, but made no move to leave, its head bobbing up and down as it focused on Diana and her group still clustered on the termite mound.

One by one the mongooses retreated inside until only Twin, Scar and Whitethroat, together with Rusty and Blackie, were left to keep an eye on their unwelcome visitor. The minutes dragged by and the huge bird still made no move to leave, looming above its tiny prey like a nemesis. Each time its head moved in the up-and-down fixating movement there would be a twitter of excitement from the mound and an explosion of *tchrrrs*. The hornbills were all squatting in trees nearby, hard against the trunks or under a thick protective covering of thorny branches. The minutes dragged on into hours and the huge bird had still not moved. Vigilance on the mound seemed to have relaxed, for the rest of the group emerged to join the watchers, and bouts of grooming and trotting here and there were interspersing the stock-still, strained postures which all the watchers had kept up at the beginning. The drongos had long ago given up their divebombing attacks and had vanished amongst the thorns. Soon it looked as if only Blackie and Scar were keeping the big bird under constant surveillance; the rest of the group was now busied with other things, only freezing and clumping together or diving into one of the holes in the mound when one of the guards gave warning that the eagle had moved.

After nearly three hours' waiting, I had almost forgotten that the bird was still sitting there, being busy making notes on social interactions between members of Diana's family. Moja and M'Bili started to play, wrestling with one another on an even stretch of the mound's top. The game became more hectic and the two started chasing each other round and round the top of the mound. Then Moja galloped down it, M'Bili in hot pursuit, watched by the rest of the group. This must have been the moment the eagle was waiting for; a cracking of twigs, a beating of wings, and he stooped . . . but too late. Scar had spotted his first movement, given the warning and the two playmates had broken off their romp immediately, scuttling full-tilt for safety again. The eagle's huge wings beat the air, breaking its descent and, just before it touched ground, it heaved itself upward to disappear over the treetops into the distance. It looked as if Moja and M'Bili were well aware of the danger they had been in, for the two of them sat huddled together, tails bottlebrushed, on top of the mound just afterwards. At the instant of the huge bird's stoop, the top of the mound had been swept bare of bodies, mongooses vanishing like lightning into the safety of the mound's interior. As soon as the eagle was gone, however, they popped back up like little jack-in-the-boxes and, when the hornbills fluttered down to the ground again, the troop was off foraging once more.

Although, in the case of real predators like the larger birds of prey, it was easy to understand the mongooses' behaviour, it was less easy when it came to the European kestrel and the little Shikra hawk. Both are primarily insect-eaters in the bush and very fond of locusts. A pair of Shikras lived near Dragon mound and, when the mongoose group was foraging through that area, made several attempts to join it but without success. Every time one of these miniature editions of a Pale Chanting goshawk, but with short legs and no white rump, turned up, birds and mongooses would flee although the Shikra was much smaller than the hornbills.

After the short rains, many birds of prey which winter in Africa start their return flight to Europe, amongst them the kestrel. I was amazed one day to see six of these birds suddenly appear and join the mongoose troop on the forage. The first reaction was flight by both hornbills and mongooses but then, one after the other, the hornbills flew down and the mongooses joined them, more or less ignoring the kestrels which swooped down right and left on the jumping locusts the mongooses disturbed. This completely amazed me. The kestrels were much bigger than the Shikra and, being birds of prey, should have been responded to just as violently, as an enemy. Here, however, was the proof that they were not – six kestrels flying in amongst the hornbills and mongooses as if they had been at it all their lives! I had difficulty trying to work out how it was possible for the mongooses and hornbills to distinguish between the kestrel and similar indigenous birds such as the Grasshopper buzzard, which was always considered as an enemy. If there was such a thing as an innate recognition of bird of prey form, why was an exception made for the kestrel? I began to think that this concept should be modified somewhat. Maybe the mongooses and hornbills actually *learned* which species is danger-ous and which not dangerous.

What was important to remember here was that the Grasshopper buzzard and Shikra were there when the mongooses had small babies, the only time of the year they would be vulnerable, while the kestrels arrived much later, when the young were half-grown and no longer in danger of being considered 'prey' by them. This meant that mongooses must be able to tell birds of prey apart even to species. What I thought especially curious was, although the hornbills were very much larger than both the Shikra and Grasshopper buzzard, the hornbills always considered these birds as enemies as well, although they could never be of any danger to them or their young. Hornbill females during breeding wall themselves up in hollow trees with mud and the males feed them through a narrow crack they leave in the wall, in this way preventing predators, especially snakes such as cobras, from reaching them and their brood, which stay walled up until each in turn is old enough to break down the wall and leave the site. This means that these little birds of prey would never have a chance of seeing a hornbill small enough for them to attack. Yet because the mongooses said 'These raptors are dangerous', through their warning cries, the raptors were accepted as being dangerous by the hornbills while the kestrels, which were not dangerous to the mongooses, were also considered not dangerous by the hornbills – an interspecific tradition!

The concept of a simple and rigid 'innate recognition system' for birds of prey in mongooses and hornbills seemed doubtful under these circumstances. It looked almost as if the information transfer in the mongooses might even be traditional, handed down from one generation to another, the youngsters noting the older animals' responses, which might be based on their own experience or even on their parents' experience, and simply copying them. My admiration for their intelligence was getting greater and greater, yet everything here was adaptive. If the mongooses were to fly to safety every time they saw a bird of prey then, in this bushland where birds of prey simply abounded, it would mean that they would spend most of their day in hiding if they weren't capable of distinguishing real enemies from non-enemies. The only curious point about the whole thing was that, once you were labelled 'enemy' you stayed 'enemy', for the Shikra and Grasshopper buzzard could no longer be a danger now the three juveniles were so well grown. They were only enemies of the small babies.

I had noticed this discrimination of enemies even in my tame group. I once had to catch one of them, which had an abscess on its throat, to take it to the vet. The rest of the group never forgave me and it took weeks of patient 'friendliness' before they stopped giving their warning calls whenever they saw me. I learned a lot from this lesson and now make sure that, if I have to remove one of the group members for some reason or other, I get someone else to do the catching! That person is then mobbed if he or she is seen again but I am still considered a friend.

It was while the mongooses were spending the night at Turret mound that I saw something which, for me as a zoologist, made it very difficult to believe in

M'bili's playmate, the Tawny Plated lizard, was almost twice her length

the intelligence (or non-intelligence?) of lizards. One of the Tawny Plated lizards lived here and, after eating some of the mongooses' faeces in the morning and having a short bask in the sun, suddenly heaved the forepart of its body upwards and stared down into the grass at the base of the mound. Then, with a waddling, sliding gait, it was down the side of the mound as fast as its legs could carry it, watched by several interested mongoose faces. I saw it snap at something in the grass and then it emerged, waddling towards the mound again with a locust clamped in its jaws. Although the rest of the mongoose group had turned their attention elsewhere, little M'Bili was still watching the reptile and, once she saw what it was holding in its jaws, ran down the mound towards it, tiny feet flying, to stop right in front of the lizard. Both animals seemed to pause for a second and then, to my amazement, M'bili started to nibble at the locust the lizard was holding and the lizard simply let her do it! At first it turned its head this way and that to try and avoid the little mongoose but M'Bili took no notice of this and just followed the lizard's movements with her own. Then the lizard seemed to give up on the whole thing and just stood there while M'Bili carefully nibbled away all the bits of the locust that were protruding from its jaws. The poor beast had almost a stoic air. The final act of cheekiness was that M'Bili, once she had nibbled off all she could, gave the lizard's scaly jaws a good lick before trotting back up the mound to join the rest of the group. The lizard then gave a big gulp and what little was left of its prize vanished down its throat.

M'Bili was still young and not much past the stage of begging food from her parents and the sight of the locust in the lizard's jaws might have been a stimulus that triggered off juvenile begging behaviour. She behaved towards the lizard as if it were a mongoose bringing food. The lizard, on the other hand, had no behaviour patterns in its behavioural repertoire to deal with an animal that came and nibbled the food out of its mouth and thus just stood there, unable to do anything.

Another denizen of the bushland mounds was the little African Ground squirrel which, at first glance, could be taken for a mongoose but has a plumper body, more rounded head and a tail with long hair and a white fringe. These little creatures usually live in the termite mounds. They eat all sorts of roots, berries and seeds and, although mainly ground-dwellers, can climb quite well.

The squirrels were usually most active when the mongooses were sleeping, around midday. Sometimes they would come in their hesitant run-and-stop gait to the mongooses' siesta mound, peer inside and sometimes even go in for a closer look. The older mongooses just ignored them when they arrived but, for the youngsters, they were something new and strange and would be head-flagged at and approached hesitantly. Sometimes the squirrel would even get a pat on its rounded nose with a gingerly outstretched forefoot but that was all. I thought these creatures were completely neutral and that the mongooses had nothing to do with them from the point of view of interaction. If the mongoose group approached a squirrel mound, the squirrels would just leave in a leisurely way and wander back again once the mongooses had moved on, for they never slept in mounds inhabited by squirrels, although they sometimes went inside to investigate them. Whether the squirrels would leave so unconcernedly when they had babies in the mound, however, I did not know, for I never saw mongooses visiting mounds lived in by squirrels when it was the squirrels' breeding season.

One afternoon when the group had just got up from their siesta and were having a quick groom on the mound before leaving on their foraging, one of these Ground squirrels came hopping up to the mound's base and started scrabbling around there in the remains of the few dried Boscia fruits that the stunted tree topping the mound had managed to produce. Moja and Tatu were having a game and their twittering play call floated through the bush.

The squirrel seemed to have found a nut which still had something in it and stood on its hind-legs, nut clasped in its forepaws and teeth working away at the hard covering. Then, to my surprise, Moja, still twittering away, came running down the mound towards the squirrel, stood up on his hind-legs too and this ill-matched pair then went into what could be termed a very clumsy version of the 'Viennese Waltz', the squirrel still grasping its nut tightly in both paws. Moja turned his partner this way and that and the squirrel, looking rather startled, obediently complied. In mongooses, the 'Viennese Waltz' type of play usually ends with the partners making playful, open-mouthed feints at each other's necks, the whole thing developing finally into rough-and-tumble wrestling. Moja tried to animate his playmate but the squirrel didn't seem to know much about mongoose play and still stood there passively while the little mongoose jabbed at its neck with its open jaws and even now and then gave its fur a playful bite and shake. Still grasping its nut, it remained standing while Moja batted its tail with one paw and finally succeeded in pinning this elusively jerking object to the ground with both paws before giving it a bite. This last act was too much for the squirrel which, taking the nut in its mouth, hopped off a few paces before squatting again and getting on with the serious job of opening it. Moja watched it intently and seemed to realise that his play partner wasn't really in a mood to play, so attacked a twig waving in the wind instead.

Most of the occasional relationships that I saw between the mongooses and other bush-living animals came about through the medium of play. The mongooses were inveterate players, only Diana holding herself aloof, but the rest of the family would play with objects in the environment or other bush animals whenever the mood took them. From the way the other bush animals responded, it looked as if there was some kind of 'metacommunication' – communication on a level higher than signals that could be understood by the animal's own species – between them. I have watched mongooses leaping about in small flocks of White-headed Buffalo weavers, jumping at the birds and jumping away again, twittering their 'play call' at full speed while the weavers just hopped out of their way and hopped back again to continue with what they were doing (which was usually picking seeds and insects from the ground) as soon as the little mongoose whirlwind had passed by. I gained the very firm impression that they were not at all afraid of the mongooses in this situation, they were just to be avoided for their nuisance value rather than their danger value. On one occasion Tatu chased a White-headed Buffalo weaver from bush to bush for almost three minutes before giving up the game. During the whole of this time, the bird did not rise more than a foot above the ground. It must have realised that Tatu's playful jumps at it were not dangerous for it made no attempt to fly off and would even skim low over the little mongoose's head to land on a twig behind it, and the chase would go on until Tatu finally lost interest and went to play with something else.

Not all the bush birds took to being played with. On one of my first trips to Kenya to look at the mongooses I spent some time watching a group in Tsavo West National Park. One evening, one of the juveniles of the group, while playing, met up with a family of Yellow-necked spurfowl, one of the larger ground-living birds of the bush country, but which did not occur in the Taru desert. Mongoose and birds met on a narrow game trail through the grass and, once it had spotted the Yellow-necks, the little mongoose was in amongst them with a bound, leaping from left to right, pushing against them with both forelegs before rebounding like a rubber ball to push the next one in line. The spurfowl made long necks and stared at this little creature which, twittering away, was bounding amongst them like a dervish, ricocheting from one bird to the next. The Yellow-necks stayed stock-still, necks craned, the little mongoose in the middle of the flock of five. Then a very imposing Yellow-neck gentleman stalked along the trail in the wake of his harem. The mongoose made a dash at him and then froze in its tracks, literally pinioned to the ground, all four feet spread and tail bottlebrushed. Five yards away from me, the cock had started to sing! Head cocked and eye fixing the little brown body at his feet, the Yellow-neck male gave vent to the call of his kind, the most ear-splitting, teeth-on-edge-setting call I have ever heard issuing from a bird's throat, with a volume that made the bustards look weak in comparison. I remember I clapped my hands over my ears. There is quite a difference between a Yellow-neck's call in the distance and a Yellow-neck's call from five yards away, and what the poor little mongoose thought of it all, only a few inches from this incredible noise, was unimaginable. But once the noise stopped, the little creature, all its fur on end, dashed full speed for the next termite mound and disappeared inside. The Yellow-neck looked around and then continued down the path as if nothing had happened, his wives in tow, and vanished into the grass.

One of the funniest play episodes I ever saw occurred in this group – but it certainly didn't start as play. I watched one of the low-ranking adult males fishing around with one paw in a small hole in the side of a termite mound. His fishing became more and more agitated until finally it drew the attention of one of his older sisters who trotted over and shouldered him out of the way with a growl and began to fish for herself. This attracted one of the younger males who came over to find out what was going on; shouldering his elder sister out of the way he dug *his* paw into the hole as well, lying flat on the ground, paw stuck in the hole up to the shoulder. The 'possession of the hole' went up the whole rank of the mongoose family until the matriarch finally unearthed the treasure it held . . . an empty African Land snail shell, bleached white with the weather and filled with tamped red earth! After sniffing at the opening a few times and sticking her paw inside it, she lost interest and trotted off. This was the chance the juveniles had been waiting for and they swarmed over the shell, growling and shoving until all had given up except one who was now in possession. He tried to drag it away from his competitors in the 'egg-carry' method but an African snail shell is even more unwieldy than an egg and this specimen was especially large, a good eight inches in length. His siblings gave him no peace however, so the little mongoose glared and growled at them and again tried to carry off his prize but this time in his mouth. He grasped the spindle of the shell in his jaws, lifted it off the ground and, just as he got it to the balance point, the thing turned in his mouth and the opening of the shell fell over his head like a trap and, like Tatu with the egg-shell, he couldn't see a thing! He seemed determined not to let go of his prize now he finally had it and made an effort to walk off with it. I had to bite my lip to stop laughing out loud and disturbing everything. He looked like someone with a huge pillowcase over his head playing 'Blind-Man's-Buff'. Two steps forward, one back and the shell waved back and forth. He gave a quick little run of five steps and collided with a bush, remaining absolutely still until he had worked out what was wrong, then reversed carefully backwards to take a few hesitant steps at an angle until he had finally negotiated the obstacle. The other two juveniles just stood there shoulder to shoulder, watching this strange performance. Then, shell still held high, the little creature vanished round the back of the termite mound, still performing his tottering dance. Later he dropped the shell on the slopes and, when the group had moved on, I went to retrieve it and have it still, a souvenir of one of the most amusing moments a wild animal has ever given me.

6   Mongoose Talk

Although I knew several of the calls the mongooses made from observation of my tame animals in Europe, it was not until I lived with them in their bush home that I came to realise that language for them was all-important. During the process of evolution the Dwarf mongooses had been faced with a serious problem that they had had to solve in order to survive – how to communicate with each other without being so obtrusive that they would attract enemies. In this bushland jungle with its hundreds of predators (I once counted twenty-three birds of prey of ten different species in a single day!) it would be tantamount to a death warrant for a small animal which is day-active and must forage in the open for its food to develop flamboyant colours and eye-catching postures. Some animals in other habitats have done this, like the brightly coloured coral reef fish and the forest-inhabiting pheasant-like birds, but these both live in a habitat where shelter is close at hand and they are not likely to be suddenly plucked out of their homes by death descending on furled wings from the heavens. Dwarf mongooses could not even afford a loud, raucous language like many of the larger animals, especially the monkeys and apes, for that would attract predators as well. What they did develop was a complicated and intricate speech which, although it contains vocalisations like the warning calls, which have a high carrying power and alert everything in the surroundings, consists mainly of quiet calls which the animals use amongst themselves not only to transmit the mood they are in to other group members but also information as to where they are going and what they have found.

Even their body postures are subdued and subtle, and it took me a long time to be able to interpret this 'body talk'. Again they have been forced to adopt this unobtrusive means of communication to prevent attracting enemies but, although the gestures they use are not flamboyant, they tell a whole story in themselves if one can read what they are saying. Then there is scent. This was the most difficult of the 'languages' that the mongooses used for me, as a primate shaped through evolution to respond to visual and auditory cues, to understand. Many times I wished that I had a nose like the mongooses so that I could understand what the marks they left on objects and on each other really meant, for I was only able to infer their meaning from watching how they responded to such marks. The usual response was just to sniff them and then move on, and I had no idea what was going on in the sniffer's brain, in short, what the mark *told* him. Only rarely was the response to the mark more than this, behaviour patterns that let me infer what the mark meant. I tried sniffing

As soon as the mongooses discovered the new marking post, they marked it wildly

the marking posts of the mongooses to try and find out if there was much difference between freshly marked posts and old ones, but my nose was not fine enough to tell me much. After they had been marked thoroughly, the marking posts were covered with a waxy substance which looked almost like a varnish and smelt strongly of musk. Old posts had only faint waxy signs and the musk smell had almost vanished from them. I knew, though, that they still left a message for visitors, for the mongooses always knew exactly where on a particular mound the traditional marking post was positioned and would go over and mark it as soon as they arrived.

One day, I decided to do a little experiment to see if I could confuse them. I took a marking post from a mound in another mongoose territory far away from their area and put it right next to the mound they were sleeping in but on the opposite side to their traditional post. Then I sat down to wait. I wondered whether they would ignore the strange post, or mark it and their own, or just mark the one so as to obliterate the smell of the strange group that had used it. It turned out that, once they had found the new post, they marked it madly, ignoring their old one completely. Not even George went over to sniff it. I decided to leave the post there now they had covered the strange secretions with their own, and see what would happen in the future. I had to wait for weeks before the mongooses wandered in that direction again and I was very excited when I noticed one evening that they would be moving into the area where I had constructed my experiment weeks before. Maybe now I would get an answer to my question.

The group foraged towards the mound, called Volcano, and looked as if they were planning to spend the midday rest period there. The vanguard of the group trotted finally up the slopes of the mound. They had still not made any move to mark or visit the posts so I had to be patient. Then George sauntered down the side of the mound, directly towards the new post, sniffed it and started to mark. Not a single animal paid any attention whatsoever to the old traditional post. It looked as if Volcano had now a new tradition. This gave me an insight into what the mongooses selected as marking posts – places which had the strongest scent remains. Whether or not a strange group had headed through while Diana and Co. were gone and had marked over their marks on the new post because they were fresh or whether George and his group were just freshening up their old marks I did not know, but it was significant that the old post didn't even get a sniff!

Mongooses are always talking. This continual chatter starts on the day they are born from the first gulp of air that enters their lungs. I had raised enough mongoose babies from birth onwards to realise how nerve-racking an ordeal it could be to have a group of discontented and wakeful babies (although their eyes are not open at this stage) in close proximity day and night. Unless they are in continual contact with something with which they feel 'safe', this cheeping 'nest twitter' continues unabated and is enough to drive any human babysitter to distraction, especially at night! I finally solved the problem of keeping my European babies quiet by sleeping with their box and its heating pad near to the head of my bed and dangling one hand into it. The youngsters seemed to be quite content with this and would cuddle up under my fingers and I would be able to get a night's sleep, although I had to pay for it the next morning with a totally numb arm which had to be rubbed vigorously to get the circulation going again.

The noise got even worse if one of the youngsters had strayed out of body contact with its littermates or me, its surrogate mother. Then the plaintive and very penetrating 'Baby lost!' call would start, almost a falsetto version of the 'Where are you?' call of the adults but delivered at a volume that was totally out of proportion to the tiny body producing it. The lost baby would stagger around until it finally found something with which it felt safe again, on which the ear-splitting squeaks would subside into a purring grunt. Strangely enough, only some of the animals I raised really purred like cats; others never did so and there was no reason behind this that I could detect. Maybe it was just a question of individual differences.

I wondered what processes in evolution had shaped this strange vocal behaviour of the mongoose young. Most nestlings are very quiet when their mothers have left them, lying almost noiselessly until her return. Not so the mongooses! They seemed to be the exact opposite and kept up a terrible racket as soon as they were alone. This would mean that they would attract every predator within earshot if the group foraged away from the litter in its termite mound. Although the mongooses have adapted their social behaviour to deal with this emergency, babysitters staying with the young when the mother is away, this still didn't explain why the babies were so noisy.

I spent a great deal of time thinking about this problem and came to the conclusion it could be adaptive in two ways. Since the mongooses have such a complicated language, they must have some 'starting-point' for the vocalisations, something like the human 'baby talk' which blazes the trail for the later development of words. This mongoose 'nestling talk' could be functioning in the same way, acting as the precursor of the adult vocalisations, many of which were developed directly from it. The other thing that struck me was that mongooses are very fond of small mammals like mice and will catch and kill them whenever they get a chance. A baby mongoose is just the right size to be mistaken for a mouse or baby Ground squirrel and maybe the continual cry that the babies keep up just means 'I am a mongoose baby' and prevents them from being eaten. In most animal societies it is the mother that usually has close contact with her young and she is prepared by Nature to accept them as her young and care for them. Most of the social carnivores have their litters in a hole where the mother stays with the young until their eyes open, when they emerge to greet the rest of the society. With Dwarf mongooses, however, it is quite different. The society comes into contact with the youngsters from the day of birth onwards and there must therefore be some sort of signal to tell the rest of the group, which has not the innate 'mothering instinct' of the actual mother, that what is lying there is not food but babies. I thought that the baby 'nest twitter' might be the means by which this information is communicated, so I decided to do a little experiment to test my hypothesis.

I had a litter of new-born mongoose babies to raise and decided to find out if a young male mongoose, which had never seen a mongoose baby before in its life, knew that what I was presenting him with was a member of his own species. I took one of the youngsters and held it in the palm of my hand with my fingers closed over it and in the other I held a grey mouse of about the same size. I then called him and when he had come trotting over, I opened both hands in front of him so that he could see what they contained. The mongoose baby started to cry and the mouse just sat there. He was very excited and started twittering, looking from one to the other then, with a pounce, he jumped on the mouse and killed it neatly with a head-bite but then dropped it and turned his attention towards the little naked grey thing that was turning in circles on the palm of my other hand, still calling at the top of its voice. He sniffed it carefully and then picked it up by the scruff of its neck. It went immediately into the typical *Tragesstarre* position, all limbs and tail curled up into a neat bundle ready for carrying. I was watching him carefully during all this, ready to jump in and stop the proceedings if they looked as if they were getting to be too dangerous for the youngster, but the young male had no ulterior motive in mind. He carried the baby a few paces off, let it go, sniffed it again and then proceeded to anal-mark it, squatting over it and rubbing his anal gland across its back time and time again. It was absolutely obvious to me from this that he knew exactly what it was – a baby mongoose – and was putting his scent on it to indicate that he had accepted it as such. His behaviour seemed to support my idea that it was the mongoose babies' crying that labelled them as mongooses – which would be a particularly useful label since at this age baby mongooses have no species-typical smell of their own for their scent glands have not developed yet. It was interesting to see that, even for this completely unrelated male animal, and a naïve one at that, a baby mongoose seemed to be sacrosanct and was not considered as food. This is not the case with many other carnivores where abandoned babies are often killed and eaten by the animal that finds them.

My observation of the young mongooses that lived with me in my house showed that the basic vocalisations of the species are innate. They appear in complete form at certain stages in development when the right stimulus appears, but the form of some of these releasing stimuli, as they are called, was very different with my tame animals from anything that would have been encountered in the bush. This led me to believe that, in the beginning, the animals had only very broad outlines for various categories amongst the objects and creatures that surrounded them, but even so, they were still capable of discrimination.

This was made very clear to me one day when I had visitors. I was in the process of feeding one of a litter of five I was raising from birth, giving it milk out of a pipette. The youngsters were now twelve days old and their eyes were starting to open, little slits where the baby-blue of the iris could be clearly seen, and they were starting to take notice of what was going on around them. As I was feeding one of the youngsters, the door bell rang and, without thinking, I handed it to my friend who was sitting next to me and got up to answer the door. What I had not reckoned with was the little mongoose's response to being suddenly confronted with a stranger. It took one look at the strange face peering down at it, threw itself on its back, all four paws spread, and went into a bout of furious spitting, albeit rather high-pitched and baby-like. The little creature's eyes had only been open for a day and it could already tell the difference between me, its 'mother', and a stranger, for it reacted to the strange face as towards an enemy! This made me realise that mongoose babies are well able to discriminate visually at a very early age. At first I thought it might be that my friend's hand smelt differently from mine, but when I looked closer, I could see its eyes following every movement of the strange face above it. The innate ground enemy call, the cat-like spit, was thus programmed to appear as soon as the little creature could distinguish friend from foe.

Another of these innate calls which was shown to me under rather unusual circumstances was the aerial predator warning call. This, especially, made me realise that at the beginning the little animals must only have had very fuzzy ideas as to what an aerial predator was and, comparing them with the adults, who could tell to a nicety how dangerous a particular bird of prey was to them at any moment, this meant that birds of prey as such had to be learned.

The incident occurred when I was driving to work one day, one of the baby mongooses, who was now five weeks old, sitting on the car seat next to me. On the way it started to rain and I switched on the windshield wipers. Total panic from my travelling companion who dived behind my back and started to mob the wipers at high intensity with the adult *tcheee* call! Something was moving in the sky and things that move in the sky are dangerous! From my point of view, the windshield wipers bore no resemblance whatsoever to a bird of prey but the little mongoose was convinced that they must be one. The only thing they had in common with a flying bird was that they were moving against a light background. This convinced me even more that a great deal of the mongooses' behaviour must be learned, either from personal experience or by copying other animals in the group, and this spoke for a high level of intelligence, which I had never doubted.

Another of the babies' innate vocalisations, that I again discovered thanks to an unforeseen accident, was the feeding growl. Adult mongooses give the feeding growl in response to having caught a large prey animal such as a beetle, cricket or mouse but they also use the same noise when rivalising with one of the group members over some object, whether edible or not, and also if they are in a situation where attack may be likely. From my observations of both tame and wild animals I had come to the conclusion that the deep-throated growling that was given in all these situations was associated with some wide-flung concept of aggression in which a bite or an intention to bite was being signalled, but I turned out to be wrong.

I had been getting the daily meal ready for my tame group who were having chopped heart meat as their basic dish. I had just finished cutting up the meat when I noticed that one of the mongoose babies, only ten days old, had managed to climb out of its box on the table and was now tottering towards the edge. Dropping everything, I dashed over to catch the little creature, which was wobbling blindly towards the brink, with a drop of several feet to the floor below only inches away. I literally caught it in midair but was very surprised at what happened next. Instead of a peeping, rather frightened little animal in my hand, I now had a furiously growling mini-mongoose, its blind head rubbing back and forth along my fingers, front paws grabbing at them, and the next thing I knew, it was chewing me with its sharp little incisors! I suddenly realised what had set off this whole pattern of behaviour . . . blood! The little animal had tasted the blood from the chopped heart-meat on my fingers and was behaving like an adult mongoose that had just caught prey. I decided to look into the stimuli that had released what to me seemed rather inappropriate behaviour, since at this age mongoose babies live entirely on milk!

I could not be sure if it was only the blood or my fingers associated with a blood smell that had turned this little blind creature into a parody of an adult mongoose protecting its prey, so I resolved to find out. I took a thin pipette, put a little blood in it and dropped a single drop on the baby's tongue. The whole pattern repeated itself, the excited little creature was groping around on the table top, dragging itself in circles and growling loudly although there was nothing there at all. It looked as if the taste of blood alone was all that was necessary to set the whole chain of events off. I then tried a little bit of squashed mealworm but that had no effect whatsoever. Although as adults the mongooses' main prey was insects, at this age, before eyes were opened and teeth to bite and kill had emerged from the gums, the little creatures were already equipped with an inborn knowledge of their ancestors' prey before they could ever hope to kill anything, let alone anything the size of a mouse, which would be the only animal with mammalian blood that they could find and kill in the bush. This must mean that the whole spectrum of behaviour patterns in which growling occurred in the adult animal was derived from a very basic and simple stimulus: the taste of warm-blooded prey.

Again I realised that the mongooses are not little machines which, once set going, repeat the same motions over and over again. They must be capable of modifying their behaviour to fit the needs of the moment, and whole new meanings can grow out of what is basically a very primitive response. The basic meaning of the feeding growl is 'I have found food'. As the animals grow older, this call is no longer restricted to warm-blooded prey but includes everything from insects to lizards and mice. Since the mongooses show such 'feeding envy', however, it is hard to distinguish between the simple message of finding food and trying to warn away rivals. Although *my* ear was not tuned in to the differences between growls, the mongooses seemed to know exactly what the growler was saying. I had a very clear example of this in my tame group.

The leading female had just had a litter of young which I had wanted to hand-tame, and I had taken them from her the day after birth to raise on the bottle. I had scattered some mealworms on the enclosure floor for the animals to find and was watching them feed. The female dug one of these out and held it in her mouth, growling softly. To my amazement her youngest daughter, who by this time was almost a year old, came rushing over to her giving the juvenile food-begging call and tried to take the mealworm out of her mouth! It was at least nine months since this youngster had begged food off her mother and at first I could not understand why she was doing so now. Her mother stood, looking a little perplexed, turned and stared at her daughter who, by this time, was looking just as perplexed herself at her unusual behaviour. Then she calmly swallowed the mealworm and trotted off.

It dawned on me later that what must have happened was that the mother, having just had babies, was acting as if they were still there. Somehow or other, the wires must have got crossed and she had given the special soft growl that meant 'I have found food' to attract her non-present young to take it from her. All she had succeeded in doing, though, was to attract her older daughter and I had the impression that both of them were rather embarrassed about what had happened – their responses had been automatic!

As I watched my little family of mongoose babies grow up, I began to realise how short the steps were between what seemed at first to be two completely different things: 'taste of blood' and 'abstraction of an enemy'. The first step in the chain was only a little one. Owing to the feeding envy, the growl started to be used in aggressive encounters. If one of the young animals found something to eat and ran off with it, it was almost always pursued by one of its littermates who tried to take the prize away. The animal with the food would be growling but when the littermate tried to push its way forward, the defending animal would block its path and the growl would be given at even higher intensity. Here its meaning had been expanded from 'I have found food' to 'I have found food – keep away'. This message was taken a step further when it came to squabbles about play objects which were never edible. One animal trying to take an object away from another one would be treated in the same way, as if the object were food, and here the same sound meant 'This is mine – keep away', all food connotations now being lost and the vocalisations being almost purely threatening.

From there it was just a small jump again to the next rung in the ladder, aggression towards outsiders. My mongoose babies were imprinted on humans and thought that humans and mongooses were the same species, something that puzzled and still puzzles me for, apart from the fact that we are both mammals, there is very little similarity between us. Visitors evoked an intense excitement twitter interspersed with growls which, in the case of some of the bolder members of my group, could even end up with the visitor getting a smart nip on the ankle. The 'Keep away' was here directed to strangers but when it reached the point that, whenever the doorbell rang, the mongooses would run growling towards the door, I realised that they were even capable of abstracting. The sound of the doorbell was now equated with the appearance of an enemy to be attacked and I realised that these little creatures were at least as clever as dogs and that they must have a very high degree of learning ability indeed.

I never heard young babies giving the adult protest scream but they had a whole series of noises they produced which were its forerunners, short, high-pitched squeaks which could be repeated or lengthened to give a whole spectrum of nuances to their meaning, depending on the severity of the situation. It was no great step from the longer of these squeals to the protest squeal itself, but the first time I heard this amongst the youngsters was when they were almost three months old. One of them had stolen a ball, with which the group loved playing, from its brother who was larger and stronger than itself. The brother ran over to reclaim his property and the little fellow who had stolen the ball crouched over it, head turned away, and started to protest loudly, his voice breaking into the more baby-like squeaks interspersed with the full-throated adult call, a very strange mixture indeed!

The most complicated complex of social calls, however, is derived from the babies' 'nest twitter', the series of little staccato peeps which very rapidly, within the first ten days, develops the hollow, more resonant tones of the adult contact call. Each animal has its own special frequency at which it 'transmits' and, like the baby nest twitter, the adult contact call is given almost continually, speeding up when the animals are on the move and being given only at intervals when they are sitting resting. From this single sound, a short 'beep' at about the two kHz level, a whole language has developed.

It was apparent even to my ear, unschooled in the niceties of mongoose language, that every mongoose had a slightly different call, some differing in the frequency level at which they were given, others in the length of the beep itself. At first, I thought this was simply an innate individual difference but once again the mongooses proved me wrong. I was trying to find out exactly how the voices of the different animals differed from one another and was making recordings of them so that I could measure exactly at what tone frequency they were being given, using a sonograph, a piece of equipment that transforms sounds into pictures. I got recordings from all the members of my tame group and found that they showed practically no variation in the tone

'Let's play!'

Tatu, 'mother's darling', remains close to Diana's side wherever she goes

The Yellow-billed hornbills wait impatiently for Diana's 'moving out' signal for the daily forage

Diana and Co. on the alert

*M'bili and Tatu gambol in the vegetation surrounding the termite mound in which
the group has spent the night*

Diana and George sit on a termite mound surrounded by their children, basking in the sunshine

frequency for each individual and that there was very little overlap between animals. Each animal had its 'note' and stuck with it. Then I came to take a look at the calls my hand-raised youngsters, some of which had been raised in groups and some singly, were making. Here I had a surprise, especially with regard to the youngsters that had, for some reason or another, been raised isolated from the rest of their kin. Instead of having a 'special note', these little ones were calling all over the range of frequencies that the group as a whole was using. Later, when I introduced them into other groups, I thought no more about this but, some months later still, I recorded their voices again and, to my surprise, things had changed completely.

Now, instead of calling all over the place, each one had a certain small frequency band in which it 'sang' and hardly deviated from this in the slightest. When I came to look at the calls the rest of the animals in their group were giving I found that, like my original tame group, each animal was singing a different 'song'. Somewhere between the point of my introducing them into the group and the later recording of their voices they had 'decided' on one particular frequency and stuck with it. This meant again that the mongooses must be highly intelligent, for it would mean learning the whole range of voices and then picking an empty frequency to sing in. How this learning came about, though, I had no idea. It was, however, of paramount importance to the group to be able to distinguish individuals by voice alone as I had often seen in Diana and Co.'s family for, when foraging, they were almost invisible to one another. In this way they could tell if the voice they heard belonged to their family and they could also tell exactly where each member of the family was at any particular moment. This could be very helpful indeed, as I was to see later.

A single short beep is a very useful sound. There are lots of ways an animal can vary it to change the message it carries. It can repeat the beep faster or slower, lengthen it or shorten it, keep it at one tone level or jump up and down the scale, and it can modulate it, changing the tone level in the middle of the beep so that the tone either rises or falls in the course of the sound itself. This rise or fall can be slow or so rapid that the human ear cannot resolve it in detail. Finally it can join beeps together to make a single sound or overlay it with noise, making it sound harsh and loud. The mongooses did everything! The sonorous 'moving out' call, for instance, was just a contact call that was repeated so rapidly that the individual beeps were no longer distinguishable as such, for they were all run together to make a call much longer than the contact call itself. Its meaning was 'I am leaving – come with me!' It was interesting to note that the mongooses were very particular as to which member of the group was listened to with this call. If one of the low-ranking group members wanted to leave but the high high-rankers did not, then the group stayed where it was!

I watched a lovely example of this one evening. Diana and Co. had foraged off towards a mound called Pyramid in which it looked as if they were going to spend the night, for they reached it just as the sun was setting. Diana peered into the holes in the mound but seemed rather nervous as she dashed from one hole to the other without going into any of them. The rest of the group copied her. Then finally, she decided on a particular hole and went inside. I expected the other family members to follow her example but they were still rather excited. It looked as if something was either living there or had been living there which the mongooses were not too happy about. Then Notch started down Pyramid towards Cake mound, only a short way away, and some of the younger animals, Rusty, Goldie and Vanessa, followed. The rest of the group just sat on Pyramid and watched her and her little party beeping the 'moving out' call as they trotted through the grass, but no one else moved. Notch stopped, listened – the rest of the family were not with her! She turned and led her little band back to the others on Pyramid again, trotted round them, giving quick nibbles in neck-ruffs, and began the 'moving out' call once more, trotting round and round the top of the mound before moving down its sides in the direction of Cake again. This time no one at all followed her and, after she had gone about fifteen yards, she suddenly realised this and came bounding back to the mound. A third time she tried but again with no result. The family were staying put! Then Diana emerged from the hole into which she had vanished and, without a glance towards the rest of the group, headed down the mound, beeping the 'moving out', and the group, to a man, stood up and followed her. It looked as if orders were accepted only from the 'boss'!

The 'play' call was one of the most complex ones that derived from the simple beep; it could be a short beep repeated very quickly, which was its least intense form, but when the play really got going, the mongooses would jump the beep up and down the tone scale or modulate it so rapidly that it sounded like a rapid staccato rattle. To date, Dwarf mongooses seem to be the only animals known that have this special call which means 'I am playing' and is given continuously whether or not the animal is playing with a partner or with an object. I wondered how such a call could have evolved but then I remembered two things – first, the mongooses had to be careful not to attract predators, and secondly, being so aggressive, they had to have some way of telling other animals in the group very clearly 'What I am doing now is play, don't take it seriously!' Owing to their facial muscles, which are not as flexible as those of monkeys and apes where a 'play face' or 'smile' can indicate the animal's intentions, they had had to use another method to show the same thing and this was the play call, which left no doubt at all as to the animal's intentions. When the play call was given, the animal could do almost anything it wanted, even bite its partner's neck-ruff, and it would not be attacked in return, something that would never occur if there were silence when the bite was given.

The 'excitement twitter' was just a rapidly repeated contact call that jumped up and down the scale and could easily turn into the 'panic twitter', a rapidly descending series of beeps so run together that they sounded almost like a single cry and where I could only distinguish individual beeps with difficulty. Between the two, there were all levels of gradation so that I was able to tell whether the animals were just noticing something interesting and telling the others about it or whether they had decided that whatever it was was probably dangerous and should be fled from immediately. If the sighted object was *known* to be dangerous from prior experience, then the descending twitters were run together so fast that they were barely distinguishable and preceded by an explosive, attention-getting noise, the warning *tcheee* resulting. If the object was *very* dangerous and all animals should note it, the mongooses said this simply by covering the *tcheee* call with a noise component – the mobbing *tchrrr*. This vocal warning system was more than effective as it allowed the mongooses to tell each other exactly what was happening, what they had sighted and how dangerous the object they had sighted was. In time I was able simply to close my eyes and listen to what they said and knew then what they were talking about – what sort of an animal they had spotted, how far away it was and whether it was in the air, in a tree or on the ground. It had taken me years to 'learn Mongoosese' but the problem was that I was not equipped by Nature to speak it, although I could understand everything they said!

Unlike human language, however, where subtleties can be expressed in different words, and actions are of secondary importance, in animals, especially the mongooses, what the animals do as they say something is just as important as what they say. This I found to be very obvious in the 'greeting' call which, again, derived from the basic beep, being simply the beep repeated very rapidly at a higher pitch. Although it sounded superficially like the 'Where are you?' the movements the mongooses made while saying it allowed no confusion as to its meaning. The body pressed towards the ground and one forefoot extended left no room for misunderstandings – the animal saying it was being submissive and very friendly. This was the mongooses' 'white flag of truce' and I was often amazed at how potentially dangerous situations were completely eliminated by one animal giving this cry which I interpreted as 'Please don't attack. It's me and I didn't mean it!' The youngsters greeted more than any other members in the group and, apart from using the greeting to save themselves from attack, they also used it to stop fights between other group members. In this they acted as 'peacemakers'. They seemed to switch this behaviour on immediately they saw that a fight was imminent between two animals in the group. I was able to watch how potential internecine war was

The youngsters' greeting 'Please don't attack me' prevented any potential aggression between group members

stopped dead by my mongoose children on many occasions.

One of these sticks in my memory as it could have developed into a nasty situation. The leading female of my tame group was about to come into heat but was not yet at the point where she was prepared to accept her husband's attentions fully. He, however, had other ideas about this and followed her about continuously, trying to mount until, in desperation, she fled into one of the nestboxes and blocked its entrance with her gaped mouth and started to protest. After several fruitless attempts to get into the nestbox with his wife, who was still closing its door with her jaws gaped wide, ready to snap at him if he got too close, he went into an absolute orgy of threat-scratching right in front of her. She promptly stopped protesting, and I could see from the way she was looking at him that this was too much. Any moment now he was going to be attacked. I wondered what the outcome of this fight would be for I had never seen any kind of aggression between the leading pair before, the male always deferring to his wife when she imposed her rank status on him by taking food away or nudging him out of a favourite resting-place. I should not have worried, though, for the mongooses had their own way of dealing with such problems. Before he knew what had hit him, the male was surrounded by a mass of flattened, madly greeting mongooses who rushed to the scene and tapped him all over the head with their forepaws to the point where he just had to close his eyes and retreat. The children would not allow any fights in the family! After this, he gave up pestering his wife until she was ready to accept him.

The 'body talk' the mongooses use in conjunction with the vocalisations gives the sounds a deeper meaning. There is a great deal of difference between a protest squeal given with the head turned away and the same squeal uttered with the head lowered and looking towards the opponent. In the first case this means 'All right, you win!'; in the second, 'If you get any closer I'm going to attack!'. Just a subtle turn of the head or a raised forepaw or hunched body can make a different message of the same noise. Some of these signs are so subtle that it took me years to realise what was going on for I was not as tuned to these nuances of communication as the mongooses. Just the lift of a head from the horizontal position by about fifteen degrees is sufficient to stop all action if the leading male does it, and a great deal of information is simply passed through looks.

Something like a glance is difficult to measure. There is a world of difference between an animal staring hard and one just letting its eyes skim over the partner. I came to realise in time that, like many of the Great Apes, the mongooses speak volumes with their eyes. An angry look . . . and the miscreant will drop his head and turn away; a 'soft' expression . . . and the partner will come over and groom the animal, which will half-close its eyes in pleasure. The mongooses struck me from the beginning as being 'eye animals', their quick, intelligent glances took in situations immediately and there seemed to be nothing going on around them that they missed. I often had a hard time keeping up with what was going on in the group for I missed much of this 'eye talk' that, had I been able to see and interpret it, would have made puzzling situations very much easier to understand. On one occasion two youngsters were playing with a small pebble, shooting it behind them like an egg, each then running to be first at the point at which the pebble had landed. This ultimately ended in a squabble over the pebble's ownership. The protest screams were being interspersed with growls and then, for no reason whatsoever, the two squabblers broke off in mid-growl and trotted back to the mound, heads and eyes dropped. I took a quick glance round at the other animals and saw the lead male just relaxing from what must have been an intense stare. Just his angry look had stopped them cold!

Nearly all 'animal languages', however, concern themselves only with momentary things – how an animal's present mood is, what it has found, what it intends to do within the next few minutes. As far as we know, animals cannot 'tell' others about things that have happened in the past – they have no detailed 'history' in the human sense of the word. Past experience cannot be transmitted directly from one individual to another. Or can it? The mongooses made me wonder sometimes.

It was approaching evening, and Diana was leading her family towards the sleeping mound. Little Rusty was on rearguard duty, sitting on the trunk of a fallen tree across one of the game trails. His family was almost sixty yards away, only Goldie, who was busily grubbing away in the roots of a shrub about fifteen yards from where Rusty was sitting, being still visible. I saw the forerunners of Diana's group trot up the slopes of the mound and, out of the corner of my eye, also saw a flicker of movement from a mound far to my left. I turned to look and saw the head and shoulders of a magnificent Blacktip male sticking out of the hole's gloom. He emerged and, after him, his wife with a half-grown youngster in tow. The three sat there, grooming each other in the last rays of the setting sun. Rusty was still on his perch and Goldie still grubbing away like mad – she must have discovered something very good!

Suddenly the Blacktip male stiffened and stared off into the bush towards Rusty. His flanks glistening like liquid silver, he was off down the mound at a trot to vanish in the silvery grass at its base. I lost sight of him for the moment but then his bobbing black tail-tip appeared like a little signal flag moving through the grass. *He* was almost invisible but his tail-tip betrayed his actions! He was running forwards, stopping and running forwards again and then I realised with horror that he had spotted Rusty and was stalking him, using every bit of cover available to creep up as close as possible. He was now only feet away from the little mongoose, who was still oblivious of his presence and looking at Goldie whose digging was now reaching frenzy pitch – the prey, probably a mouse, could only be inches away. Then, before Rusty knew what was happening, the Blacktip was on him with a rush.

What happened next was so fast that I had trouble keeping up with it. What started as an attack by a Blacktip ended up with the Blacktip being attacked! Before the Blacktip had a chance to make contact, Rusty had seen him and was off. Goldie looked up from her digging, saw what was going on and dashed to the rescue. The next thing I knew was that the Blacktip was being chased round and round in circles by two furious bundles of golden fur. The Dwarfs, all their hair on end and growling horribly, were galloping full speed after the other mongoose which was twisting and turning through the bushes, trying to shake off its pursuers. Finally the two little ones reckoned they had chased him far enough away and, beeping loudly, trotted off down the game trail towards the mound where the rest of the group were about to go to sleep, only a single animal sitting on guard and, from the way he was looking about him, he had not even noticed what was going on between Rusty, Goldie and the Blacktip.

This incident would have just been an interesting case to illustrate the enmity that existed between the Blacktips and Dwarfs if what happened the next morning had not put a completely different light on mongoose communication. Twin got up early and sat on top of the mound looking about; within a short while, the entire family had assembled there and they were all acting rather excited. After marking and giving each other a quick nibble in the neck-ruff, they were off, Diana in the lead, the whole group close-ranked in Indian file behind her. I noticed, to my surprise, that Diana was headed directly towards the mound the Blacktips had emerged from the night before, a mound that was usually bypassed when the Dwarfs foraged in that direction. The little band looked as if it had something definite in mind, for this was not the lazy foraging that usually happened, in fact, no one foraged at all. Nose to tail, they trooped through the grass until they reached the base of the Blacktip's mound where they halted.

The group then fanned out and Twin, Whitethroat and Scar, tails bristling and bodies stretched, approached the mound's opening where the Blacktips had emerged the night before. Heads flagging, they crept forwards step by step and then Scar finally reached the hole and peered down it. Ever so hesitantly he crept inside followed by the other two. I expected to hear the sounds of fighting from within but all was quiet. After what seemed an eternity, Scar's head appeared in the opening again and I could tell by the way he was standing that it was all right, the Blacktips were not at home. The 'all clear' being given, the rest of the group stormed up the mound, and then followed the most amazing episode. The only interpretation I could put on it was pure revenge. George began threat-scratching furiously and then started to mark the sides of the hole entrance, followed by the rest of the family. They smeared their anal secretions all over the mound around the hole and on all twigs anywhere near it and cheek-marked the ground thoroughly. Then came the final indignity. Diana squatted right in front of the hole and defecated, promptly being copied by everyone else until the Blacktips' front doorstep was covered with Dwarf mongoose droppings! After controlling the marks, Diana gave 'moving out' and the whole bunch trooped off into the grass and set off on their usual morning foraging.

It only dawned on me later that what I had seen was something extraordinary. It was interesting enough that the Dwarfs had made a vendetta out of the attack on two of their family. I would not have been surprised if this had followed directly after Rusty and Goldie's return to the mound the night before – but it hadn't. The return attack had followed the next morning, which was unusual enough in itself: but the question that kept buzzing through my head and to which I could find no answer was 'How had Diana *known*!' It was *she* that led the group and not Rusty or Goldie who had actually had the experience of being attacked. She could not have seen anything the evening before for she was already in the sleeping mound at the time the incident occurred. Rusty and Goldie would have arrived back at the mound very excited, which would have told the group that something had happened, but not exactly what. Diana, however, had acted on very detailed information – *what* had attacked her two children and from *where*! The answer to the riddle of 'where' could simply be that she knew that the Blacktips usually frequented that particular mound but I still could not get around the problem of 'what'! There had been no physical contact between Rusty, Goldie and the Blacktip male the night before. They had just chased him away, so it was unlikely that they had got any of his scent on their bodies that could have given the clue as to the 'what', Diana then extrapolating from this sign 'Blacktip', to 'Blacktip that lives in that particular mound'. It was all very curious and I was left with a sneaking feeling that maybe there was such a thing as abstract communication amongst animals – or at least amongst Dwarf mongooses!

In any case, 'mongoose talk' is one of the most complicated of any of the animal languages known to date.

7 Family Life – and Intrigues

When I first met the family, they were just a group of mongooses as far as I was concerned. Now, after months of watching them day after day, the animals were as different to me as individual human beings are. A few of them, such as Diana and George, were easy to characterise right from the start but it took a long time before I was able to fathom the depths of some of the shyer of the group members such as Victoria, Vanessa and Goldie who seemed to keep more in the background. Little by little, however, a picture of their family life started to appear, a family life which, on the surface, seemed tranquil enough, but which was seething with undercurrents whose cause was not far to seek. Sex . . . or rather the lack of it!

Probably the most important social behaviour pattern from the mongooses' point of view was grooming. This was used in practically every social situation when two family members met each other on the mound, or sat next to one another. There were three types of grooming which were easily distinguishable and which meant different things. The most common was the 'neck-nibble'. One animal would walk under the chin of another, turn its head and nibble its partner in the neck-ruff, its own neck being thus conveniently placed directly under the chin of the other, and this was then promptly nibbled in return. Licking the partner's fur was a rarity and seemed to be reserved for special occasions. The third type of grooming was also very common and seemed to be indulged in with gusto when allowed. This was anal grooming. The ano-genital region of the animal would be licked by the partner and it appeared that eversion of the anal gland was important here, for I often saw animals literally scratching the anal gland of their grooming partners to open it, presumably to imbibe the partner's smell.

Anal grooming, however, seemed to be a privilege accorded only a few, for not every animal which stuck its nose under the hind-leg of another to initiate this behaviour was accepted. If the groomer was going to be allowed to groom, its partner would then roll its hind-quarters over and rest half on its back and open its back-legs to expose the gland. If its attentions were not desired, the groomee would just stay put or sit down to prevent the groomer going any further. This was quite a contrast to neck-nibbling where anyone could more or less groom anyone else at any time, although, here again, there were differences and close friends groomed each other much more frequently than other animals. Anal grooming, though, seemed almost to be a status symbol, for all the animals wanted to groom George and Diana but some were always

Anal grooming was a privilege accorded only to special friends in the group

allowed to and others could never do it. Of course George and Diana came in for the lion's share of grooming as of everything else, and when they were not grooming each other, which they did most of the time, someone was grooming them. It was curious that, owing to this very stylised grooming posture, only two animals would neck-nibble at the same time and 'chains' of groomers, as is found in many monkey and ape societies, were never formed.

Another social behaviour pattern that revealed the relationships between individuals was mounting. Although this is of course basically a sexual act, subordinate mongooses are very much indifferent as to whether the partner is of the opposite sex or not. At first I thought that this behaviour, like similar mounting in monkeys, apes, horses, cows and many other bovine animals, was just an indicator of rank, the higher-ranking mounting the lower-ranking animal to show that it was superior to it. This was not true of the mongooses, though, and mounting here meant something quite different, as long observation showed.

Then there was play. Mongooses play whenever they can and if they can't

Moja and M'bili still played together frequently even at eight months old

find a group member to play with them, then they will play with other animals or objects. Who played most with whom also gave me a clue as to what was going on in the group behind George and Diana's backs.

Some of the first friendships that took my eye were those between Rusty and Moja, and Scar and Notch. They were, however, completely different in their type. Rusty looked to be almost exactly a year older than Moja, probably from Diana's litter the year before. Right from the beginning I noticed that these two would often sit together and groom one another. The basis of their friendship, however, lay in play. Both of them were rather boisterous individuals, always in the fore of things, but so was Blackie. He, however, judging from his size and the thickness of his neck-ruff, looked to be a year older than Rusty and, although he sometimes played with the two of them, his mind was already on other things. Rusty and Moja's friendship seemed especially strange since M'Bili, Moja's sister, was also a rather boisterous character but somehow she was never invited to join them when the fun started and rarely sat with her brother on the mound now she was getting older. At the beginning, when they were smaller, I reckoned about four months old, the two were practically inseparable but four months later their close companionship had started to wane and, although they still seemed to play very frequently together, Rusty's relationship with Moja deepened and seemed to eclipse that of M'bili's. M'Bili, on the other hand, was now tending to spend more time with Goldie with whom she would also play, and she would sit by her side and groom her very often when the group rested.

Tatu interested me particularly because she was an exception to the general rule of things; she always stuck close to her mother and had little contact with the rest of the family. She was still much smaller than her brother and sister. Frankly, from the state of her coat and her thinness, I thought she might have some kind of intestinal parasites which could account for her stunted growth and lack of general vitality. I kept a sharp eye on her during the months in which the youngsters started to spread their wings on the social scene. She stuck to Diana like glue, but there were other animals in the group who would make tentative approaches towards her and she did not rebuff them. These approaches, however, were restricted to simple neck-nibbling that sometimes went into anal grooming but little else. In the case of Moja and M'Bili, the friendships also included mounting and play but Tatu rarely played except with her littermates and I gained the impression, seeing how she would break off a game with one of them when one of the older siblings came to join in and would run back to her mother, that she was a little afraid of her older brothers and sisters. This was also reflected in her greeting behaviour, the mongoose's 'white flag of truce'. Although Moja and M'Bili practically only greeted their parents, Tatu would also greet Twin, Scar, Blackie and Rusty if they startled her or she thought she had been driven into a corner by them. I once saw her catch a cricket right next to Blackie while the group were foraging early one morning near the base of the mound. At her growl, Blackie turned towards her and instead of dashing off with her find, she dropped it and ran towards him, greeting loudly. Blackie seemed a little nonplussed, not to say embarrassed by this, for he turned away quickly and left. She greeted the other males in similar situations and I had the feeling that, because she was so small, she felt inferior to them. The time of her baby 'food-begging' was long past and she could no longer approach them with impunity and, whereas M'Bili or Moja would have just intensified their growls and gone into a hipslam if they had been in the same situation as Tatu was with Blackie, Tatu did not seem to want to take any chances and became submissive immediately. Hers was the only case I had ever seen of a youngster acting submissively towards elder brothers and sisters.

Two of the group, however, seemed to act with friendship towards her and those were Fleck and Notch. Although this friendship never reached the intensity of that between her brother and sister and Rusty and Goldie, a certain sympathy was there which expressed itself in cuddling close to her when Diana was not around and grooming her, both of which Tatu accepted and reciprocated. It seemed strange that the oldest female in the group, apart from Diana, should pay so much attention to the youngster, and she had also taken especial care of Tatu when she was younger. Now, however, I began to have a feeling that Notch was more or less 'using' Tatu as a means to an end, and that end was George! Where Tatu was, Diana was somewhere in the vicinity and where Diana was, George could not be far behind. I frequently saw Notch suddenly stop grooming Tatu when George put in an appearance and she would then run towards him and, after a quick neck-nibble, would invite him to be groomed anally, which he very rarely refused! Diana would just lie there and watch the other female but I never saw her act aggressively towards her.

Fleck's friendship with Tatu, however, was more difficult to explain. He did not seem to 'use' her to get near Diana or any other of the group members, nor could it be simply written off as 'teenage club' friendship, for Fleck and Tatu, besides being several years apart in age, were also of opposite sexes. Fleck, however, would sit and groom her and lick her face and sometimes invite her to a game, although she rarely joined him. It seemed that here was really a case of personal involvement between the two animals but what it was based on, I could not tell.

Fleck's other friend in the group was also atypical, when one considered the usual constellation of male–female friendships, for his greatest friend of all was Blackie. The two of them were the same age and probably littermates and the friendship that had existed between them as small babies had probably been prolonged into sub-adulthood. There were no other such friendships between members of the same sex in the rest of the family, although Scar and Twin, when they were not on duty guarding, seemed to show more affection for each other than they did for Whitethroat, the other adult male of the trio. It was possible that littermates of the same sex kept a special bond between them, even when they were adults, but I needed many more years of watching groups where I knew the relationships between the individuals before I would be able to tell for certain.

Fleck and Blackie seemed almost inseparable and often did things together, like guarding simultaneously or relieving one another of the guarding duty. They also spent a great deal of time resting in contact with each other and grooming and playing. What was very surprising, though, was their relationship in mounting, for they preferred mounting each other to mounting any of the low-ranking females, even though the latter were ready and willing if not downright promiscuous!

The female that dominated the latter category was Notch. I think if she had been a human, one would have termed her a nymphomaniac. She seemed to take every opportunity to make herself noticed by the rest of the males in the group, even George, and sometimes it was almost embarrassing. She would run up to Scar, who was a special favourite of hers, throw herself on her back and open her legs to be anally groomed, clasping her grooming partner round the head with her forepaws and licking and nibbling him while he was busy. If George was not there she would quickly mount Scar, or whoever it was that she was flirting with at the moment, and then go and stand in front of him, asking to be mounted in turn. She seemed to have taken a shine to Blackie and would sidle up to him and start flirting with him as well, but I never saw anything that looked like jealousy on Fleck's part. Although he would reciprocate Notch's advances, he did nothing to encourage them.

Blackie, on the other hand, was much more willing and when he saw an opportunity, he would sidle up to Notch, if she had not sidled up to him first, and start grooming her, this ending in the inevitable mount as long as Dad wasn't looking. I knew about the mongoose 'moral code' of no sexual relationships between low-ranking animals and that the leading male of the group was the one that enforced this, from observations on my tame group. It seemed to be the same with Diana and Co. as well for, as soon as George came on the scene, all illicit goings-on stopped immediately. I think this was the whole basis of the tension within the group, the females trying to form special friendships with certain males and vice versa – but on the sly. Notch, however, sprang all the bounds of common decency and tried it on with more or less any male that was willing to reciprocate. In this, she was a great contrast to her younger sister Vanessa.

Vanessa seemed to have found a partner in Twin, although the relationship was a very subtle one and not at all obvious like Notch's frantic efforts. She and Twin would often 'just find' themselves sitting together and groom each other as a matter of course. Although Vanessa played most with the youngsters and her sisters of about the same age, Victoria and Goldie, the only male of the group she invited to play with her was Twin. This did not mean that she did not play with other males for, if they invited her, she would join them, but with Twin she took the incentive. She, like Notch, would let Twin anally groom her and sometimes mount her, and with him, in contrast to the other males of the group, she would not protest.

Although play and grooming gave me indications of what active relationships were present amongst the group members I think the most useful indication of these friendships came through animals simply sitting together. Play and grooming were things that would be actively initiated by one individual and their reciprocation was, in most cases, automatic and refusals (exceptions being made for George and Diana) were rare. In sitting together, however, one animal could just walk off and leave the partner if it wanted, so I kept a careful watch on who sat with whom. This was difficult in many cases for the mongooses would form resting groups of six to eight animals and I would have to see how these groups were built up. Who came to sit next to whom first and who joined the group afterwards? This gave me a very good insight into what was going on.

The first thing that struck me was that, with the exception of M'Bili and Goldie, females almost never came and sat next to each other. There seemed to be no 'friendships' between members of this sex, not even between Victoria and Vanessa who looked to be sisters from the same litter. Notch seemed to be part of almost every resting group but, here again, careful observation showed that she usually butted in. As time went on it became clear that the females would try and sit next to their favourite male whenever possible and it was through working out who sat with whom that the very subtle friendship between Rusty and Victoria came to light, and it was Victoria that seemed to take the initiative. The problem was that Rusty's friendship with Moja often obscured the issue for Moja would come and sit next to his elder brother as well. Rusty was also the only member of the group that I ever saw Moja mark anally and this occurred in a situation where I was not sure if I could consider his behaviour jealousy or not. Usually, anal marking, which occurred rarely, was almost always directed towards George and Diana so it was with great surprise that I saw Moja one day put his scent firmly on his friend.

The two of them had been sitting together on guard, bodies close-pressed, when Victoria came sidling up and pushed herself between them and started to groom Rusty's neck-ruff, then turning on her back to expose her anal gland. The invitation could not have been more clear and Rusty complied with her request. Moja sat watching the two of them for a second and then stood up and walked towards his friend, and as he passed him he lifted his hind-leg and rubbed his everted anal gland along his brother's flanks, repeating this three times. He then sniffed his mark and pressed between Rusty and Victoria, breaking off their grooming of each other by doing so. At this, Victoria stood up and walked away. Was she trying to form a friendship with Rusty? It looked like it, for she and Goldie had no special friends at present amongst the males of the group and this, her first tentative attempt to approach one she liked, had been broken off by what looked like a jealous younger brother. I saw her trying to involve Rusty in close physical contact on three subsequent occasions but each time Moja was there and interfered, and after this she stopped.

Although Notch would often lie in body contact with Scar, it was Blackie who was her favourite partner for whenever she saw him sitting, usually with Fleck, she would come over and join the two of them and begin her rather blatant attempts to start an affair with Blackie. She also did the same if Scar and Twin were together and would push between the friends in both cases. It

Diana, the 'queen' of the group

George, her Prince Consort

Vanessa, Chief Babysitter

Twin, the image of his father

Goldie, the prettiest of the family

Moja, always ready for a game

was quite obvious who her special friends were from which of the two she groomed first, and these were Blackie and Scar, but the other usually got a quick nibble as well. It was obvious that she wanted to be loved by somebody but, to date, she had not found anyone who was interested enough in her to form a close partnership; however, she kept trying.

Whitethroat was an enigma. He seemed to have no special friends amongst the other group members, not even his age-mates, Scar and Twin. None of the females paid him much attention and he more or less ignored them. There was one female in the group, however, who had caught his eye and this might have been the reason that the other females kept away, for his special 'friend', although the friendship was rather one-sided, for she never sought him out but would accept his advances when he approached her, was Diana. Whitethroat was aiming his sights high! Not only would he sit next to her when the chance arose but he was the only one of the adult males – apart from George – who attempted to mount her. As far as Diana was concerned, however, this was taking things too far and she would protest loudly, which was usually enough for Whitethroat, who would then dismount and placate her with a meek neck-nibble. It almost looked as if he was aiming for George's position should anything happen to the Old Man and was trying to develop a bond between Diana and himself. Only very careful observation over months revealed what was really going on for it seemed that, under normal conditions, George held a very strict watch over the goings-on in the group. Diana, on the other hand, seemed rather oblivious of everything and more or less let things take their course. Her only interest was George and vice versa.

Of all the relationships in the group, though, only Diana's and George's could be termed really close, for there was no one there to say them nay in contrast to the subordinate males and females who continually had to keep an eye open for George when they were breaking the rules. I think the closest one could come in describing the relationship was a 'love match', with most of the loving coming from George's side. The way he danced attendance on his wife would put most human husbands to shame for she was the 'only mongoose in his life', and he would try and sit next to her and groom her whenever he could. Diana would accept this with good grace and return the favour but she never sought him out as often as he did her. If he had been off performing one of his 'duties' like the occasional times he guarded or went to break up something going on amongst the rest of the family, as soon as he returned, he would run to Diana, sit next to her and groom her. If she moved position on the mound, he moved too, just to keep near her. This bond between them, however, was not purely one-sided, as I was to see on many occasions, and Diana had a real fondness for him and would look for him if he had been absent long. The bond had grown up over years of friendship between the two of them and might have been a 'teenage romance', such as I could see the beginnings of between Vanessa and Twin. The importance of such early social bonds was once shown clearly in my tame group.

My old leading male was ill and I decided to take him out of the group and put him in a smaller pen during the time he was undergoing treatment. So that he would not be alone, I put his wife in with him. The rest of the group seemed stunned and for four days practically all activity ceased. Then two females which, owing to their rank and age, would contend the place of lead female, started a 'grooming tournament' which went on for six days until the younger of the two emerged as victor. She then chose as her consort from amongst the males the one with which she had been having an 'illicit affair' for years beforehand. Curiously enough, the other males showed no rivalry regarding her choice of their future leader and did not fight amongst themselves for the privilege. It seemed completely up to the female whom she chose – and she chose her best friend.

George and Diana were the hub around which the rest of the group wheeled; it became very obvious that all the group members continually had their eyes on their parents, watching what they were doing and taking their cue from this. If George was in a bad mood, which he sometimes was when he came out of the termite mound in the morning, I didn't know why, everyone was very nice indeed to him. His bad mood could be inferred by the violence of his threat-scratching and sometimes the youngsters would run over to him when he looked as if he was really furious, greeting madly, on which he would subside to normal again. The younger animals were especially obsequious towards their parents and would try and cuddle close when they got a chance and groom them. Victoria, Goldie, Vanessa and, of course Notch, were very fond of anally grooming George and sometimes all four of them would be at it at the same time, George just lying back and enjoying their attentions but rarely returning in kind. It was interesting to note that when the whole group was around George like this, Diana would just sit and watch them, making no move to interfere. It looked almost as if she was so sure of him that the other females were wasting their time in trying to usurp her position.

It was quite different from George's perspective, however, for he hardly tolerated such associations between his wife and other members of the family. Whitethroat, Diana's secret admirer, seemed to know this, and it rarely came to a confrontation between the two adult males for Whitethroat would slink off as soon as he saw George coming. Diana would enjoy being anally groomed by the rest of the group as well, especially Blackie, Fleck and Rusty, and sometimes two or three of these would be busily licking her, only to creep off, bodies flattened, when George approached or stared at them hard. Blackie, however, seemed less intimidated by George than the other two and would just turn away and walk off normally as if there was nothing wrong. Scar and Twin, although they groomed Diana frequently, did not seem to be as active at it as the younger males, neither did they sit with her as often. Of the two, it was Twin who seemed to have the closer connections with the leading pair and, strangely enough, not with Diana but with George. He and George would sit together much more frequently than did Scar and Whitethroat, but they did not groom each other much; it was Blackie and Fleck amongst the males who seemed to be Twin's main grooming partners while Scar, on the other hand, never seemed to groom these two at all. The only one of the older males that he seemed to groom was Whitethroat. These 'wheels within wheels' were very confusing for it looked almost as if the males all tried to be 'nice to father' and some of them would sit with him far more often than they did with Diana, but Diana was the one who got the most grooming. I sometimes wondered, especially in Twin and Blackie's case, although Twin had a special friend in Vanessa, whether this friendliness towards their father was just a means of getting close to Diana and trying to win *her* friendship. Diana, however, did not seem to be playing.

The youngsters' relationships with their parents were especially interesting. Although Tatu was rather an exception owing to her strong bond with her mother, the other two youngsters, Moja and M'Bili, were more than friendly towards them, but it seemed that their affections were more or less equally divided between the two, in contrast to their older brothers and sisters where the parent of the opposite sex seemed to be preferred. Apart from sitting next to them and grooming them, the two would also mark them anally quite frequently although they never once mounted either of them at this stage in their development. I was not sure what the marking here meant: whether it had the same meaning as in George's case when he marked his wife, more or less 'She belongs to me', or whether these youngsters, who were marking very frequently in general at this time, were just trying to strengthen the bond between themselves and their parents and imprint their personal odours on the 'family smell' which was constantly being maintained by animals rubbing up against each other or anal-marking passively by just walking under the tails of their partners and thus smearing their flanks with their secretions.

The friendship between M'Bili and Blackie took a sudden turn when M'Bili was almost nine months old. Up until now, the two had mostly played together and groomed each other. Blackie and Fleck, however, were indulging in a spate of mutual mounting which, in contrast to their mounting of the females in the group, George turned a blind eye to. M'Bili came trotting over to her friend who promptly stopped mounting Fleck and mounted her instead. This was the first time I had ever seen her mounted by anybody and she stood absolutely rigid, eyes straight front, not certain what she should do. When

Blackie dismounted she was still standing there, looking a bit bewildered, while Blackie went back to mounting Fleck again. M'Bili stayed as if thunderstruck, body rigid, for almost four minutes and I wished I could know what was going on inside her head, but her face and posture betrayed nothing. She tended to avoid Blackie for a few weeks after this occurred and it required some effort on his part to get back into her good graces again. I was of the firm opinion, after seeing her response to this 'rape', that she had not found it at all pleasant and maybe, amongst mongooses, sex is also something that does not just 'come naturally'.

It seemed that, since George kept a firm hand on what was and what was not allowed in the group, the group found their outlet for 'illicit contacts' in play, for mongooses are the most playful animals I know and play even when they are full grown adults. The most prominent of the players were the females, although even the adult males such as Scar, Twin and Whitethroat would play frequently, but rarely with each other and usually with one of the ladies of the group. It was interesting to notice the difference in the 'play invitation' between these older players and the youngsters. The youngsters usually started their play bouts with a tapping towards the head of their partner, one forefoot extended; for the older players, the play usually arose out of grooming or mounting. After watching the animals playing on many occasions I began to have the feeling that this was not just an expression of high spirits as it was amongst the younger animals, but that again, there was an ulterior motive behind it.

Something that happened between Vanessa and Twin set me on the track of what was really going on. The two of them were sitting round the back of the mound, out of George's sight, and were grooming each other intensively. Vanessa lay there, legs spread, and let Twin groom her anal gland. This led one step further to Twin mounting Vanessa and, while he was clasped firmly around her flanks, George suddenly came round the side of the mound and, I could tell by the way he was standing and staring at the two, he was not at all pleased at what he found. Instead of slinking off, Twin then did something which surprised me greatly. Instead of dismounting, he started beeping the play call and pushing Vanessa from side to side with his forelegs still clasped around her flanks, making playful bites towards her neck. Vanessa immediately got into the spirit of things and, beeping herself, threw herself onto her back and started to wrestle with her partner. Twin reciprocated and then Vanessa tore off, still beeping the play call loudly, Twin close on her heels. Once the play call had started, George had subsided and, when he saw the two of them wrestling, had turned to go back to Diana. It was almost as if the miscreants had told him 'Look, Dad, we're just playing!' As I kept a special lookout for such occurrences in the future, I found that they were very common, only I had not really noticed them as such at the beginning. The subordinate males and females were more or less using play as an excuse to come into close social contact with their friends, a social contact which seemed to be 'allowed' by their father, for he never tried to interfere except in cases where the play became too wild or the players went too far away from the mound. Then he or another member of the family would go in and stop it. This seemed to be a way in which the mongooses 'cheated' by using a juvenile behaviour pattern for a completely different purpose. Often, when George had been pacified by their good intentions, the players would suddenly break off and go back to mounting and grooming again.

It was not only these forms of social behaviour that gave an insight into the workings of the group. The commonest group duty, guarding, in which all the group members took part to a greater or lesser extent, showed that there were relationships present here as well. Some of the group members were much more avid guards than others. Here it was obvious that it was the young males that took the brunt of the burden upon themselves and, of these, it was Blackie and Fleck who guarded more than the rest of their brethren. The older males, Scar and Twin, only seemed to go on guard frequently when there was something dangerous in the offing and, when I had joined the group for the first time and they were not quite sure how they were going to consider me, friend or foe, Scar and Twin were the ones that had usually remained near me, keeping an eye on what I was doing. As their fear of me waned, things got back to normal and Blackie and Fleck took over. Only Whitethroat, of the adult males, showed anything like the level of guarding that Blackie and Fleck did and Rusty, their younger brother, although he often guarded as well, was not such an avid guard as these two. Why Whitethroat, of the adult males, still kept up his very frequent guarding, I had no idea, but it might have had to do with the fact that he was 'unattached' and I sometimes had the sneaking feeling that he was doing it to impress Diana, for he would go on guard rather ostentatiously when the group was leaving the sleeping mound in the mornings or later afternoons, as it were doing it 'under her nose', but anything like his 'showing off' would be almost impossible to prove.

There was almost always a guard up when the group went foraging but there was a tendency that, when the group was accompanied by a large number of birds, the guards would be fewer and not stay at their positions as long, in contrast to times when there were few birds around. It almost looked as if the mongooses were depending on their feathered friends in this case. Blackie and Fleck would leap-frog mounds and points of vantage as the group moved past. If Blackie was on guard, Fleck would go up on a mound ahead of him and take over until the group and Blackie had passed, on which Blackie would go up on a guarding post in front of Fleck and Fleck could then go off

Rusty keeps guard while the others sun themselves and the youngsters play

duty, repeating the favour further along if nobody else took over in the meantime. Strangely enough, most of the other animals seemed to take over from Fleck on such occasions, he seemed to be the main guard in this respect while Blackie's relief was either his brother and friend or Whitethroat. I wondered if this friendship between Fleck and Blackie was somehow associated with their close sharing of this, one of the group's most important duties, and asked myself if they had just 'grown into' this arrangement or whether it was deliberate. There were so many unanswered questions that the mongooses brought up, as I watched their lives starting to unfold before me, questions to which I would probably only get an answer in the future by finding out whether similar things happened amongst the youngsters that were now growing up and whose life histories I knew.

Although my first impression of the rank order existing within the group, that of the younger animals being higher-ranking to their older brothers and sisters, still held when it came to important priorities such as food, now I had come to know the group better and understand the machinations that were going on within it, I realised that there was more to a rank order than meets the eye. It must have been necessary for something like the 'priorities rank order' to have evolved simply to make the youngsters a focus for the attention of the rest of the group and ensure that they thus got a high degree of protection and, of course, the most food. When it came to more subtle things like 'who likes whom?' and 'who is the most active socially?' a very different picture emerged. Since many of the mongoose social activities like grooming and playing were reciprocal, one animal initiating and the other responding, I had to be careful to distinguish between who started an encounter and to whom the social action was directed. When I began adding up all these 'social points', something rather surprising emerged, something that gave me a completely different picture of the mongoose society and how it functioned.

When it was a question of social activity – grooming, playing and sleeping near other animals, it was, surprisingly enough, Fleck and Blackie who won first prize, Notch coming a close second. Only then did the youngsters Moja and M'Bili come into the running, followed by George, then Diana, the older males next and the females of the group coming a poor last. This meant that the young males were the ones that spent most of their time interacting with other group members and not their sisters, although I had the impression that *when* their sisters initiated an interaction, then it meant much more from a social point of view. When I came to look at which group members were receiving the attention, it was as I had expected, Diana and George led all the rest with a large majority, then came Vanessa, Victoria and Notch followed by Fleck and Blackie. Only then came the youngsters Moja, M'Bili and Tatu, and their eldest brothers Scar, Whitethroat and Twin once more tailed the list. Not only were they not very socially active in themselves but they did not seem to be very attractive for the rest of the family either.

This started me thinking. Maybe how active an animal was in making social contacts also influenced how attractive it was for the other group members, a system of 'one hand washing the other'? In order to compensate for this, I decided I should subtract the 'social points' given for social activity from those that indicated the animal's 'attractiveness': how often other group members would contact it. In this way I could get at the 'surplus': how often a social interaction was started with an animal over and above what it initiated through its own actions. This would give me a far more accurate view of what was really going on in the group. The results were quite different from the simple 'priorities rank order', and they gave me an insight into the social importance of various individuals.

Right at the top of the list, as expected, came Diana and, close on her heels, George. The next one in rank was a surprise for it was Twin and, after him, Vanessa, Notch coming in a close fourth. Then it seemed that Scar and Whitethroat were the most popular, followed by the youngsters and, right at the bottom of the list, Rusty, Blackie and Fleck. It was almost a reversal of the priorities rank order and the social activity one as well. Viewed subjectively, it looked as if the younger animals spent all their time running round being nice to the older ones and the older ones were just accepting this but giving little back in return. I had seen how the youngsters used the 'greeting' call to prevent aggression breaking out within the group and these findings made me wonder if it were not the younger animals, especially the subadult males, who were responsible for group cohesion, for they were the ones being actively 'useful' and 'nice' and, in doing so, it might be that they held the group together.

I was especially surprised that Twin and Vanessa headed the list right behind their parents and wondered if their stable friendship might have something to do with this, and if they might be the 'Prince and Princess', groomed to take over if something happened to their parents. The rest of the group seemed to be very aware of their position as 'important people', as my data showed, and it almost looked as if they were being 'toadied' to by the rest of the group, just in case. Notch's high position I considered as being the result of her playing the field, especially amongst the males who were yet unattached, although Scar's position right behind her made me also wonder whether her 'friendship' with him had influenced both their social positions in a similar way to the case of Vanessa and Twin. Victoria and Goldie were also important as potential partners, but as neither of them had yet formed a close alliance with one of the males, their position was more open. It seemed, from the fact that Rusty, Fleck and Blackie were so low-ranking in this respect, that their high social activity level might simply be directed towards attracting one of these unattached females while at the same time placating the higher-ranking animals, especially their parents. Things were getting more and more complicated!

As far as attractiveness went, it looked as if the youngsters did not count for much at present but they still ranked above their elder brothers, the subadult males, probably because so many of the group members played with and groomed them. There was still a shimmer of their 'baby attractiveness' left and I wondered how things would develop when Diana had a new litter. Would the youngsters then be the centre of attraction or, when it came down to brass tacks, would they be just as low-ranking as her present youngsters? Only time would tell.

8   Love, Marriage
and the Wages of Sin

The Commiphora trees were anticipating again. Although I could tell no difference between the weather of the week before and this week's – both weeks were equally hot and dry – the Commiphoras said rain was on the way, for each thorny branch now had a faint shimmer of light green. The buds were opening. Other than this, life was much the same as ever in the mongoose family: a daily wander in search of food from one termite mound to the next, marks on marking posts freshened up, little family squabbles and occasional meetings with various enemies to liven things up a bit, in fact, 'business as usual'. The youngsters were now almost nine months old and had started to take part in the group 'duties', like taking their turn at guarding when the group was foraging. I had thought that something as complicated in its organisation as the guarding behaviour that the mongooses performed would be preprogrammed, but again the mongooses proved me wrong.

It all started when Moja and his sisters were about six months old and literally into everything. This is the age at which mongoose children are at their worst when it comes to a peaceful life for the rest of the family. When they were not playing they were continually bothering somebody or trotting off and getting lost or sticking their heads into places where they shouldn't. Moja, the most precocious of the three, had even got to the point where he would try and climb into the car to have a better look at me. I would watch him clambering with difficulty up the side of the tyre to sit, wobbling, on his precarious perch on top of it, from which point his little face with its two beady eyes would peer at me from around the side of the mudguard. Ominous scratchings would come from beneath the car as busy little claws worked away at interesting things like the differential and fuel lines and I never knew when one of the three would be balancing on my front axle. I was very tempted to try and be friends with them, attract them to me by giving them titbits, but decided against it. I wanted them to accept me but not change their behaviour because of me. I was enough of a disturbance in their normal lives as it was and I did not want the disturbance effect to increase by my actively trying to change things. Just providing an animal with a regular supply of food can change its usual habits completely, bringing it into situations which would rarely if ever occur under undisturbed conditions and thus giving an observer a biased view of the animal's normal life. I was quite content to watch and wait and let Nature take its course.

It was about this time that I noticed that Moja, especially, was not always with the family when they went foraging. Quite often he would remain behind with the guard of the moment but when I started counting how often he sat with different guards, I found out that he had one especial favourite, his friend Rusty. Moja would sit close to him, bodies touching, and stare seriously off into the bush, but he could never keep this up for long. Within a minute or two he was off, scrabbling about at a fallen leaf that had caught his attention or poking his nose and claws into a crack in the bark of the tree above the mound. Gradually, however, his periods of careful watching grew longer until he could manage as much as three minutes sitting still and looking about. Quite a feat for an active little mongoose! Then started the real training. One day, while Moja was sitting pressed close against Rusty's flank, staring with him out into the bush, Rusty just got up and left him – wandered down the mound and started to hunt about in the grass at its base. Moja wasn't too sure how to react to this. He stared hard at Rusty, made a quick move towards him, looked around – there was no one else guarding! I could almost see the conflict mirrored in his face – to go or to stay? Moja stayed. I don't know where this 'honour system' that the mongooses have with regard to guarding has its roots but it is present even in the young animals. If you are on guard you stay on guard until you are relieved by someone else. In this case, there was no one and Moja stayed.

Rusty did not leave him alone for long, though, and within a minute he was up the side of the mound again and squatting next to Moja who, with what appeared to be almost relief, began to potter about on the mound again. Later, when Victoria took up the guard office on a mound ahead, the two of them shot off towards the rest of the family, tails out like little pokers, Rusty in the lead and Moja close behind. This became a common sight as Moja's sojourns with Rusty when he was on guard duty became more frequent. Rusty continued to leave Moja stranded every now and again but always only for a few minutes. Then he was back again and Moja could go 'off duty' and attend to more important things like playing.

As the weeks went by I noticed that Rusty was leaving Moja alone on the mound now for longer and longer periods of time. Little Moja seemed to take his job very seriously for he was even more assiduous than the experienced animals, warning whenever he saw something move, whether it was a flycatcher or an eagle, and trotting to take up his position on the other side of the mound every now and again, just in case something was creeping up on him from behind. At first the group would react to his almost continual warnings by dashing into hiding but I noticed that, with time, they would scan the heavens first and decide for themselves if what Moja had seen was dangerous or not. Sometimes I felt rather sorry for Rusty, for at each of Moja's warning calls he would come dashing back to the mound, looking about him wildly, trying to spot the enemy. In most cases there simply wasn't one and the panic had all been for nothing.

When Moja was finally at the point where he could guard alone for up to ten minutes, Rusty keeping a sharp eye on him during this time, the baptism of fire came. Instead of trotting back to the mound to pick Moja up and go with him to join the rest of the group, Rusty just kept on the way he was going and Moja, for the first time in his life, was literally on his own. When he saw Rusty leaving, he started to trot up and down, giving the 'excitement twitter', but made no move to follow him. He sat down again and waited, peering carefully off into the bush all around. I sneezed and the next thing I knew, Moja was over on my side of the mound, body flattened and staring hard at me as if he had never seen me before in his life! He glanced continually towards his family in the grass and kept up an almost paranoic search of the surroundings for the least thing that might be out of place, but all was quiet. Then, finally, Fleck took over on a log in front of the foraging group. Moja needed no second invitation! All his hair on end, he headed full tilt, little feet scampering so hard they almost looked a blur, towards his family. This was the first time that he had ever crossed open space all by himself and he was very frightened – but nothing dived on him from above. The first thing he did when he joined up with the group again, however, was to run to Diana and give her a quick nibble in the neck, which she reciprocated, an almost unheard-of thing when the mongooses are foraging, for then their whole concentration is fixed on finding things to eat and there is very little social contact between them. Maybe Moja needed this reassurance after the ordeal he had been through.

After a few days, however, he was no longer so frightened and would race after the group like any normal guard. Rusty now regularly left him alone and Moja fitted himself into the scheme of things quite easily. The final step came almost two months after he had started his guard duties. Rusty only sat with him for a moment once the group had left the mound and Moja was left to do an entire guarding stint all by himself. By this time, however, he was relatively seasoned and it did not bother him, as far as I could see. He had stopped warning at everything that moved and was now restricting his calls to things he didn't know or things he knew were dangerous from the way the others would mob them if they appeared. The next thing I knew was that Moja now even started 'volunteering' for guard duty, simply staying behind when the group moved on. He was growing up!

At about this time I noticed a change in George's behaviour. His anal grooming of his wife was getting rather obvious, both in the frequency with which he did it and the length of time he spent doing it, when Diana allowed him. Sometimes, however, she was not in the mood and would just stand up and walk away but if George persisted, he would be rebuffed with a little squeal and a push of the forepaws. It was Blackie's behaviour, though, which struck me as curious. He seemed to take every chance he could to sit near Diana when George wasn't there and nibble her neck, which was reciprocated, for I had the impression that Blackie was one of Diana's favourites amongst the group members. Then came the first tentative mounting attempts, Blackie delicately resting one forepaw on Diana's back. She would glance at him and usually stand up and walk away at this but these gentle rebuffs did not deter Blackie from trying again. Diana must be coming into heat for George too would attempt to mount her after they had groomed each other for a little while, but got the same treatment as Blackie. Diana wasn't ready yet!

Soon the situation between George and Blackie started to get strained. It became rather funny to watch the little cavalcade walking round the mound when the group was resting; Diana in front, followed nose to tail by George, with Blackie only a pace behind. Diana was completely oblivious of all this, or acted as if she was, but the glances that George shot his son every now and again were enough to shiver him in his shoes, had he been wearing any! Blackie was not to be intimidated, however, and persisted in his attempts to get close to and, if possible, mount his mother. The nearer Diana approached her oestrus, the more attentive Blackie and her husband became. Finally Diana even allowed her son to mount her, at first protesting – which she also did in George's case at this time as well – but later quite silently.

Things could not go on in this way, for George's aggression towards his son could almost be felt as a palpable wave by this time. Blackie, however, avoided all eye contact with his father and poor George was left fuming. Finally things came to a head and Blackie's challenge of his father's supremacy was answered.

Diana had just trotted down the mound and was grubbing in the grass at its base. Blackie saw her and trotted down to grass-grub right next to and parallel with her. George spotted this and was down the mound in a flash to stand parallel to Blackie but on the other side. I think it was at this point that Blackie realised that he had gone too far, for I saw him falter, drop his head as if to stare hard at something on the ground, and make ineffectual little scratches with his forepaw in the dirt. He was watching his father out of the corner of his eye and his father was staring quite deliberately towards him with no pretence as to the challenge in that look! Blackie should have turned and run, but he didn't. He just stayed there, scratching, head bowed. Since Blackie was not to be cowed so easily, George went one step further and stood in front of him, sideways on so that Blackie's further progress was blocked. There was absolute stillness for a moment and I could almost feel the tension between the two but Diana, as usual, was oblivious of everything. Then, with an ear-splitting scream, Blackie flew at his father, both forepaws outstretched in front of him, and rammed him in the side. With a lightning movement George turned and the next thing I knew was that he was standing over Blackie, who was lying on his back on the ground, pressing George's body away from him with all four feet and screaming bloody murder! I have never heard such terrific protest screams issue from a mongoose's throat before or since. George ignored them completely and just stood there, head raised, pinning his cheeky youngster down so that he could not move. Blackie's screams went on and on and the rest of the group peered down at what was going on but not a single animal made a move to come to Blackie's rescue. Finally, after almost thirty seconds, George let Blackie go and Blackie dashed, all his hair on end, into one of the holes in the mound and did not emerge for a long time afterwards.

George could easily have fought Blackie and bitten him severely, for he was much older, stronger and more experienced than his son, who was only just getting on for two years old. Despite this advantage, he had done nothing of the sort, but had just threatened the forward youngster with an extremely severe form of punishment, one which I had never seen before but what one could term a 'psychological thrashing'. He had taken pains not to hurt Blackie but, at the same time, made it absolutely clear who was the boss. He seemed to have succeeded, though, for Blackie left Diana alone after this and George had her all to himself.

The days that followed were an absolute torture for poor George. It was then I realised that his 'job' in the group was more than just 'Keeper of the Peace' and 'Commander-in-Chief' in battle. He was also in charge of the mongoose moral code! It was now obvious that Diana's peak oestrus was not far off for she was accepting George's tender advances with little or no protest by this time and would allow him to mount her, gripping her around the flanks with his forepaws, but I did not think that he had mated with her yet.

The problems came from another side. I began to notice that Notch was tending to lag behind the rest of the group when they were on the forage but she rarely lagged behind alone! Within a few minutes, one of the older males – usually Twin or Scar – would decide to keep her company. The two would find some sheltered spot and Notch would then play the coquette, sidling up to the male, rubbing her body against his and nibbling him in the neck-ruff, this turning into anal grooming and the inevitable mount. In contrast to Diana, however, Notch never protested, and seemed to be enjoying every minute of it!

George, while all this was going on, would be following Diana faithfully, as

Diana's oestrus reaches its peak and she allows George to mount

During this time, George hardly leaves Diana alone for a second

if tied to her tail by a piece of string, literally dogging her footsteps and keeping other animals in the group at a distance with his angry stares. On one of the first occasions I had noticed that Notch had lagged behind and Scar with her, George had suddenly appeared out of nowhere and stared hard at the two of them, who broke off what they were doing immediately, Scar turning his head away, his body pressed to the ground and uttering little protest squeaks. Notch, on the other hand, acted completely nonchalant, just giving George a glance and then trotting past him to join the rest of the group. Scar was still hunched up submissively under a bush and, after another angry look thrown in his direction, George turned and hurried after his wife, casting furious looks right and left and growling softly.

I wondered how George had known that Notch and Scar were missing. It was impossible for him to have seen them from his position right behind Diana in the fore of the group but it was very clear that he had noticed that something was wrong and had turned back to find out what was going on. It was equally clear from his behaviour and Scar's response to it, that illicit sexual behaviour was not going to be tolerated in the group, for Scar had responded immediately to George's threatening stare. What interested me, though, was how did George know about it? He was a good forty yards away and could not have seen it. I decided to watch carefully the next time the same thing happened.

I did not have to wait for long, for within the next half-hour Notch was at it again. This time she made the pretence of having found something in the roots of a small Grewia bush and was digging around there as the rest of the group passed her by. I could tell by the way she was scratching, though, that this was all an excuse. She was hardly looking at the place she was actually digging in, her eyes were flicking this way and that, looking to see if anyone was coming. It was Twin that appeared this time and, without much ado, promptly mounted her, Notch standing tail to one side and back slightly arched, with a rather placid expression on her face. I kept a sharp eye on George, who was still glued to Diana as the group slowly moved off. He didn't seem to have noticed anything but then he suddenly stopped. I saw his head lift as if he was listening, and then he was galloping back along the track the group had used and finally stumbled upon the two miscreants. He halted about a yard away from them and began his aggressive stare again. Twin slunk off around the back of the Grewia bush and made a wide circle around his father, keeping a low profile until he was finally behind him, at which he set off at full gallop towards the rest of the family again. Instead of showing submission, Notch trotted up to where George was still standing, staring at her, and calmly nibbled him in the neck-ruff before trotting on to join the rest of the group, as if nothing had happened at all! George stood still for a moment, as if not quite knowing how to react to all this, then turned and galloped at full speed back to his wife who was assiduously being followed by Whitethroat. When Whitethroat saw his father approaching, he slunk off before it could come to a confrontation.

When I thought back on the incident it had looked as if George had *heard* something, and had known then that Notch and Twin were up to no good. I, however, had heard nothing, and I was pretty sure that the two of them had been as quiet as mice while they were having their illicit tryst. It took me a while to realise what exactly was going on. I was right, George had *not* heard anything – that was the whole point! Notch and Twin's contact calls were *missing* from the chorus of little beeps that surrounded him. It was not the presence of a noise but its absence that had given him the clue, and he had dashed off to find the two and stop what was going on between them.

As Diana's oestrus reached its peak, George was literally run ragged. Not only did he have to take good care of his wife – for as soon as he left her side for a moment, one of the other males would take his place – but he also had to keep an eye on Notch and her doings. Notch restricted her activities to the time the group was foraging, however. It almost looked as if none of the males would dare to do it directly under George's nose when the family was resting on one of the mounds, and Scar and Twin even seemed to keep a distance from her when they were there. Whitethroat showed practically no interest in Notch whatsoever. He was more interested in Diana and tried to get close to her every time George was out of the way – which was never for long!

George's courtship of Diana was touching. He would nibble her neck-ruff until it stood out in little wet spikes, bore his nose into her anal gland as soon as she gave any sign of stopping and mark her continually, rubbing his scent over her back by lifting one hind-leg and sliding his scent gland along her flanks. Diana would reciprocate the grooming but I never saw her mark him in return. She gave me the impression of being a real queen in this respect, accepting the obeisances of her courtier but holding herself aloof. George's mounts were, at the beginning, rather violent, for he would grab Diana around the flanks, swing her round and try and pull her onto his lap, rolling backwards to rest on his sacrum with her sitting on top of him. Then he would gently move her up and down with his forepaws. It was curious that this was not the typical copulation behaviour found in most male mammals where the male performs thrusting movements of the pelvis. Here there was no thrusting at all. The fact that a male mongoose's penis is only about three-eighths of an inch long even in the erected state could explain the adoption of this alternative method of copulation. It all looked very gentle and Diana accepted George's advances at this stage without even a squeak.

George tolerated absolutely no one near himself and his wife, chasing all of the other family members away irrespective of age and sex. He spent his time almost continually in action, either mounting his wife or dashing madly at the row of interested little faces who were watching what was going on from a safe distance. Even when the group was foraging, he had no peace for he was continually dashing between Diana and Notch as soon as he realised that the latter was out of earshot again. It was exhausting for him for even when foraging, he stuck to Diana like glue, stopping when she stopped to grub in grass tussocks but hardly grubbing himself – he just stood behind her casting furious glances at any of the group he could see and dashing towards them to chase them off if he thought they were getting too close.

It was amusing to watch George on the mound when Diana was with him. He spent almost his entire time lying on top of his wife, his forelegs clamped around her flanks, only breaking off to chase away one of the group members that had dared to approach. Tatu, who had always been mother's darling, suffered especially from his attacks since she continually tried to take up her position as usual near Diana but George would not tolerate this and chased the juvenile away as soon as she came near. Tatu seemed to be getting very depressed and would often sit by herself somewhere as far away from her mother and father as possible and showed little interest in joining the rest of her family. This was the first time that she had been seriously attacked by one of the family members and she seemed to be taking it hard. Even the rest of the family seemed to feel the tension that Diana's oestrus, and Notch's as well, was building up amongst them, for they no longer played around the base of the mound in the mornings as they usually did. They kept their eyes glued on George to make sure that they did not approach him too closely inadvertently and thus release his rapid darting attack in their direction.

By the second day of Diana's full oestrus, George was beginning to show the strain, for his attacks against the rest of the group decreased in violence and even Notch got away with her illicit affairs more frequently. George still followed Diana as if tied to her with a piece of string and groomed and marked her whenever an opportunity arose, but usually he contented himself with just slinging one forepaw over her back whenever she stopped whatever she was doing, as if demonstrating his rights. She did not appear to be too pleased with this slackening of his attentions for she would tear herself away from him on occasion, run behind him and mount him vigorously, then run and stand in front of him, her tail held coquettishly to one side, and George would mount her in turn, being a bit more attentive about it this time.

It was on this day of her oestrus that one of the funniest things I ever saw happening occurred – funny to me, but very embarrassing for George! Diana was standing, tail to one side, inviting George to mount her, which he did. He must not have noticed, however, that his back was towards the slope of the mound and, as he pulled his wife onto his lap in the usual way, he lost his balance and came hurtling backwards down the side of the mound, Diana on top of him, to land in a heap at its base. She was furious! She leapt up, dashed at George, who struggled to his feet a little dazed, and then shot off round the side of the mound, Diana in hot pursuit, ending up in a hole at its base where he started to protest-scream at full volume. Diana stalked over to the hole and stuck her head inside. George's protest screams redoubled. Diana went and stood a few paces away and George hesitantly stuck his head out of the hole and looked around. He took one glance at Diana, who started to move towards him again, eyes glaring, and subsided back into his retreat, protesting violently. Diana kept him pinned there for the next half-hour. Every time he stuck his nose out she would dash over and George would start screaming again. Finally she gave up and left him in peace, and a very abashed George crept out of the hole to fling himself on Whitethroat who was sitting next to Diana, grooming her neck by this time. Whitethroat took off as soon as he saw his father approaching and George went and sat next to his wife, who threw him a rather cold glance, and he took over where Whitethroat had left off, nibbling Diana's neck in a rather chastened mood. It took a while before George was finally in her good graces again!

On the third day of Diana's oestrus, George had just about had it. His steps started to drag, it was only with an effort that he sometimes managed to heave himself up onto his wife's back and there he would promptly fall asleep, his head nodding and his eyes closed. Diana would not tolerate such slacking on the job, however, and would tear herself away from beneath her snoozing lover and run behind him, mount him vigorously and then run to stand in front of him again. George would comply, but very much lacking in the vigour that he had shown at the beginning. Within a few moments he would nod off again and lie there, spreadeagled over his wife's back.

Notch was now taking every opportunity for her clandestine meetings with Twin and Scar while this was going on and even the youngsters now seemed to be getting into the spirit of the thing and would mount each other on the other side of the mound, out of George's sight. I did not think that these mounts were real copulations, for females would mount males as frequently as the other way around. George's grip on the rest of his family seemed to be slipping!

Finally there were signs that Diana's oestrus was ending, for she frequently started to protest when George tried to mount her. Notch had also lost interest in trying to attract Scar and Twin to secret meetings and would protest if they tried to mount her and tended to keep with the rest of the group when they were on the move instead of lagging behind. It had been five days now since the two females had started their ovulation cycle – five days which

George was really starting to show the effects of. He was much thinner than usual and would nod off at every opportunity, usually on Diana's back, for he was still not letting any other males get anywhere near her. The life as consort to the queen was a hard one and, when Diana finally started to protest every time he slung an exploratory paw over her back, he managed to catch up on the thing that he had been sorely lacking in over the past days – sleep! George just flopped out at every opportunity he got and slept and slept for the next two days!

I had counted how frequently he had mounted Diana in the five days of her oestrus and came to the astounding total of 2,386 times! No wonder he was so exhausted! But not all of these mounts were true copulations with ejaculation. It was very difficult to tell exactly when George had ejaculated but I noticed that sometimes his thighs would quiver and his eyes half close at the end of the mount, and both partners would lick their genitals immediately afterwards, sometimes each one their own but just as often, they would reverse the roles. Even when I added up just the cases where I was certain that George had ejaculated they were over ten per cent of the total mounts, 286 times! This was a tremendous feat by any standards and, when I considered all the other activities he had been involved in during this time – chasing off the rest of the family and keeping an eye on Notch – I could easily understand why he was so exhausted.

During the time the two females were in oestrus, the group had not moved far in their daily foraging excursions and were literally 'mound-hopping', moving only one or two mounds further each day. Once George seemed to have recovered from his exertions, however, the usual daily wanderings resumed. The tension between group members now seemed to have been lifted and they began their usual play sessions around the base of the mound in the mornings. I even had the impression that they were making up for lost time, for sometimes as many as ten of them would be playing at once. Only Diana held herself aloof as usual and George didn't quite seem to be able to muster the energy to join in at present. It was a delightful sight seeing the little creatures, all twittering like earth-bound birds, leaping around and chasing each other or playing at mock battles, or having a game of 'King of the Castle' – one of them climbing onto a log or sitting in a hole in a termite mound and trying to keep the others from usurping its position. Once it had 'lost', however, the 'winner' would take its place and the game would start all over again. Sometimes these games would go on for half an hour or more and I noticed that it was the females, especially Goldie, Vanessa and Victoria, which seemed to be the most active. They would go up to one of the males, usually Rusty or Fleck (Blackie was still not in the mood to play; his recent bad experience with his father seemed to have rather taken the wind out of his sails!), but even asking Twin, Scar and Whitethroat to join in. The youngsters, however, needed no invitation to a game and would start playing whenever an opportunity presented itself. Sometimes there would be as many as three pairs of animals all turning slowly, arms around each other, in the stately 'Viennese Waltz', beeping the play call at full volume in the rays of the rising sun. Diana always kept a sharp lookout, however, and if she saw that the players were forgetting themselves and getting too far away from the mound or making too much noise, she would dash down the mound and stop them. Although, chastened, they would trot back after her, it was only a matter of seconds before they would be at it again!

In the weeks that followed, I began to notice a slight but obvious change in Diana's usually slim figure. She looked as if she was definitely pregnant. At this time she had an enormous appetite and poor George had to suffer. It seemed as if, every time he managed to catch something good, Diana appeared as if out of nowhere and relieved him of his meal. He tried to run off as soon as he had found anything but it was usually too late – Diana had spotted him and once that happened, he could forget about retiring to some quiet corner to enjoy the spoils of the chase.

The heat was building up again and the whole atmosphere of the bush spelt rain. The dust-devils in the afternoons were getting more frequent and started to become a nuisance. I often returned to camp covered with a second skin of red dust and bits of dried grass all nicely cemented together with a liberal application of sweat. The huge cumulus clouds were slowly becoming more common, replacing the 'snowy sheep' that had been the only source of shade up until now, and I was thankful for them. Sometimes it would get so hot in the car at midday that I would feel dizzy and nauseated. The only thing that made it bearable was the sweeping line of shadow cast by these giant aerial galleons as they swept by under full sail. There was still no rain.

Diana and Co. completed another round of their living area and were headed towards the Dragon section again. Diana was now very rotund and Notch did not look much less so! It seemed as if her illicit love affairs were going to bear fruit. I was very concerned as to whether Notch would have a chance to raise her youngsters or not. The group's daily foraging excursions were becoming more and more curtailed and Diana had a tendency to lead them back to the same sleeping mound that she had used the night before. They were not travelling half their usual distance and it looked as if Diana was finding the pace hard, for she would usually flop down as soon as the resting mound was reached and just lie there, her swollen belly resting on the ground, and snooze whenever she had a chance.

The group finally arrived at Dragon and I thought that Diana was very near her time. She still led the family foraging, though, but their trips only took them for short distances away from the mound. Then, one morning, she led them off, away from Dragon to Log, a mound almost two hundred yards south of it and, after searching every hole and crevice, went over to the marking post and marked. The rest of the family sniffed this mark carefully and then followed an orgy of marking that was quite new for me. The group spent at least half an hour marking and remarking the post. Diana by this time had vanished into the depths of the mound and that was the last I saw of her until the next morning. When she emerged, I hardly recognised the portly lady of the previous day in the slim sylph of today. She had had her young! Now I could understand what the orgy of marking the day before was all about. Something in Diana's anal secretion must have changed and signalled her family that this was the place where she had chosen to have her babies. They responded to this signal by putting their family signature well and truly on the marking post of the mound, so that there could be no mistake as to who was inhabiting it.

On looking closer, I could see that the hair around Diana's nipples was wet and that all her six nipples had been sucked, so she must have a large litter, at least more than one or two. George was very excited and the rest of the family as well. They kept dashing back and forth, peering into the holes in the mound and vanishing inside only to pop up again a few minutes later. I could hear protest squeals coming from inside the mound as various family members tried to get close to the youngsters and investigate them, only to be shouldered out of the way by others who wanted to do just the same thing. Diana seemed rather unperturbed but it might also be that she was tired after the birth. George kept running between her and the babies and spent a great deal of time licking her anally, which she seemed to relish at this point. I was hoping to catch a glimpse of the babies for I knew how active they were, even right after birth, and since the mongooses build no nest for their young, it was more than possible that one of the youngsters would come crawling out of the mound when no one was looking – but I was to be disappointed. The group stayed near the mound the whole day but of the youngsters, I couldn't see a thing. Every now and again the faint chirping of the nest twitter could be heard when the wind dropped but, apart from that, nothing. Finally the group retreated into the mound for their daily siesta and I scanned the heavens in the hope of some sign of rain, but apart from the cumulus clouds, there was nothing.

Scar finally took up his post on the top of the mound at almost five p.m., but the next animal to emerge was Diana, holding something in her mouth. At first I could not be sure what the little bundle was, it looked like a little grey ball, but when I peered closer, I could make out that it was a tiny baby

Two-week-old youngsters with an eager babysitter

mongoose, all 'packed up' in the carrying position. I was worried in case my being so near was disturbing her and that Diana was going to transfer her young to a safer place but, instead of that, she ran down the mound to the marking post, Victoria, Vanessa and Goldie in close pursuit, and deposited the baby on the ground near the base of it.

The three 'aunties' crowded round and Diana sped off into the depths of the mound again only to reappear with a second baby an instant later. By this time the whole group was in turmoil and running hither and thither and I had a hard time trying to keep up with who was doing what. Some animals were crowded round the babies at the marking post, others would dog Diana's footsteps as she darted into the mound and emerged again with yet another youngster to place it with the first ones. Finally all seemed to have been brought out. There were five of them, mewing little bundles which kept running round blindly in circles giving the 'baby lost' call. Vanessa tried to run off with one of them only to be promptly stopped by her mother who took the baby out of her mouth and returned it to the pile. Then Diana marked the post and each of the babies in turn, sliding her anal gland across them. This was the signal for the rest of the group and, once that had been given, I felt sorry for the youngsters, for they were marked, along with the post, by all the family members, and some of them none too gently!

When the mass-marking was finished, Diana picked one of the babies up and vanished with it back inside the mound. Vanessa, who had been just waiting for this excuse, grabbed one and followed. Goldie took her example and, by the time Diana emerged again, there were only two left. She looked from one to the other, and took one in her mouth, but then the crying of the other attracted her attention so she dropped the one she was holding and tried to grasp the other. In the meantime, Vanessa was back and, without more ado, she picked up one of the youngsters and went racing off with it into the depths of the mound again, so Diana's problem was solved. She picked up the last little one and vanished in turn.

It almost looked as if this was a 'public introduction ceremony' for the young, who were more or less presented by their mother to the group as a whole. It was particularly important that all the group members marked them, putting the family 'seal of approval' on the offspring, saying 'They belong to us!' The older sisters seemed to be just dying to mother the little ones but Diana, at this stage, seemed to want to prevent it, for she had taken the baby away from Vanessa. Although Scar and Whitethroat appeared briefly on top of the mound about half an hour later, that was all that I saw of the group for the rest of the day, although protest squeals came from inside the mound every now and again, so I knew they were still busy there with the babies.

Notch had more or less kept out of things up until now and I had not seen her all day except for a brief appearance at the marking post in the afternoon. She had shown a great deal of interest in the new family members but did not seem to be as fascinated with them as the younger females were. She had vanished into the mound with the rest of the group and, from her size, I realised that it could not be long before she brought her young into the world as well.

Finally dusk fell, the sky a blaze of crimson. Huge clouds were rolling in from the north and the air felt moist on my skin. The first rains could not be long in coming now and I wondered what the mongooses would do when they fell. Twin took the late-night guard and, as the last rays of the sun disappeared behind the thorntrees and the shadows grew long, he too disappeared into the mound with the rest of his family and I set off back to camp.

During the night I was awakened by a tremendous roll of thunder, and then the first drops hit the roof of the tent like lead shot. After this prelude came the deluge and I lay awake in my camp bed listening to the thunder of water outside. It sounded almost as if someone had turned a fire-hose on the tent and, on both sides of the flysheet, the water poured in little waterfalls to the ground. The shower was just an introduction to the main act, though, for by morning the sky was clear and all that was left of the rain in the night was a thin layer of mud and trees, twigs and grass sparkling in the morning sun as if hung with diamonds. I hurried back to the mound as fast as I could in case something was going on in my absence, but all seemed to be still. The mongooses were not up yet, although the hornbills had already taken up their station on the trees around, preening their bedraggled feathers.

I had to wait more than an hour before the first little head stuck out of the top of Log and looked around. The family still seemed to be staying close to the youngsters. Then the morning ritual started and I waited expectantly for Notch's appearance. When she finally did come out, one of the last of the group, she was thin as a rake – she had had her babies during the night or in the early morning! I waited all day for some sign of her bringing them out to be marked by the rest of the family, but there was nothing. I didn't even know if the youngsters were alive or not for, although I could occasionally hear nest twitter coming from inside the mound, I did not know if this was from Diana's babies or Notch's. The rest of the group more or less ignored her and, although I tried to see if she had the tell-tale marks of being suckled around her nipples, I could not make out anything.

The group stayed close to the mound during the day. One of the first things they did in the early morning was to go down and lick the raindrops off the grass stems and grub around in the moist earth for creatures that had been washed out by the rains. Diana went foraging with them but her babies seemed to be in good hands as Vanessa remained behind – after some dispute as to who was going to be allowed to do so!

I heard loud protest screams coming from a hole in the side of the mound and could make out two little figures, Vanessa and Victoria, who were standing there shoulder to shoulder, heads raised and screaming at the tops of their voices. It took me a while to work out what was going on but then it became clear that they were having a fight – but a very stylised one indeed. The two of them stood rigid, heads raised, and tried to push each other out of the way with their shoulders. Neither would budge an inch from her position and, after about a minute of screaming and shoving, Victoria gave up and trotted down the mound after her departing family and Vanessa vanished inside to where the babies were chirping shrilly – I could finally hear them, fifteen yards away, now that the screams had stopped! Rusty stayed with her and, while she busied herself in the depths of the mound keeping the children quiet, he sat on the top on guard. Diana and her group went wandering off through the grass and I lost sight of them.

Vanessa remained hidden and it was all quiet in the mound; even the chirping of the babies had ceased. Rusty seemed to be taking his duties very seriously for he was very much on the alert and every time something moved, he would stare towards it, warn and growl, and dash into the mound at the slightest excuse. As the hours went by and still nothing was to be seen but

Rusty keeping watch on top of Log, I began to wonder what was going on in the mound's depths; there was not a squeak to be heard. The sun was beating down out of a clear sky washed clean of its dust by the rainshower the night before and the day was getting very hot. It was almost ten-thirty, however, before I heard the beeping contact calls approaching through the bush and saw Diana in the vanguard of her little family trotting back towards Log. Rusty rushed towards her and followed her as she immediately vanished into the depths. Again I heard protest screams coming from inside but had no idea what was going on there, for the rest of the family had trooped in after Diana and anything could be happening. A few of them came out to sit on top of the mound afterwards before the midday siesta and I saw that one of these was Vanessa. As she turned to groom herself I noticed telltale suckling marks around her nipples as well, although she did not have any young! This was a great surprise to me but it meant that she had spent the whole time curled up in the mound with the babies and the babies, in rooting around, had found her nipples, though milkless, and had suckled. It was all very strange indeed. At least her behaviour had kept them quiet, for all the time I had sat in the car, I had not heard the youngsters crying once.

As I drove back to camp that night, after having watched how Victoria and Twin had taken over the task of guarding the babies in the afternoon while the rest of the group were away, I began to wonder how something like babysitting could have arisen in the mongoose family. It was extremely altruistic behaviour, if one regarded it objectively, for an animal babysitting cannot feed and it is thus robbed of a certain amount of energy intake. On the other hand, my impression to date had been the opposite of any form of reluctance on the babysitters' parts to do the job. On the contrary, Vanessa and Victoria had even fought over who was going to be allowed to take care of the babies first! To date, Notch had not remained with the babies in the mound but had gone foraging with the others and I was still not sure whether her babies had survived or not.

9   The Rains Come

The next morning I was wakened by the sound of something gently scrabbling on the walls of the tent. It was dark outside and I could see nothing but thought that it might be drizzling. I had left the roof-hatch on the car open, so decided to get up and close it before everything got wet. Taking my torch, I opened the tent flap and the next thing I knew was that a river of shining black things poured into the tent, the river finally resolving itself into thousands of large black ants – *Siafu!* The Driver ants had hit the camp! I tried to brush the things out of the tent as fast as possible but only succeeded in scattering the army, which seemed to be crawling everywhere – up my legs, all over the floor and into every crack they could find. I woke Danson and Sammy and, between us, we managed to get the tent more or less free of the insects. I was already a mass of bites and the boys were leaping about slapping themselves. It wasn't until the sun rose, however, that I realised the extent of the 'army' we were battling against. The whole side of my tent was a mass of seething black bodies and thin strings of ants wound their way up guylines to the flysheet where they seemed to be drinking the little drops of dew that had accumulated there. I tried banging against the tent walls from inside to dislodge the beasts but it only made things worse, for they started milling around and getting into everything. Furniture and stores were hastily moved and, before I could do anything about it, I saw the little gecko that lived on my tent wall above the entrance smothered in a sea of black and fall, wriggling, to the ground to disappear under the wave of shining black bodies. I told the boys that, now we had got the creatures out of my tent, we should leave them alone as they would clear the camp of all other insect visitors but, as a precaution, we rescued Fred from the potato box and put him in a jar inside my tent so that he would be safe from the marauding jaws. I had never seen so many ants of such large size in such a small area in my life. Now the sun was up, they seemed to be lethargic for they remained hanging to the tent walls and made no move to go. The boys wanted to evacuate the camp but I persuaded them to stay and wait until our unwelcome visitors left of their own accord.

I was late getting back to the mound that morning thanks to the ants, so did not see who remained in there with the youngsters when the rest of the group went foraging. Twin, however, was guard for the day and reacted very strongly to me just driving up in broad daylight. When I stopped the car and cut the engine, his head poked out of a hole in the mound and he started warning loudly at me, flagging his head up and down. A dark head showed next to his in the hole – a head with a tell-tale mark on its ear. It was Notch! It looked as if she was taking over the babysitting duties for the day for, after a quick look at me, she disappeared back into the mound again. Twin soon calmed down and sat on top of the mound, gazing around. Every now and again he would vanish inside for a few minutes and reappear later to resume his duties. This was not the only time in my life that I wished that termite mounds were made of glass. It was very frustrating to have to sit there and know that some of the most interesting aspects of mongoose behaviour were going on only a few yards away and yet be able to see nothing.

To the north a blue-black cloudbank was approaching, its veil of rain sweeping behind it. Of Diana and Co. there was no sign and Twin had retired into the mound to join Notch, so I was left with an empty landscape. High above me in the blue, the eagles were sailing southwards, out of the path of the storm that was approaching, minute dots in the azure of the sky. I counted fifteen of them. All was still around me as if the world were holding its breath waiting for the life-giving water. The rain's smell preceded it for miles, borne on the wind. The hot, metallic air of the Taru was now replaced by the smell of wet earth. The clouds swept closer, obscuring the sun, and the air went suddenly cool. The first ragged fringes of the storm groped through the sky above me. I rapidly closed the roof-hatch and wound up the windows and waited. Twin poked his head out of the mound, looked around and then submerged again. Then the first raindrops hit, making sharp pings on the metal of the car. Within seconds, the deluge started and my range of vision was cut down almost to zero. Diana and her family had still not returned and though I peered through the streaming windows, there was nothing to be seen.

The force of the rain was astounding. Within minutes pools of water had formed in every hollow and the orange-red of the earth had taken on a deeper hue. Water started flowing past the car and I realised that Diana and her family must have gone into hiding – they would certainly not be out in this if they could help it. I spoke too soon, though, for, through the water streaming down the windowpanes, I saw a little figure headed full tilt for the mound, its hair in wet little spikes all over its body and its scampering feet throwing up showers of water as it ran. It stopped briefly at the top of the mound, looked behind it the way it had come, shook one forepaw delicately and then vanished into the mound's depths. It was Diana, although barely recognisable as such, for I had never seen her soaking wet before. Within a few seconds a stream of little bodies followed in her wake, eyes almost closed against the pounding of the water. Fur plastered and tails rat-like, they vanished like lightning into Log, not to emerge again. The rain must either have caught them unawares or Diana had insisted on coming back to her babies despite the weather. I had

The bushland waiting for the life-giving rain

The force of the rain was astounding and my range of vision was little more than a few feet

A fortnight after the rains, the Taru bloomed and the grass seemed to shoot up overnight

never seen mongooses out in the rain before, they usually disappeared into the shelter of the mounds long before the storms hit.

It was raining so hard that even with the windshield wipers on at full speed my range of visibility was little more than a few feet. It was far too dangerous to attempt driving through the bush in this weather, so I decided to wait until the deluge had abated somewhat. As I was sitting there, I wondered what would have happened if Diana had not come back, if she had got stuck for days in some öther termite mound. The rainstorms sometimes went on for a week or more and the whole place would flood, then there would be practically no chance of her getting back to Log. It suddenly dawned upon me that the babies would probably have been all right for, of all people, Notch had been with them. I remembered seeing Vanessa's nipples yesterday and how the babies had tried to suck from her. In Vanessa's case, it would have been a waste of time – but Notch! She had had babies the day before and there would have been milk in her teats. I put two and two together and began to have other thoughts about the practice of killing another female's young, as I had seen in my tame group. Maybe it was a sort of insurance for the mongoose family, that these childless females could then take over nursing the babies when the queen was not there. If I had managed to get a good look at Notch before the rain had started I should have had proof of my theory, but she had only stuck her head out and nothing more.

After two hours of pounding rain with no sign of it abating, I decided to chance driving back to camp. The water was now inches deep around the car and if I waited any longer there was the probability that I would get bogged down. It was only with some difficulty that I got the car to move, for the wheels had already sunk into the mud and started spinning wildly. Finally, with a lurch, I manhandled the car out of its self-dug grave and headed cautiously in the direction I hoped the camp would be, for all my landmarks had been blotted out by the teeming water. Trees loomed in front of the car's bonnet and I had to reverse to avoid them; what once was a little dip in the ground had now become a pool that had to be driven through at speed to prevent the car from bogging down and stalling. I twisted and turned back and forth between the bushes and suddenly realised I was lost! I had no idea where the road lay and the leaden sky gave me no clue as to the sun's position. I could be driving round in circles for all I knew! At this point I almost panicked but, pulling myself together, I decided I would just try and drive straight ahead and keep one direction steady as well as I could, for somewhere I was sure to run up against a bush road.

The next half-hour was torture. I could hardly see through the windows and, despite my efforts to keep driving straight ahead, I had the sneaking feeling that, what with the frequent reverses and bends back and forth to avoid obstacles, I was drifting off to one side or the other. The rain was still pelting down and looked as if it was never going to stop. When I finally reached the road almost an hour later, I nearly missed it for it no longer looked anything like a road and I was miles from my starting-point. The road had become a river, and at first I did not know whether to turn right or left along it. My 'bump of direction' was completely useless. The water flowed past me in a torrent, creaming against the wheels of the car. As I watched it, I suddenly realised the answer. My camp was on higher ground than the mongooses' homeland and if I drove upstream, I would finally reach some point I knew and from there on I would be all right.

I had never driven in a river before and it was no pleasant journey, for the numerous potholes were hidden under the brown torrent that was now my sole means of getting home. I jolted from one hole to another and every now and again the car would go into a skid, that threatened to hurl me amongst the trees, when it hit a patch of subaquatic mud and the wheels could get no grip. Yard by yard I crept forward, cursing myself for staying out so long and not getting back to camp at the first signs of the storm. I gritted my teeth and drove onwards, only seeing about a yard in all directions. The drive went on for what seemed to be an age and I began to think that my clever idea of driving uphill had been wrong and that I was now headed in a completely different direction. Then something pounded on the window and I turned my head. A pair of startled eyes peered through the streaming glass and then the door opened. It was Sammy, soaked to the skin! Panting, he threw himself into the seat next to me and then asked me where I was going. When I told him 'Back to camp' he started laughing. It turned out that I had driven right past it in the rain and had not noticed it! The boys had heard the car and, when they realised that I was not going to stop but was carrying on along the road at a crawl, Sammy had come chasing after me.

Back at camp, things were in chaos. The kitchen roof had sprung a leak and everything was swimming in water. Even the little gas cooker was flooded and just made gurgling noises when I tried to light it to make a cup of tea to warm us all up a bit. To light a fire was ridiculous. Our fire pit was now just part of a torrent running through the camp. All that remained to tell where it had once been were a few charred pieces of wood that had drifted against twigs and tussocks of grass which protruded out of the swirling water. I looked at my last packet of teabags and realised that the thought of tea would have not been much good anyway, for they had been left on the kitchen shelf and had now all exploded in the deluge of water that was pouring over our rough plank table and gurgling out under the sides of the hut. Danson and Sammy and I, water streaming off us, tried to get as many things off the floor as possible in the storehouse and a whole variety of creepy-crawlies were washed away with the flood of brown mud that swept over the place where they had been. When we had got everything possible under cover, I went over to my tent. At least the rain had done some good after all, for the Driver ants were all gone.

Squatting, dripping wet, under the flysheet, I looked across what had once been a neat and clean camp and came to the conclusion that the only thing it resembled at present was a paddyfield during the monsoon. The water was at least six inches deep everywhere and the rain showed no sign of letting up. Danson and Sammy crawled into their tent and lay on the bed, out of the wet, and I thought it was a good idea too. I opened the tent door and almost had a fit! My house had turned into a river – there was water flowing in one end and out the other! I rescued my clothes, books, mats and sundry other objects that were plastered or bobbing in a row along the back of the tent and all of which had seemed to be dyed red-brown instantly, piled them, sopping wet, on a table, and dashed out to find our *jembe* – the broad native hoe. I remembered from my Girl Guide days that, in case of rain, one should dig a trench around the tent to drain off the water. Ten minutes later, dripping with perspiration as well as ordinary rain water, I surveyed the results of my handiwork that were just at this point submerging under the flood again. I realised that Guides had never camped in the African bush during the rains. All I had succeeded in doing was make a long pool in front of the tent which the water seemed now to be using for a mass assault on my bush home! I went back inside and sat disconsolately cross-legged on my bed. I was wet, my bed was wet and I didn't even have a dry change of clothing. The water had knocked over the little stand with my suitcase on it and suitcase and contents were now mud-logged, for it seemed to have acted like a very efficient settling tank and everything was covered with a thin slimy layer of red-brown muck. The force of the rain pounding on the roof, despite the double protection of the flysheet, resulted in a fine mist of water that settled on everything. The few plastic bags I had were rapidly turned into safe hiding-places for my precious field notes and films – there was nothing left over for personal belongings.

Since I was so wet anyway, I decided at least to try and get some food into myself, so floundered over to the kitchen to see what was still edible. I emerged with a can of corned beef and some cold macaroni that had been left over from the previous day's supper. As I was squatting on my bed, devouring these finds, I suddenly realised – it was Christmas Day! I have never had such a miserable Christmas dinner in my life. Since there was nothing else I could do and I had started shivering with cold, I decided that the best thing was to get into bed and stay there until the rain let off a bit. It was then that I found my Christmas present from the bush animals. Hardly had I crawled under the clammy covers when I was out again like a shot and scratching like mad. Six Driver ants had had the same idea as I had! After removing the insects from myself and the bed, I crawled back in again and lay there, shivering, listening to the pounding rain and feeling a bit like Noah. The torrent of red mud still swirled round the legs of my bed, bringing with it twigs, insects, dead grass and other rubbish which slowly piled up around me, but I was past caring. At some point I must have dozed off, for the next thing I knew, it was morning.

The rain had now slackened to a drizzle and, as I squelched through the layer of mud and muck now covering the tent floor, I wondered whether the camp was still standing. My clothes had more or less dried on me during the night but it looked as if I was going to be stuck with them, for there seemed to be no chance of drying off my other things if the rains continued.

I crawled out of the tent and, in doing so, released a deluge of water from the bulging flysheet, and all hopes of remaining half-way dry died as I took my inadvertent shower. I decided to take my shoes off and go barefoot to the kitchen for the mud was so thick they would have been ruined in no time. Slipping and sliding and sloshing through the puddles, I finally reached my goal but the rain had done its work well. The kitchen lay under a blanket of mud and rubbish from which all sorts of bush denizens were slowly untangling themselves. Huge millipedes, ground crickets and beetles struggled out of the rows of flotsam washed against the kitchen walls. I tried to get the little gas stove started and managed it after almost half an hour of blowing through it and drying it off as well as I could. Judicious application of my lighter flame finally did the trick and within no time, the kettle, relieved of its mud and inhabitants (a large, half-drowned spider and a millipede), was soon singing merrily. Exploded or not, the teabags were put in and I hunched on my wet camp chair under the flysheet sipping my tea and surveying the scene of devastation around me. The camp looked literally as if a hurricane had hit it. Whole branches had been swept through by the flood and the thornbush *boma* had been carried almost into the middle of the central space. I could read the height of the water level the night before from the telltale tideline of grass caught in the branches: at some points, a foot or more.

As I sat there, staring out into the grey drizzle, I saw what I took to be a grey mist rising from the ground beyond the ruined *boma* wall. The mist grew thicker and rose, through the drizzle, towards the open sky. It was only when I could see it against the relative brightness of the heavens that I realised what it was. The termites were flying! Thousands and thousands of these insects, which had been waiting in their tunnels in the termite mounds for just this moment, were now on their nuptial flight. For almost an hour I watched as they fluttered on grey gauze wings through the falling rain, up into the sky on the only day of their lives that they would see the sun – and even then it was hidden behind the thick grey clouds! As king met queen, the two of them would spiral to earth to begin their new family. Several pairs had landed near me and I watched, fascinated, as the founders of a new dynasty broke off their wings with a curious jerky sideways movement of the wing muscles, helped by the hind-legs, and then began the important task of getting underground as fast as possible, digging little tunnels in the wet earth, both the female and the smaller male busily excavating what would be their future abode. In no time the wet ground was littered with the iridescent shimmer of cast-off wings and their owners had dug themselves to safety.

I decided to try and get back to Log to see what the mongooses were up to but when I reached my car, I realised that it was hopeless. The wheels had sunk in the soft earth almost to their rims and it would be a hard job jacking each one up and filling the holes so that I could get moving. Danson and Sammy seemed to have thought better of things and were staying in their tent out of the rain and, without their help, it would take me hours to get the car started again. I decided to wait until the rain had stopped as it would be very unlikely that the mongooses would be out in this weather anyway, so I set about trying to get my muddy clothes clean and tidy the camp up a bit. After a quick breakfast of cracker mush with condensed milk and sugar – a sort of bush muesli – I set to work. The fire pit was now a mud pool which had to be shovelled out and I rinsed my clothes as well as I could and hung them under the flysheet in the forlorn hope that they might dry some day.

About mid-afternoon, the drizzle died down although the sky was still threatening more rain. By this time the boys had emerged from their cocoon and, together, we jacked up each of the car's wheels and stuffed the holes with twigs and grass. I then tried to get the engine going but all that happened was that a weak grinding noise emerged from under the bonnet. Water must have got into the distributor head! Almost half an hour later, after drying the points and checking the carburettor intake, I tried again. This time it was better and I got a splutter for my efforts. With choke full out, the engine finally roared into life and I slowly let in the clutch.

It seemed to take an age to get back to Log and there were many occasions when the car's wheels started to spin and I thought I would get bogged down. The drizzle had died off by this time and I parked the car directly on a patch of Grewia bush to make sure it would not sink in while I was waiting to see what the mongooses were doing. All was quiet on the mound and there was not a bird to be seen in the trees. I finally spotted some busily picking things up off the ground not far from me – the hornbills seemed to be having a feast despite the mud! A pair of Yellow-bills fluttered down next to the car and started eating busily. Heads moved up and down with pendulum rhythmicality – the termite marriage had lasted only a few hours for some of the insects! High above me the storks and herons were circling in to join in the feast. I saw them land, one after the other, legs stretched to the fore and wings back-beating in the air, at the nearby waterhole that now really earned its name. Before the rains came it had been just an area of dry, cracked mud, but now the water was brimming over its banks – subsistence for the bush animals for the months to come.

I kept a close eye on the mound but nothing stirred. The mongooses seemed to be enjoying the weather as much as I was and were staying safely inside their snug quarters. It was almost an hour later before I saw a little head appear in one of the holes and a delicate paw scratch at the wall of one of the mound's entrances. A little nose bored into the hole it had made and seemed to be satisfied with what it had found for the nails of one forepaw were inserted into the slit. The mongoose, it was Fleck, waited a few moments and then withdrew his paw again, and attached to the nails were three or four fat white termites which he delicately removed with his teeth before plunging his paw back into the hole to repeat the process. Fleck was fishing for termites like a chimpanzee! But he didn't need a grass straw, he had his long claws already built in. The versatility of the Dwarf mongoose seemed to know no bounds. As soon as the rain had softened the cement-hard mounds to the point that they could be broken into, their inhabitants were on the menu! The termite mounds were not only shelter.

Although I waited until it was almost dark, the mongooses did not leave their termite castle and, when it started drizzling again, I realised that they were not going to come out that day if the weather worsened. Again the slalom drive back to camp and we quickly made what preparations we could for the threatened deluge. The clouds to the north were almost black by this time. I managed to fry some corned beef and potatoes on the gas stove, the first warm meal we had had in two days, and then we retired to our beds, which were just as damp and soggy as we were, and hoped for the best. The wind started up and my flysheet cracked like a whip above the tent. An eerie howling filled the air and the sun set behind the bank of cloud, only a red shimmer showing through the black of the heavens. I felt nervous, for it looked as if we were in for a bad night. The boys vanished and, after a quick look around the camp to make sure that everything that could be tied down was, I crept into bed again, still fully dressed, and hoped that the storm would not wreak too much havoc. I lay there, listening to the crack of the flysheet and the wind moaning through the thorntree branches.

It was almost impossible to sleep with the drumming rain and howling wind, but at some point in the night I must have done, for the next thing I knew, the sun was shining and I was once more sleeping in a mud-pool. The rain had stopped and everything looked bright and clean – if one could call a campsite under about a foot of mud clean! All the work of the day before had been undone and even added to by the elements. The kitchen hut was standing askew with its roof hanging down on one side, and branches were littered everywhere, broken off by the wind in the night. Heaps of rubbish had gathered at every point that blocked down-hill progress.

The rubbish was a zoologist's treasurehouse. Baby tortoises, half drowned during the night, struggled ineffectually to crawl out of the heaps of water-born jetsam. Huge mole-crickets, swollen with water, lay lifeless amongst the sopping wet windrows of dead grass. I even found a tiny baby antelope – a little dik-dik – that looked as if it had been carried away by the flood before it was strong enough to flee. Then there were the termites; thousands of water-bloated bodies lay amongst the rubbish and, with them, the corpses of millipedes, scorpions and even the huge Scolopendra centipedes. Although the ground was very wet, I decided to try and get the car going and head to Log for, now the sun was out, maybe the mongooses would be out as well.

At Log, the family was already up and about, busily sorting through the bounty the rain had washed to their doorstep. Storks and herons trod their way daintily through the mud and grass, picking drowned bush denizens up in their beaks and swallowing them. A flight of Marabou storks came gliding in to join the Europeans and the Black-necked herons who were filling their crops as fast as they could. The mongooses were nose down and gobbling greedily but I could see that they were not too fond of the wet, for forepaws would be delicately raised and shaken vigorously to dislodge the mud attached to the claws before being put to work again to dig out the next titbit. Vanessa pounced on a drowned scorpion and dashed back to the mound with it clamped fast in her jaws. Most of the group, however, was gobbling up the remains of the termites' nuptial flight – the families which had not made it. I saw M'Bili digging around in the opening of a small tortoise shell. Every time the tortoise gave a defensive hiss, M'bili would spring backwards only to approach again and poke her inquisitive forepaw into the shell once more. Finally, however, she left the poor thing in peace and went back to gobbling termites again. After almost two hours the group was replete, in fact, to look at them, one would think that they were all pregnant! With huge fat tummies they waddled back to the mound and went inside, giving themselves and each other a quick lick before disappearing, removing the drops of water clinging to their fur and using their teeth to pick off clumps of mud from their forepaws.

Now the sun was out, the bush started to steam, and inside the car it felt like a sauna bath. Flocks of the brilliantly coloured Regal starlings and the Fischer's starlings, in their neat grey and white suits, were carrying on where the mongooses had left off, peering into the lines of washed-up grass and extracting the tasty insects that were tangled amongst it. They kept up a continual harsh chatter and sometimes I thought it was a pity that their voices didn't match their dress! The Marabous were stalking around like ugly old

The marabous, with wings outspread and head sunken, reminded me of Flying Fortresses

men in evening dress, delicately picking out the drowned insects with the tips of their huge bills and tossing them backwards into their throats, their swollen, naked throat sacs swaying to and fro as they walked. As it got hotter, they gathered near the bank of the waterhole which was just visible from the car, and stood there, wings outspread and heads sunken like a row of Flying Fortresses about to take off. The shadow of their wings covered their bald pates and their throat sacs hung in the wind. They were cooling off!

Midday came and went and the bush continued to steam. It was almost four o'clock before the mongooses emerged again but they didn't seem very hungry, which was no surprise to me. They pottered around the base of the mound and out into the grass a little way but made no move to go foraging far off. Diana was out on the mound with George but there was such a coming and going that I had no idea who was staying with the babies. The stormclouds were rolling in again from the horizon and I realised that the second part of the cyclone would not be long in hitting. I was wondering whether to go or not, for the family was just pottering about, when I heard the plaintive *tseee* call and Goldie, who was sitting on top of the mound, stared off hard into the bushes behind. The rest of the group were there in a flash, a crush of bodies on top of the mound blocking my view. I saw Twin and Scar dash down the mound towards something but, whatever it was, it wasn't going to be stopped so easily.

Mongooses dashed up and down the mound and inside it and I stood up to see what it was that was getting them so excited. Something that looked like a long length of grey hosepipe was sticking out of the hole at the mound's base and the mongooses were darting in to nip it in the sides. The hosepipe withdrew with a jerk and I found myself staring at the head of a huge Black mamba! The head disappeared into the mound again and a good portion of body after it, the mongooses going almost frantic, leaping at it and biting any part of its body they could reach. George was threat-scratching and cheek-marking like a little fury while the others were dashing around ineffectually.

The babies! I had almost forgotten about them in the surprise of seeing this giant of the snake world, but the mongooses certainly hadn't. Diana appeared with a little grey ball in her mouth and set off at full gallop towards Big, followed by Vanessa, also carrying a baby, and Notch. The three of them were running full belt and within minutes they had reached the mound and vanished inside. Diana reappeared and came galloping back. Three were now in safety, but what about the others? Diana rushed up the mound and disappeared inside again only to reappear a second later with another baby – that was four! Again she galloped off towards Big and I wondered why none of the others were helping to transport the little ones. The males of the group seemed to be inside the mound, for only George and Rusty were now outside, George cheek-marking and threat-scratching but seeming to be almost useless in an emergency. Then a little head appeared holding number five. M'Bili had come to the rescue! She galloped off after her mother, the baby in her jaws looking totally out of proportion. She must only just be about a year old but nevertheless, she was doing her bit in taking care of the young.

I waited for Diana to return, thinking that maybe Notch's young were still in the mound, but no one came. The spits were becoming more furious than ever and mongooses were popping out of one hole only to disappear into another. The snake was still inside and the family was getting frantic. The ladies, Diana included, had now retreated completely to Big with their charges and the field had been left free for the fighters. I still couldn't make out what George was doing for, instead of going into the mound where he could do some good, he was still demolishing soggy grass tussocks, stopping every now and again to pick the mud off his claws with his teeth. No one was there to watch his display – he must have been doing it for himself!

A flurry of mongooses appeared on top of the mound and peered down the holes, then, from the side, a grey-black, scaly head appeared, looked around, retreated with a jerk as it was spat at by a furious Whitethroat and then the snake sped off, the whole mongoose bunch chasing after it. I was amazed at the speed at which it could move. The front third of its body seemed to be held above the ground and was propelled forwards by powerful thrusts of its tail end. The animal was a good three yards in length and could move faster than a man could run. It sped through the grass and bushes, the bunch of furious little mammals close on its heels, looking almost as if they were surrounded by golden halos in the rays of the setting sun, for all their hair was on end. Diana, Goldie and Notch were standing in high sit on the top of Big, staring after their retreating family. M'Bili and Vanessa seemed to be inside with the babies. Then, one by one, the warriors returned, peered quickly into the holes on Log and then trotted off to join their womenfolk who rushed down the mound to meet them. The episode was followed by a spate of neck-nibbles and George anal-marking his wife.

I wondered what they were going to do next – stay at Big or move back to Log. As usual, I was wrong. They did neither. Diana appeared with a baby in her mouth once more and sped off towards Dragon, followed by the faithful Vanessa who was also carrying one of the offspring. Notch joined them and the males of the group were still milling around, very excited, and getting in everybody's way. M'Bili didn't do any baby-carrying this time but galloped off in the wake of her mother. As soon as she had deposited the youngster, Diana was back again for a second one and she and Goldie between them rescued the rest of the brood. I think the majority of the group did not know what was going on at all, because mongooses were dashing to Big from Dragon and vice versa. The episode seemed to have upset them more than I had ever seen them upset before and it was almost an hour before things started to calm down again and the group ended up on Dragon. The grooming that went on that evening was the most intensive I had ever witnessed, and the mongooses really needed it! Most of them were wet and muddy after their exertions and just sat there, letting themselves be cleaned by their friends. One thing was certain though, something must have happened to Notch's youngsters, for there had been no sign of them and I still didn't know if they had been killed at birth or whether the mamba had stumbled upon them first and eaten them. I rather inclined towards the former hypothesis.

I wondered why Diana had decided to move the youngsters out of Big. Maybe it was still too near to where the snake had been sighted for her liking, or maybe Big's architecture was not her ideal of a nursery.

The first thing on the agenda, once things had calmed down again, was marking the marking post at Dragon, which the whole group did with gay abandon. Once they had cleaned themselves up, it looked as if it was time for the old rituals to be paid attention to again. When this task was finished, the group dribbled, one after another, into the depths of the mound. The western sky was a blaze of fire; one of the truly magnificent sunsets which seem to be purely Africa's was filling the sky with crimson, gold and blue. I glanced up at the dark rainclouds which were still rolling in from the north and decided to get back to camp while I could. It looked as if Diana and Co., for the time being at least, were going to stay put.

For the next two days it was totally useless to think about mongoose-watching for the rain teemed down without a break. The camp was transformed once more into a paddyfield, and I became resigned to living in sopping wet clothes and sleeping in a sopping wet bed. My feet started to suffer from the continual damp and with horror one night, as I peeled off my wet socks, saw all the skin on the soles of my feet peel off with them! I had been hoping for weeks that it would rain but now it was the other way around – I couldn't wait for it to stop and the sun to start shining again. Despite precautions, our meagre supply of potatoes and other keepable vegetables started to rot and even the macaroni was covered with a thin layer of mould. Mould sprouted on every leather object I possessed and I was giving up hope of rescuing some of them, especially my shoes, which had taken on a pretty green-blue tinge despite vigorous rubbing. I spent most of my time pacing up and down in my tent, impatient to get back and find out what the mongooses were doing, but at this stage it would have been hopeless.

Finally, the morning dawned bright and clear. The cyclone had passed and the air almost seemed to be glittering. The whole bush was hung with dewdrops like a crystal chandelier and everywhere was a slight shimmer of green – the grass was sprouting. The Commiphora trees now started to look like trees instead of reminding me of a blasted heath – and even the buds on the Grewia bushes were starting to open. I am always awed by the rapidity with which Nature immediately takes advantage of the life-giving water. It almost looked as if everything had been ready and waiting for the first raindrops and, once they had fallen, life could begin again. After an hour of jacking up, filling in and pushing, the car was finally disembogged and I crawled off to Dragon. A huge monitor lizard waddled through the grass, speeding up as he saw me approach, to disappear into a nearby termite mound. The impala were there in full force, nibbling the fresh green as soon as it started to sprout. I even saw a herd of Peter's gazelles, a subspecies of the ubiquitous Grant's, cashing in on the first fruits of the season – antelopes whose preference is the young green grass blades and which I had not seen before. A pair of gerenuk were standing on their hind-legs, long graceful necks stretched to their utmost to nibble the bursting buds on an acacia bush. The Taru was coming to life again.

At Dragon, the mongooses were already up and about and only Goldie and Blackie were on the mound itself; the rest of them were grubbing about looking for drowned insects of which there were still hundreds littered through the swathes of soggy grass that lay everywhere. The storks and herons were making their stately way through the area, picking left and right as they found some tasty titbit. I saw a Marabou pick up a small puff adder which must have got drowned during the flood and, before it could swallow it, all its companions in the area came dashing over, looking highly comical as they tried to hurry as fast as possible to steal the find, their wings beating the air and their legs looking like someone trying to run on stilts. Goldie and Blackie watched the ensuing squabble as well as I.

As I was observing the ungainly birds, from behind me the *tseee* call came from Dragon loud and clear. I whipped round and saw Rusty and Goldie, all their hair on end, staring towards a Black-necked heron which, with a stabbing motion of its bill, impaled something on the ground behind the mound and swallowed it. It looked like a mouse. Then came the stab and swallow again. The third time the beak stabbed downwards, though, I thought this was too much of a coincidence and, as I focused the binoculars, I saw with horror that it was a baby mongoose that was vanishing down its throat! Goldie was calling '*Tseeee*' at full power and then the rest of the group arrived through the bush at a gallop, just in time to see the third baby end up in the heron's crop. With furious growls the family attacked and the heron turned to run, trying to pick up enough speed to take off. The bushes were so thick, though, that it could hardly spread its wings and before it knew what had happened, the mongoose army was upon it. As it ran, I saw little brown bodies attached by their powerful jaws to its legs. They looked almost twice their normal size with their hair on end and I realised that the heron had better get off the ground quickly if it was not going to be badly bitten by the furious family. It struggled through the last patch of bushes and reached open ground, the mongooses still hard on its heels and holding fast to its legs whenever they could get a grip, their teeth clamped in the vicious bite I knew so well having been on the receiving end of it on many occasions and only managed to prise the locked jaws apart with a knife. A few powerful wingbeats and the bird was airborne, but attached to its right leg was a furry bundle – the last mongoose was not going to give up so easily! The bird was almost two yards in the air before its dogged attacker finally released its hold and fell to the ground. I heard the mobbing *tchrrrs* as the heron circled above, gaining height, and a dozen pairs of eyes watched its every movement until it was out of sight. Then the troop headed back to the mound.

Goldie had gone in to the youngsters as soon as the rest of the family had appeared, although it was a case of shutting the stable door after the horse was gone. Instead of staying inside the mound with them as she should have, she had been on top of it, watching the Marabou squabble with Blackie, and during this time the babies must have crawled out of their hiding place and been spotted by the heron, which was stalking around on the lookout for a quick meal.

I felt shocked and somehow horrified that it had all happened so quickly

Vanessa runs full tilt, the baby a little grey ball in her mouth, until she reaches the safety of Big mound

and there had been nothing that the mongoose family could have done about it. Diana was acting frantic, dashing into one side of the mound and out of the other, and the rest of the group, their hair still on end, was rushing hither and thither, cheek-marking the ground and the marking post and anal-marking and nibbling each other. Then Diana appeared once again with a youngster in her mouth and I could see now that its hair had started to grow somewhat, for it was covered with a fine light-brown down, but its eyes were still closed. She trotted with it up and down the mound but seemed to come to no decision as to what to do. I expected her to head off towards another mound after what had happened, remembering her reaction after the mamba had invaded Log, but finally, baby still clamped in her mouth, she vanished inside Dragon again. Vanessa appeared a moment later with the remaining youngster and took off towards Big with it, galloping full speed with all her hair on end. When she reached Big, she vanished inside, baby with her.

Diana had come out again in the meantime and looked as if she was searching for something: I didn't know if it was the lost babies that the heron had eaten or whether she realised that one of the remaining two was missing as well. There was no sign of movement from Big and Diana searched the grass surrounding Dragon, every now and again dashing inside it to have a look around and appearing out of a hole somewhere else. Then she suddenly shot down the mound, dashed at full speed towards Big and vanished inside, to reappear a moment later with the missing youngster in her mouth. Vanessa was hard on her heels and trying to take it off her again, running parallel and making quick darts towards it. Diana avoided her as best she could and the two of them, baby included, disappeared into the depths of Dragon.

I had watched this 'baby-stealing' by subordinate females in other groups, for all the childless 'aunties' seemed to want the youngsters for themselves. Vanessa had been rather prominent right from the first in her solicitous care of Diana's babies and I had more or less expected her to try and steal one of them at some point. Sometimes this 'baby-stealing' could have tragic results. I had once seen a catastrophe happen in my tame group that could have been avoided if the female in question had just kept to the role she was supposed to – that of guarding and warming the youngsters.

It had all started when a young female stole one of the babies and carried it into a nestbox with only a small entrance hole which she was able to guard very effectively against any attempt of the frantic mother to retrieve her offspring. I expected her to carry it back again some time later, but she had no intention of doing so. She stayed where she was in the box all day. The next day, the baby was still there, being jealously guarded by the young female who, since she had no milk, was unable to suckle it. The mother would come dashing over every time the baby started to cry and try and reach it, only to be rebuffed by two jaws full of teeth and violent protest screams from the female within the box. This went on until nightfall, and the baby's calls were getting weaker and weaker. Finally I decided to intervene and went to retrieve the youngster before it starved to death, for it had had no food for almost two days now. As I opened the box, the female, instead of fleeing, leapt out at me and fastened herself on my hand, her teeth clamped in a locked bite and I couldn't budge her. While I ran out of the enclosure, the mongoose still clamped to my hand, trying to find something with which I could prise its jaws apart, the mother saw her chance and took it. She was in the nestbox like a flash and carried the baby back to the rest of the litter, while I rid myself of the over-assiduous babysitter. As soon as she was returned to the enclosure and I had staunched the flow of blood from my hand, she dashed to the nestbox and peered inside. The youngster was gone! She shot over to the box where the mother was with the litter and emerged with another one clamped in her jaws and looked as if she was going to repeat the whole process, but this time the mother was after her, with catastrophic results. The mother grabbed the back end of the dangling youngster and the young female had its neck in her jaws. Then followed a tug-of-war, both of them growling horribly, the little worm stretched to breaking point between them. Finally the young female let go her hold and the mother was left with the corpse of her baby dangling lifeless from her jaws. Its back had been broken in the struggle for its possession. The mother trotted back to the box, still carrying it, but that was the last I saw of the little body for, a week later, when the rest of the litter emerged and I went to clean out the box, there was no sign of its corpse. At some point it must have been eaten.

Such accidents were, however, few and far between and usually the babysitting system functioned with well-oiled precision, although baby-stealing was a favourite pastime amongst the younger females. In this, they reminded me a bit of many monkey and ape societies where the younger daughters can hardly wait to get their hands on the new-born babies. I realised that, if such a tendency was not present in the mongooses, then the babysitting system could not function at all. It was essential that the young females take an interest in the youngsters if they were going to act as 'temporary mothers' while the true mother was away feeding. Without food, she would have no milk and the babies would surely die for, true to mongoose tradition, no food would be brought to her. In this way, she could make sure that she was well nourished and rest assured that the youngsters were being well taken care of in the meantime. I had the impression it all hung together with the fact that mongooses build no nest for their young, the reason for this being not far to seek.

I had had a horrible example of the consequences of nest-building when I was hand-raising youngsters. In order to keep them warm and quiet, for unless they had something to cuddle against the babies were continually on the move and crying, I made a nest out of paper wadding that could be changed and thus kept clean easily. The youngster in question was almost three weeks old and eating meat and insects by this time. I put some chopped heart-meat in a little dish in its box. In its greed to gobble up the contents, the baby overturned the dish and, before I could intervene, it had eaten the blood-soaked paper together with the meat. It was obviously unable to tell at this stage what was real food and what was just a blood-soaked substrate. The result of this mishap was a complete blockage of the intestines and I had to put the poor little creature out of its misery, for no medicine helped in the least. This taught me a lesson, however, and, from this point on, the mongoose young were kept on the bare floor of their rearing boxes.

Since they had to keep moving house, the mongooses didn't build nests, but the result of this was that the youngsters kept wandering about unless they had a babysitter in attendance. I had seen what had happened when Goldie had not been with them. They had wandered out of the mound and ended up as a heron's dinner. It all fitted together beautifully. How such a system as the babysitting had been selected for in evolution was still a mystery but it was the ideal solution to the problem, for it kept the youngsters warm and quiet and at the same time, the danger of their eating nest material was avoided. I wondered how many years of evolution were required to perfect the system – for it *was* perfected and accidents happened only rarely.

10 Growing up in the Taru

Within a fortnight of the rains falling, the Taru seemed to blossom. Yellow flowers appeared on the acacia bushes and the buds were bursting everywhere. Grass seemed to shoot up overnight and many of the animals that I had rarely seen for weeks beforehand suddenly appeared again – zebra, impala, gazelles and Kongoni antelopes. Flanks rounded and coats started to shine as the fresh green was fed into stomachs that had lived for months on nothing but dry grass and twigs. Occasional bands of elephants would wander past but we only heard them in the distance at night, their trumpeting squeals and the cracking of branches like pistol shots marking their passage. With the game, though, came the predators. Lions roaring in the distance were almost a nightly chorus, as was the eerie *whooo-oop* of their spotted followers, the hyenas. Everything seemed to have timed its breeding season to fit the yearly cycle of abundance. The jackal family which lived near the camp, and which I often saw in the evenings on their visits to our rubbish pit, now had a pack of round-bellied jackal babies following them, looking like little beige-grey puppies with long ears. They were still having difficulty in negotiating the grass and twigs that littered the ground, for I would often see one stumble and fall as it gambolled after its parents. It was a time of life – and death.

Diana and Co. had remained at Dragon during the past week despite the heron's attack. The storks and herons had long left, following the rainclouds to feast on the bounty they would produce elsewhere with their life-bringing floods. Only a few stilts and Egyptian geese now inhabited the waterhole and I watched the geese leaving, heading north early one morning, the white patches on their wings flashing in the sunlight as they flew with loud, harsh honks. With the rains had also come the insects, especially the flies, and I would almost be driven mad by them settling on me in their hundreds as soon as the car stopped, their buzzing so loud that I could hardly hear what the mongooses were saying. As the insect life began to swarm, the smaller birds of prey came in in their hundreds to fill the bushlands. It almost seemed as if every second tree now had a Grasshopper buzzard perched on it ready to pounce down on anything moving below.

By this time the babies' eyes were open and, with the usual mongoose irrepressibility, they seemed to take every opportunity to crawl out of the termite mound and go exploring on their own, much to the babysitters' consternation. There were usually three or four of the mongooses left at the mound at this stage, the group usually comprising one of the older females, an older male and a younger male or female or sometimes two. Vanessa was still playing her role as 'Babysitter-in-Chief' and took charge whenever she had a chance. To date, however, the young had not left the mound to forage with the group but when Diana returned with the family after a session of foraging, the young would now run towards her to greet her, twittering, and nuzzle her flanks to get at the milk. Usually she would disappear into the mound, the two babies trailing after her, but sometimes she would lie down in some sheltered place on top of it and let them suckle. I watched their little feet pushing rhythmically in the 'milk tread' typical of nearly all carnivores and their little snouts would nuzzle to and fro, going from one teat to another. Both the young looked very healthy and fat and I was still not sure if they were not getting some milk at least from Notch but, strangely enough, she did not appear to be such an avid babysitter as Vanessa was. It might simply have been that Vanessa, being higher in rank than she was because she was younger, was preventing her from staying with the babies as much as she would want to.

The whole group seemed to take a great deal of interest in them and Moja, especially, would try and get them to play with him. He would come bouncing over to the little ones, giving the play call and tapping at them with one forefoot – which usually had the effect of toppling the youngster concerned, still none too steady on its feet, over sideways. On one occasion one of the little ones even ended up, after what must have been, for it, like falling down a mountain, head over heels in a heap at the bottom of the mound. Goldie and Vanessa were after it like a flash and I thought that a tug-of-war might result as both 'aunties' tried to rescue the youngster simultaneously. But Goldie stopped at the last moment and Vanessa picked it up, cheeping loudly, in her mouth, on which it curled itself into a quiet little ball once more, and she headed back up the mound to vanish with it to safety.

The young at this age looked really ugly, as their coats were sparse and the greyish skin beneath shimmered through. Their heads were much too big for their bodies and their short legs, along with the little pot bellies and rat-like tails, were hardly anyone's conception of a 'cute little baby'. It seemed that, when the youngsters were awake, the babysitters had more than their hands full, for at some point or another a cheeping little head would appear in one of the holes, to scrabble with difficulty out of it and then go slipping and sliding, sometimes even somersaulting head first, down the side of the mound to end up in a furiously cheeping heap at the bottom, and someone would have to go and retrieve it. I began to realise why the babysitting contingent had been doubled and wondered how they would have managed if the heron's attack had not been successful. Two little bundles of energy were bad enough – but five?

I had always believed that one of the basic reasons that the mongooses had

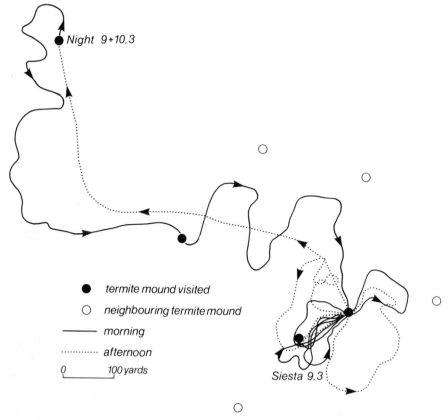

Night 9+10.3

● termite mound visited
○ neighbouring termite mound
——— morning
··········· afternoon
0   100 yards

Siesta 9.3

The babies remained with the babysitters in the termite mound while Diana and the rest of the family went foraging. They only returned in the evening and Diana suckled her young

'invented' the babysitting system was because they did not have the innate tendency to bring food to other family members. It was with great surprise, therefore, that I saw Diana approaching the mound at a gallop one day with something large dangling from her jaws. It turned out to be a young Multimammate rat and, as she ran up the mound, the youngsters staggered out to meet her as usual, twittering wildly. She stopped in front of them and, after they had sniffed what she was holding, suddenly two friendly little babies were turned into two little horrors. They flung themselves on the rat and Diana let it go and sat next to them, watching. The two of them grabbed opposite ends and started pulling and tugging at this creature which was as big as they were, worrying it and growling furiously. They were making absolutely no impression on the rat, however, for their baby teeth did not seem to be strong enough at this stage to break the skin. The two of them went through all the typical behaviour patterns one would see in two adult mongooses squabbling over prey; trying to pull it under their bodies and stand over it, trying to 'shake it to death' – rather feebly for their necks were not strong enough at this stage to lift the rat – and pushing and shoving at each other in the typical mongoose hipslam. Finally, it seemed, they had had enough, or maybe they even realised that the rat was not going to be of much use to them as they could never manage to get into where the meat was at this stage, their teeth and jaws were just not strong enough. They trotted back to where their mother was still sitting, watching them carefully. I wondered what would happen next, if Diana would go over and open the rat for them to get at the insides, but before anything could occur, a brown body, flattened against the ground, flashed round the side of the termite mound, a quick snap and the rat vanished. If the babies didn't want it, Moja certainly did!

The mongoose babies seemed to attract almost every predator in the neighbourhood. It became a daily occurrence for the group to be pinned down by a Grasshopper buzzard or Shikra which, although incapable of handling an adult animal, had noticed the babies on the mound and waited in nearby trees for their chance to catch one unawares. The babysitters had to keep their eyes peeled continually, for one of these birds would come twisting and turning through the branches at a second's notice. Since the hornbills were off foraging with the main group, their 'early warning system' was missing as well. In the first weeks of January, however, the Grasshopper buzzards started to leave. In their wake came hordes of Pale Chanting goshawks on their migration northwards to the Somali desert, and with them the European harriers. These birds were more dangerous to the youngsters than the Grasshopper buzzards had ever been and the bush echoed loud with the musical chiming call of the goshawks. They were so numerous that hardly a day went past without an attack taking place. It was also a common sight to see the harriers swooping past under the thorntree branches, close against the ground and moving at terrific speed, pouncing on anything that caught their eye.

One day, one of the mongoose babies was very nearly caught. The youngsters were now nearly three weeks old and this was the time that they really started to turn into little mongooses, for many of the adult behaviour patterns appear suddenly at this stage of development. I had called one of the youngsters 'Wart', because of a small lump on its nose that looked like a wart, and the second 'Pickle' because the name described the animal perfectly. When there was trouble brewing, Pickle would be mixed up in it somewhere! She was the most active and inquisitive mongoose baby I had ever seen. Pickle had her nose into everything and was forever trotting down the mound, driving the babysitter to exasperation. Vanessa spent most of her time with

A lost baby will be grabbed by the neck and dragged back to the safety of the mound by the babysitters

Pickle when Diana was away, but once she returned she seemed to be in charge automatically, for the babies would leave whoever they had been with and rush towards their four-legged milk source. On this particular occasion, Pickle had played truant again and had somehow lost her way, for she started cheeping the 'baby lost' call at full volume. Vanessa was immediately all ears and gazing wildly around but Pickle was hidden behind a thick tuft of grass. Suddenly there was a flurry of wings, pale red with a black border – a Grasshopper buzzard had spotted Pickle at the same instant as Vanessa and I. It shot downwards, talons to the fore, and Vanessa, all her hair on end, gave a tremendous leap which carried her from the top of the mound to the edge of its earth apron. A second leap and she was upon Pickle and, just as she turned with the baby in her mouth, the buzzard hit the ground immediately behind her, taking off again a split second later, leaving nothing but a puff of dust to show how near Pickle had come to being a buzzard's supper. Vanessa dragged her charge by the scruff of its neck back to the mound, Pickle's feet hanging limp and her eyes closed as she went into the instinctive *Tragestarre*. The panic-stricken 'auntie' vanished in a twinkling into one of the holes, dragging the little body after her. She had hardly been in there a few seconds when Pickle's head appeared in one of the openings again and once more she was off on her travels, Vanessa trotting after her and trying to grasp her neck to drag her to safety once again. I was wondering how long it would be before Pickle fell prey to one predator or another for, at this stage in her development, she was completely oblivious of the danger she was in. She would stare even at the most dangerous of the aerial predators with her blue-filmed eyes, not realising what they were.

When the youngsters were just over three weeks old, the first signs of the mongooses' most favoured pastime, apart from filling their stomachs, appeared. Pickle toddled towards Wart and patted him on the nose with one forepaw, the age-old invitation to play. The two of them, almost in slow motion, moved round each other, peeping the play call slowly and in falsetto, holding fast to each other's necks and turning round and round on their stubby little legs. This was their first attempt to play with each other and, although they were doing it slowly and carefully, the basic elements of play could be seen even at this stage. Wart rolled on his back and his sister climbed on top of him, their mouths gaped and little jaws fencing back and forth, a slow-motion parody of the lightning quick stabs of the older animals. Moja was watching them both and suddenly the temptation was too great. Beeping loudly, he jumped on top of them wanting to play as well, but the only result of his untimely interruption was that Wart fell down the side of the mound, Pickle staggered backwards and Vanessa had to go down and retrieve the loudly cheeping baby. After about a week, I watched Moja playing gently with the two of them, tapping them every now and again with one forefoot but mostly bounding round them like a little rubber ball, beeping loudly. I think the greatest problem he had was with the wrestling, for as soon as he grasped one of them gently in the neck with his teeth, his playmate would turn into a limp little bundle ready to be carried. The *Tragestarre* reflex was still working at full force at this time and the least touch on the neck seemed to set it off. At this point Moja would stop, look a little startled and let the baby go, on which it would immediately start staggering round beeping the play call again. I had never realised up until now how automatic the 'carrying reflex' was. Once the stimulus of the jaws on the baby's neck was gone, the baby just seemed to carry on where it had left off.

From the very first time I had seen the youngsters on the mound they had shown the typical mongoose nibble-grooming, but at that stage even this basic and important pattern of mongoose social behaviour seemed to go off automatically as if a little switch had been thrown. As soon as one of the others nibbled the youngster the youngster's jaws would start working, reciprocating the nibble. This sometimes ended up very comically, for family members walking past would often give the babies a quick nibble on any part of their anatomy they could reach. Sometimes the nibbles were given at the base of the tail and the little creature would twist round, trying to groom its grooming partner in return but unable to reach it. Then I could see the little teeth nibbling like fury in mid-air but with nothing there for them to nibble! Wart soon solved this problem by nibbling his own forefoot when someone nibbled him where he could not nibble back, but Pickle still performed the 'air nibbles' when the right stimulus came. The mongooses' grooming nibble seemed almost to be preprogrammed for partners' necks, for even the tiny babies would turn their heads on being nibbled on the neck or shoulder and reciprocate the friendly act, even though it meant they only managed to reach to the groomer's upper leg – if that!

Most of the time, however, the young were licked, Vanessa and Diana being the 'Lickers-in-Chief'. Most of the time they seemed to love having their tummies and anal regions massaged by mother and aunties' tongues. They would lie back like little buddhas, their back legs spread and their forepaws folded over their bulging bellies, and let their guardians take over.

Although George was very taken with the youngsters and would lie next to them and groom them, when he managed to have a chance of getting near them through the crowd of babysitters, he did not seem to concern himself too much about them at this stage. It wasn't until the babies were nearly a month old that he started to play a major role in their lives. By this time the 'aunties' were taking less and less care of the little ones and they were starting to wander around more on their own. One morning, I saw George come running back to the mound with a large locust in his mouth, stand in front of the youngsters and give the feeding growl. Two little heads turned in his direction and, in a flash, Wart and Pickle were alongside him and begging in high chirruping voices. As soon as they had grabbed his prize, he let go of it and, after a few furious growls at each other, Pickle won the day and tore off as fast as she could with the locust to eat it in peace, Wart close behind, squeaking loudly. George disappeared down into the grass again and was back within a minute with another large insect, a cricket this time, and this Wart got, for Pickle was still busy with the locust. Although they had still not cut their adult teeth yet, the youngsters were very efficient at crunching up insects' skeletons, although Pickle had a bit of trouble with the locust's wings as they got stuck in her teeth and she had a hard time picking them out. She was still none too steady on her feet and each time she would raise one forepaw to dislodge the stuck wing, she would fall over onto her side and have to start all over again. She finally got rid of it with a sharp shake of her head and then got back to the job of dismembering the locust.

Diana had continued to bring large prey back to the mound in the week beforehand, mostly mice which the youngsters couldn't quite manage at this age. I only once saw her tear the head off one of the captured animals and, once this was done, Wart and Pickle were on it like a pack of wolves, growling madly and shoving each other out of the way, both of them smeared with blood and sucking everything in sight, including their own paws. I almost burst out laughing on one occasion when Pickle, frantic with the taste of hot prey, pounced on her brother's forefoot which was liberally coated with gore and began to chew and suck at it. Wart just stopped dead as if he didn't quite know what to do and then shouldered his greedy sister out of the way and went back to sucking and slurping at the mouse's body.

It was significant that, at this age – they were barely three weeks old at the time – the youngsters were not chewing the mouse with their cheek teeth but were responding to the blood as if it were milk, slurping it up with suction of the lips and throat muscles. It wasn't until several days later that I saw the adult chewing movements appear. The blood lust was there long before the behaviour patterns which could be used to dismember any animal with blood in it appeared.

It was a small step from George bringing insects to the mound to the babies going with him foraging. Their first real foraging excursion took place very early one morning when they were almost four weeks old. George trotted down the mound and the youngsters followed him, keeping close to his sides and poking their snouts wherever he did. His finding of some juicy titbit was heralded by a growl from him and almost simultaneous squeaks and squeals from his children, one of which would grab the insect out of his mouth and gobble it up with much crunching of jaws. On this, their first trip out into the bush, they did not go far and George led them round in a small circle and back to the mound again.

The hornbills, especially, seemed very intrigued by the little mongooses and would hop along behind the trio, their heads cocked on one side, watching them carefully. Hornbills are intelligent birds and it did not take the Yellow-bills long to realise what was going on on these excursions. A mongoose was catching food and holding it in its mouth! It was about a week later that I saw how deep this 'friendship' between the mongooses and hornbills was.

It seemed to have fallen to George's lot to take the youngsters foraging in the morning while Diana had a 'late lie in' on the mound. By this time, they were hardly being suckled by her any more and although they seemed to prefer to spend most of their time with her when they were on the mound, in the early mornings, when they were hungry, George was most definitely their favourite person. They would give him no peace until he finally got up and led them off on a little foraging excursion all of their own. I was watching the little procession grubbing their way through the grass only about five yards from the car and recording how George would dig out a tasty beetle or cricket and hold it, growling, for the youngsters to take. Two Yellow-bills hopped in the wake of the little trio, pouncing right and left on fleeing grasshoppers. Then one of the birds moved right up behind George and his charges and the next time

It seemed to be George's job to take the youngsters food-hunting in the early morning

George caught an insect, a wicked-looking yellow bill shot over his shoulder, grabbed the madly begging Wart by the scruff of his neck and flung him to one side, to stab again immediately afterwards at the captured insect. George flung his rear end at the bird in a magnificent hipslam, growling loudly, and the bird took a smart hop backwards. By this time Wart had disentangled himself from the grass tussock in which he had landed and dashed, still

begging madly, back to his father.

It was only later, when I came to think over the incident, that I wondered what had stopped the Yellow-bill from simply picking Wart up and eating him? I had seen Yellow-bills eating quite large prey – up to the size of adult Multimammate rats. If the bird had only kept its hold on Wart and flown off with him, there was very little that George could have done. But George

A young mongoose grabs an insect from its father's jaws and eats it while he looks on

responded to the hornbill in exactly the same way he would have responded to an adult family member trying to steal food off him – with a hipslam! There was more behind this business of the mongooses and hornbills than met the eye. Later it became a common sight when the babies were older and were foraging further afield with the rest of the group, to see the hornbills hopping behind the mongoose which was leading the babies and trying to steal the insects it had caught for them. Although on other occasions I also saw mongoose babies spinning through the air, thrown backwards by the greedy birds trying to get at the insect caught in the adult's jaws, I never ever saw one make a stab at one of the youngsters, although one jab of those powerful beaks could have killed or, at the least, seriously injured them. Mongoose and hornbill really did seem to be friends.

Although their little anal glands were not even developed at this stage, this did not seem to stop Wart and Pickle from trying to use them, or their cheek glands either. I vividly remember Pickle's first attempt to mark with the rest of the family. She pushed her way amongst the crush of bodies at the marking post and started to sniff it very carefully indeed, even going into a very wobbly version of high sit to reach up a bit further. This was quite a feat in itself, for there were other family members leaping into handstands all around her and anal glands descending along the length of the post, which was a sunbleached Commiphora branch near the base of the mound. Although she got sat on three times and was knocked flying by Blackie, who had just not quite managed to make the connection between post and back legs and had fallen over sideways, Pickle persisted.

After Pickle had thoroughly investigated the post she marked. She slewed her body round, lifted her tail high and raised one hind-leg as her backside moved past the base of the branch. She whipped round to see if she had connected – which she hadn't, she had missed the post by at least an inch – and then tried again. Once more a total failure. Although she was going through the motions of the 'leg-lift' anal marking process which the mongooses use to mark each other, her aim was most definitely off! After three more tries she trotted up the mound again and I was not sure if she had thought she had marked properly or whether she had just given up. In any case, Pickle was now trying to add her name to the family signature.

Even the cheek gland marking was a total failure at this stage. The two youngsters, if they found something protruding from the ground on or near the mound, would toddle towards it and try and rub their faces along it in the typical left and right of the cheek marking movement. Even this seemed to go off almost automatically, for there did not seem to be any connection between the movement and the object. On three occasions I watched Wart and Pickle marking grass stems which, in their hurry to get as close as possible, they had bent over by treading on them, but they continued the back-and-forth head movements at the point where the grass-stems had been a moment before. Although their cheek glands were not developed at this stage, it looked as if the behaviour patterns of marking were there, though not very accurate in their aim, long before the animals were capable of putting scent anywhere at all, even if they had managed to connect.

Most of the time, though, the youngsters did nothing but eat, sleep and play. As their muscles developed and their coordination started to improve, the play sessions became wilder and more abandoned. They also spent long periods of time investigating their surroundings, trotting along one after another, usually in the wake of one of the adults, and poking their noses into everything. All sorts of things were unearthed and turned over by busy little paws, irrespective of whether they were edible or not, and the babies would watch carefully how one of their elder brothers and sisters or their parents fished tasty insects out of grass tussocks and then try the same themselves.

One morning early, George had gone off with the two of them on the obligatory 'baby-breakfast-finding' excursion and the two youngsters were following close at his flanks, just waiting for him to unearth something good. Then Pickle suddenly darted to one side, fished around in a grass tussock and, both paws scrabbling in the 'washing' movement, brought a large black ground weevil to light. The weevil struggled mightily to crawl back into the shelter of the grass but Pickle was very intrigued with what she had found and flipped it over with a deft pat of her paw time and again so that the insect had to struggle to right itself once more. Then she started to give the play call and bounce around the insect, making quick darts at it with her snout and hitting it back and forth with her paws. The weevil drew its legs close to its body and lay there like a little stone. Then Pickle jumped on it with both paws and, with a quick thrust backwards, shot it underneath her body in the typical 'egg slam' movement. The only problem was, she didn't seem to have her hind-legs coordinated with her front ones, for the weevil landed up with a crack against her tummy and it was only then that she gave a little hop with her back legs. Instead of shooting it backwards as she had planned to do, she had only managed to push it underneath her. She whipped round, searching behind her for the insect but, of course, it was not there. The weevil took its chance and started to crawl off again and its movement alerted Pickle who pounced on it and once more hit it beneath her with tremendous force for such a little creature. Again her backlegs didn't seem to take their cue, for the hop occurred after the weevil had already come to rest under her stomach. Once more she whipped round to look at the place the weevil ought to have been only to find nothing. She obviously didn't quite realise what was going wrong. It was obvious that this 'egg slam' was a behaviour pattern whose coordination had to be learned through practice for Pickle was absolutely hopeless at it at this stage.

Finally, she was just about to try again when Wart came gambolling up, having noticed that Pickle had got something, and as soon as he appeared on the scene, Pickle's behaviour towards the weevil changed. She took it in her mouth and, growling loudly, tried to turn her back on her brother, but Wart was not going to be put off so easily. He dashed forward, head outstretched, and tried to take the weevil off his sister. Some protest squeaks, a few turns in a circle – Pickle still trying to keep her find away from her brother – and then there was an audible crack. In her excitement, Pickle had bitten through the weevil's hard shell and this was the first prey I had ever seen her kill for herself. Growling loudly at her brother and hipslamming him every time he got too close, she chewed the insect up, crunching away at the hard carapace. Finally it was all gone and she trotted quickly after George, who seemed to be taking this God-given opportunity to try and get some food into his own stomach.

At this stage the little creatures did not seem to be able to make a

At five weeks old, the youngsters forage along with the babysitters and are fed by them

connection between these moving objects which they found in the grass and food, for nearly all the kills appeared to have come about through accident, when one of them had found something and the other had tried to take the insect off it. The result had been a harder bite and, once the insect had been killed, it then fell into the category of 'eatables' and was chewed up with gusto. They knew exactly, though, that what George was holding in his mouth was food, but it did not seem as if they would have been capable of feeding for themselves at first had this sibling rivalry not existed between them. It was terribly funny to watch them when they had found a small grasshopper. Each time a paw or a nose would stretch out to investigate the creature, the insect would give a jump and the mongoose baby would jump in surprise in the opposite direction only to chase after the insect and try again. Usually, these grasshopper investigations did not last long for one of the hornbills or shrikes would spot the insect and come swooping over to catch it and the mongoose baby would almost be tumbled over in the rush of air from the bird's wings, creeping away to hide in some convenient grass tussock until the thief had gone.

It took almost a week of these investigations before it seemed that the connection between something moving and food had finally been made for, although the youngsters were still begging food from George and the other members of the group until they were well over two months old, they started slowly to hunt for themselves weeks beforehand. Most of the prey they could manage to capture, though, was very small and I could only tell that they had found something by the sight of little jaws champing, but the object they were chewing was usually too tiny for me to make out what it was. It was on one of the foraging excursions that George, the babies squealing and shoving next to him, managed – despite their efforts to interfere – to unearth a rat youngster. Instead of killing it with one well-aimed bite across the head, he held it, squeaking and struggling, in his mouth and Wart and Pickle were on it in a flash. Then George just let it go and the two youngsters dashed after the fleeing rat, trying to grab hold of any part of its anatomy that they could reach. Pickle got a smart nip on the nose from her would-be prey and I could see her stop and rub the wound with one forepaw. This did not deter her, though, for she scampered after Wart, who had managed to grab the animal in the neck and was hanging on for dear life and being dragged, all four feet thrust forward to act as brakes, in the wake of his fleeing partner.

When Pickle joined him and grabbed the rat from the other side, Wart let go his hold and, growling falsetto, tried to push his sister away. In the squabbling the rat managed to escape into a thick patch of grass. The youngsters, George close behind, then started to investigate, rather nervously, their heads flagging up and down as they peered into the jungle of grass stems. George, however, without further ado, plunged in amongst them and, after a furious struggle during which the blanket of grass heaved up and down, emerged once more with the rat hanging squirming from his jaws. Again the youngsters pounced on it but it was fairly obvious to me, at least, that they were not going to manage to wound, let alone kill it. I didn't really have the impression they were trying to! George looked on alertly while the two once more fell upon the rat and tried to bring it to a standstill. Then Wart gave up the struggle and went to investigate the roots of a grass tussock, leaving Pickle to handle the huge furry object on her own.

To my amazement, once Wart had left, the growling stopped and was replaced with the unmistakable play call, and Pickle started shaking the rat to and fro, hanging on to the scruff of its neck! She let go her hold and began pouncing upon it, giving it little pushes with her forepaws. At this stage the poor rat looked completely numbed, for it just sat there, quivering, eyes staring wide, and made no move to run. Pickle pranced round her new playmate, tapping it here and there with her paws, and finally darted in to give it a quick nip in the tail. This seemed to shake the rat out of its panic-stricken freezing and it darted off, Pickle, still beeping loudly, in close pursuit. Once again George came to the rescue, pinned the rat down with a quick movement of his paw and bit it neatly through the head, returning to the youngsters with its corpse dangling from his jaws. Each grabbed a hind-leg and started pulling wildly and, in the struggle, the skin split, exposing the meat. Then the rat was buried under two horribly growling mongoose babies, each trying to shoulder the other one out of the way to get at the tasty meal. George stood by, watching them.

It was especially interesting for me as an ethologist to watch the transitions that the same stimulus 'rat' had gone through before it was finally recognised for what it really was – food. This was the first time the youngsters had seen a live Multimammate rat; all the others had been dead or partly eaten by the time they came in contact with them. At first the rat was just an object of curiosity, to be fought over as to who was allowed to investigate it first, and Pickle had won. Then it was a playmate, as far as Pickle was concerned. It was only after George had killed it and stood with it hanging from his mouth that the babies had considered it food, but I was not sure even then whether, if they had not managed to break the skin to taste the blood, they would not have gone back to playing with its corpse. At any rate, it seemed clear that there was no innate recognition of a rat as prey – at least not a live rat. Although I kept a sharp lookout, it was several weeks later before I saw George catch a rat near the youngsters again and they immediately pounced on it, tore it apart and started feeding. I still did not have the answer to my question for they were, by this time, several weeks older and maybe just simple maturation of behaviour patterns had resulted in their change of response to the rat. Or maybe they had remembered the connection between 'live rat' and 'meat' and had acted accordingly. Prey capture in mongooses did not look as if it was at all preprogrammed, at least from what I had seen. The only thing that seemed innate was the recognition of blood as food – the rest had to be learned and it seemed as if the adults, especially the babies' father, were the teachers.

It had always struck me as curious that George, of all animals, should be the one to take the babies foraging. Sometimes they went with Diana or one of the older males, especially Scar and Whitethroat, but George was the one who brought them the most food. Putting concepts of 'paternal affection' aside, it was still a beautifully arranged system. Diana had been the one who had had to invest the most energy in the children, first by carrying them in her body for almost eight weeks and then by nourishing them with the milk she produced. To have had to supply them with most of their solid food as well would have been a great drain on her resources, so, thanks to the mongoose social code, she had been spared this extra job. Her husband who, although having had a hard time of it during their conception, had now had almost two months to 'get back on his feet again', was the one to bear the brunt of feeding the offspring, the other family members lending a hand only if they were unlucky enough to be nearby and have found something. The more I watched them, the more I came to realise that the mongooses had developed a social system far in advance of any other mammal I knew of – except Man!

The babies seemed to be no exception to the rule of family toilet hygiene, for almost as soon as they emerged from their hiding-place at the age of three weeks, at which time they had started to eat an appreciable amount of solid food, they tottered down the side of the mound with the others in the morning and performed their tasks on the family midden. Up until this time, their mother and aunties had licked them clean, stimulating them to produce their faeces by massaging them with their tongues so that the sleeping hole remained spotless. It was therefore with surprise that I noticed Pickle come dashing down the side of the mound one morning and, instead of going to the family toilet, just squatting where she first landed and leaving her little sausage there, turning round to sniff it carefully in true mongoose fashion. It looked as if she had been bursting and had just not managed to reach the proper place. What happened afterwards gave me cause for thought, however, for not only Wart but George as well, when they came down the mound in the youngster's wake, stopped to sniff what she had left and promptly added their portion to it! It looked almost as if Pickle had inadvertently started a new tradition for, when others of the group met up with these fresh faeces, they promptly added their own. Only a few of them, which had not happened to pass by the site, went as usual to the traditional toilet almost on the other side of the mound.

This observation intrigued me so, when I got back to my tame group in Europe, I decided to try a little experiment. I took some fresh droppings from their toilet and put them at the opposite side of the enclosure, leaving nothing but old droppings at the original site. Once the mongooses had investigated this change in their usual furniture arrangement, they promptly left the old toilet and used the new one from that time onwards. This raised the question 'Was it important that it be their *own* fresh droppings or were fresh droppings in general a sign of "toilet"?' I removed their droppings and put those of another group in their place. This caused even more excitement and, after the droppings had been anally marked by the 'anal drag' method, the animals sliding their bottoms over them with the anal gland everted, the toilet was used as before. This seemed a very efficient method of keeping a termite mound clean, for it would mean that each group would use the same toilet and not start a new one of its own. What was so amazing, though, was that this behaviour was even present in the very tiny babies and it was only Pickle's 'mishap' that had brought me to the train of thought that resulted in finding out that something as commonplace as a toilet could have important social connotations.

Regular mound changes took place practically every day and I realised that here was another reason why mongooses should not build nests – even when babies were there, they remained nomads. By the time the youngsters were five weeks old, they did not need to be carried and would trot along after the others who would make the excursion just part of the daily foraging, moving slowly enough for the youngsters to keep up.

It was now very important for them to learn who their enemies were, for there were many of them. All they were given by Nature was a fear of something moving quickly against the sky, and it was their guardians who polished this rough image up by showing the babies exactly what was dangerous and what not. After watching how they would take in every detail of the predator and how the guardian would give the warning call continually, I realised that the learning of predators would not be difficult for the young-sters. They learned about Pale Chanting goshawks very quickly, for hardly a day went by without the group being pinned down by one of these birds. If a goshawk or other raptor caught the mongooses on their way between two mounds, which sometimes happened, the youngsters would rush for the nearest adult and stand close to it or try and get underneath, heads peering upwards at the predator from behind the grownup's legs, their little voices joining the chorus by the time they were five weeks old. Before that, they would just peer upwards at the bird silently.

This was the season, too, of happy events amongst the antelope family, which meant that ground predators were on the increase. The impala were especially numerous at this time and one morning, I was treated to a unique and beautiful sight. A herd of females without their usual male harem owner, for they had recently given birth and at this time the mothers leave the main herd and form a herd of their own, wandered slowly in front of the car and, one after another, lay down on the ground to sleep, leaving only a single member of their group on guard. Her black-tipped ears flickered back and forth, taking in every sound, but all was quiet. The rest of the company were stretched out on the ground, deep in slumber and only about fifteen yards away from me. I wondered how many other people in the world had had this experience, a herd of shy antelope behaving as if I weren't there! I wondered also where they had left their young, for impalas, like many other bush antelopes, have young which 'lie out' in the first days of their lives when they

A herd of impala wanders slowly in front of my car

are not yet strong enough to follow their mothers. At this time the young are odourless so as not to attract predators, and find some sheltered place to lie until their mother returns to the area and calls them. She never goes directly towards her baby, which could leave a scent trail for predators to follow, but waits until the baby comes towards her to suckle. When it has finished, she leaves and the baby makes its own way back to its hiding-place to wait until she returns again. I resolved to be extra careful when driving through the bush from now on just in case I ran over one of these little ones which 'sit tight' even under the most extreme provocation, expecting their camouflage to protect them.

It was two days later, as the sun was setting and the mongooses were gathered on Flat mound, one of the low *Odontotermes* ones that they favoured, that I heard a terrific yapping. Somewhere a jackal was furious about something; I had never heard such angry barking coming from a jackal before. Through the deepening shadows an object was approaching at full speed but I could not make out what it was. It was certainly bigger than a jackal but it seemed to be headless and have more legs than usual! It was only when the creature burst through a patch of Grewia right in front of me that I realised what I had been staring at. It was a Striped hyena with a baby impala in its mouth, looking over its shoulder at a Black-backed jackal which was running after it, nipping it in the heels. The hyena had its bottom tucked in under it and was running as fast as it could and, since it was looking over its shoulder at its pursuer, which was still yapping furiously, it didn't see me until literally the last minute and almost ran into the front of the car. The jackal stopped dead and the hyena whirled round and, with a tremendous leap, sailed past me to land on top of Flat amongst the mongooses, who had been all curiously watching these goings on. Total panic! The mound emptied as the hyena went bounding past, the impala baby still clamped in its jaws. Only Wart was left wandering, cheeping loudly, up and down the mound. A head and the foreparts of a body snaked out as he passed one of the holes, grabbed him by the neck and vanished with him into the mound's depths. This was the last I saw of the mongooses for the night!

Wart and Pickle seemed to have survived the dangers of baby life successfully for, by the time they were four months old, they started to look like little adults and act like adults too. They were miniatures of their parents and well capable of finding their own food and spotting dangers, though I considered it a miracle that they had survived these first four months at all. They had long given up begging food from the other group members and were now catching most of their own food themselves. But this did not mean that they never got fed, for the twittering charge of one of the youngsters promptly relieved any of the other animals of their hard-caught meal even though the necessity for this was long past. It was such an easy step from giving food to the young to them being rank-high permanently over the rest of their brothers and sisters. The transition was so gradual that it was painless. Pickle, however, was still the boss when it came to her domination over Wart and, although he would try and fight her off if he found something to eat, if she was near she would promptly take it off him. This may simply have been associated with the fact that Pickle was bigger than Wart and more precocious in general, for I had seen very much the same thing happening in my tame group but, in this case, the larger of the two littermates had been a male and he had dominated his sister until the two were about a year old. I didn't know what set the fight off but the two of them had a tremendous battle and, for the next three days, the young male just hid from his sister and protested loudly whenever she approached him. After this, he gave in to her whenever she tried to take something away from him. The tables had been turned and the mongoose rank order put back where it belonged, with the females on top. It seemed as if, should the rank system not work right from the beginning, it was made to work as soon as the animals were old enough and strong enough to take the incentive.

It was at this age that Wart and Pickle really started to integrate into the group and build up special relationships with other group members. Although George and Diana were still most important in their lives, they would initiate social interaction with their siblings whenever they got a chance.

Wart and Pickle had usurped Moja, M'Bili and Tatu's role with their parents. Moja and M'Bili, however, had gradually drifted away from this close relationship by the time they were six or seven months old; it was only little Tatu who remained tied to Diana's apron strings. After Diana's oestrus, when George had continually chased her away from his wife, she had gone into what could be termed a depression, for she no longer played as frequently and often sat by herself on the mound. Although Fleck would pay more attention to her than the other family members did, she seemed not to reciprocate his interest. When he would sit next to her flank-on-flank and nibble her neck-ruff, she would automatically nibble in return but I never saw her seek him out to return the favour. She had become almost an outsider and maybe the shock of her attacks from George, which had violently broken the bond between her and her mother, had made her incapable of transferring her affections at this time. She would play with Wart and Pickle when they invited her to but that was all. This was quite in contrast to Moja and M'Bili who would initiate games with their younger brother and sister and Moja, especially, would seek every opportunity to play.

The first signs I saw of a special friendship starting up with either of the babies were between Pickle and Vanessa. Vanessa had been Pickle's most avid babysitter when she was younger and it was she that, owing to Pickle's irrepressibility, had had to spend the most time with her just to keep her out of trouble. It became obvious as the weeks went by that Pickle sat next to Vanessa more frequently than was dictated by the laws of chance, and the two would groom each other and play together. This friendship was, however, by no means exclusive and both partners would often groom and rest near the other family members. Vanessa's friendship with Twin was still obvious although contacts were kept to a minimum when they were under George's eye, as usual. I wondered whether the friendship with Pickle was a remnant of the bond Vanessa had felt for her when she was very young, a bond that had attenuated somewhat when the youngster's dependence on its parents for food had taken pride of place in its development, but which was now being revived. Interestingly enough, Pickle seemed to sense the relationship that existed between Twin and Vanessa and was more friendly towards him than towards the rest of the adult males in the group – with the very big exception of her father – and would groom him frequently. This could just have come about, though, through the simple fact of Twin hanging around Vanessa as much as he could and, as a result, he automatically came in for Pickle's attention more than the other males did. Another curious thing was that, apart from her parents, Vanessa was the only other group member that Pickle greeted, which indicated that she also had a certain amount of respect for her friend. She would also greet Wart on occasion but only in situations in which he had something that she wanted and which he was not prepared to give up. Pickle would use this as an excuse to get near him and, once she had managed this, Wart standing almost numbed by this furious 'white flag' waving of his sister's, she would dart in and steal whatever he had been guarding. This automatically brought the truce to an end and Wart would go haring after the thief to try and regain his property. This was the first time I had ever seen a mongoose 'cheat' by pretending submission when in actual fact it wanted something completely different. If Pickle had just come charging up to Wart he would probably have fled and hidden himself with his prize in some place she could not reach, but in this way his defences were down and she could get what she wanted. I have never seen another mongoose act towards any of its family members in this way before or since.

The two friends, Rusty and Moja, had now gained another member of their club and that was Wart. Moja had always wanted to play with the youngsters when they were small and had shown a great deal of interest in them in general. It looked as though this interest was now being reciprocated, at least from Wart's side.

Although his sister and parents were still Wart's favourites his next favourite seemed to be Moja and he would often trot over to invite him to a game. As usual, if Rusty tried to join in, the game would break up, unless they were playing 'Hare and Hounds' or 'King of the Castle' where more than two could play at the same time. Wart would often squeeze between the two young males when they were sitting together and nibble their neck-ruffs and be nibbled in return, and it seemed as if they were accepting his advances for, if one of them happened to be alone on the mound, he would trot over to Wart and sit next to him and give him the nibble of friendship. It seemed significant that, at this stage of their development, the youngsters seemed to prefer the company of older brothers and sisters of the same sex, instead of the other way around. They were far from being sexually mature, however, and I did not know how their relationships with the family members of opposite sexes would develop as they grew older. At this stage they were like little human children, boys playing with boys and girls with girls.

Despite this tendency for friendships with older siblings, Wart and Pickle spent most of their time together and in the company of Diana and George. They still foraged near their mother when the group was on the move and lay next to her on the mound but George was the only one of the two who would play with them. Diana never did. Although he was now able to feed more or less in peace, George was still very concerned with his youngest children and they with him, and they would join him at the marking post when he went to mark. The first time I saw the two of them trying to mark from a handstand position they were just over two months old and their marking technique in general had improved enormously by this time. When they began handstand marking, however, I ruined several observation periods by laughing out loud. It was one of the funniest things I had ever seen.

It all started when Pickle – as usual she was the first of the two to try anything new – trotted down to the post in George's wake one morning to mark. In the weeks before her technique of the 'leg lift' had become expert and she was now making contact with the post by simply backing up to it with her tail raised once she had gone through the twist and leg lift part of the procedure. She stood on her hind-legs to sniff the marks of the others and then, with a twist and a spring, she was in handstand – but not for long! She wobbled back and forth on her forepaws, trying to keep her body in balance but inches away from where her feet should connect, and finally, after a tremendous effort to keep upright, she fell with a crash on her back. She scrambled to her feet and once again gave a mighty leap, and this time her momentum was so great that her hind-quarters made a big arc in the air and she landed on her bottom with a thump. Wart came to join her. He was even worse than she was! The two of them leapt about getting in each other's way. Once they both leapt simultaneously from opposite directions and two back-ends met with a crash in mid-air, their startled owners glancing back at them when they had come to earth again as if to ask what had happened. It took almost a week of constant practice before they finally managed the handstand. Within a few weeks, though, the two youngsters were almost as proficient at handstand marking as their older siblings. They kept to the maxim 'Practice makes perfect', marking the post much more frequently than any of the other animals. Maybe this was something like a 'coming of age' for the two little ones, a time at which they were writing their signatures over and over again in the family album to make sure no one forgot that they now really belonged.

Handstand marking was the last of the adult behaviour patterns to appear in the youngsters, at least those of the social behaviour context. Neither of them had managed to catch a mouse or any larger prey yet, although I had seen both of them digging furiously in holes where I presumed a mouse to be but, after half-disappearing inside their excavations, they would emerge covered in dust and, after a quick shake of their bodies, trot on again. They still got their share of the mice the older animals caught. But now their 'baby stage' was over, and they were about to be told so in no uncertain means by their parents.

The first time Diana refused her youngsters a bit of the mouse she had caught came as rather a shock to both of them. Up until now, they had been used to getting more or less what they wanted and Diana had given in with good grace. One afternoon, however, I saw her trot up a mound with a mouse hanging from her jaws, Pickle and Wart in hot pursuit, twittering and cheeping at full blast. Diana stopped and pinned the mouse down with her forefoot and started to growl loudly at the two of them, but they took no notice and pushed their snouts towards her prey. She growled again and swung her body round in a hipslam that took Pickle full force and bowled her over. The little one got to her feet, hestitated a second, and then dashed forwards to beg again. Once more she got a hipslam from her mother and Wart had not come off much better, for he had been on the outside edge of the mound and Diana's first hipslam in his direction had sent him flying to the bottom, but he still persisted. Finally it looked as if Diana had had enough and trotted with her mouse into the mound, still growling loudly, not at all like the 'attraction growl' she had given before to get the babies to come and take the food off her.

The youngsters' behaviour towards their mother changed rather subtly after this for they were no longer so vehement in their begging food from her and, if she growled at them, they retreated and came back again very submissive. I think that this was the point in their lives when they came to consider their mother as a mongoose to be respected and not simply a food-giver and refuge in emergencies. Although their friendly relationships with her after this incident were even more evident, their old gay abandon had been lost and they would continually keep an eye on both her and George, ready to dash in submissively if one of them showed the slightest aggression, either towards themselves or other group members. Wart and Pickle now seemed to have taken over the older trio's job of keeping the peace, their first grown-up duty in the family. Their roles as 'Peace-makers' had just grown on them as they grew themselves. They were well on the way to becoming adult mongooses.

11   The Wars of the Mounds

I was sitting quietly watching the mongooses get up from their afternoon siesta one day when I saw a flutter of black and white way off to the south of them. I raised my binoculars and could make out two pairs of hornbills peering down from some bare bushes at something on the ground. I took no more notice of them and continued my watching of Diana's group, expecting them to fly over and join the hornbills there at any moment. When they showed no sign of doing so and continued hopping from bush to bush with three White-crowned bush shrikes in tow, I began to realise that something was wrong and the one thing I had been hoping for in all these patient weeks of waiting was about to happen. It looked as if another group of mongooses was approaching!

Diana, George and the rest of them hadn't seemed to have noticed what I could see from my perch inside the car and their hornbill friends, although noticing the other group of approaching hornbills, had not said anything about them. It wasn't until the two groups were only about twenty yards apart and I could see small brown bodies, stretched to their utmost, stopping and then running with rapid rushes towards Diana's mound that Blackie, who was on guard, caught sight of one of the approaching invaders. '*TSEEEEEE!*' His call 'Come quickly!' was more than penetrating. The rest of the family gathered round him in a twinkling, all heads pointed in the direction in which he was looking. The invading group stopped dead on a fallen tree about fifteen yards away and sat there, shoulder to shoulder, watching Diana and Co. who also, shoulder to shoulder, were watching them from the top of the mound. The 'armies' started to organise themselves! There was a great deal of 'excitement twittering' from Diana's group, quick nibbles were being given in neighbours' neck-ruffs and animals marked each other with their anal glands, either rubbing them over each other's backs or rubbing themselves under the uplifted tails of their neighbours. The opposing army was doing much the same. Then George gave the 'Charge!' and the group headed down the mound as a body, George to the fore, Moja, M'Bili and Tatu close behind him, Blackie, Rusty and Goldie in the middle and Diana, the other subadults and females behind them. Bringing up the rear came Whitethroat, Scar and Twin. At the instant George had charged, the other group made their advance as well and both armies met on the battleplain, an open stretch of grass between the two positions. The hornbill friends of both groups were skimming around low through the trees almost as if they did not know how to react to this sudden change in their peaceful day's foraging.

Shoulder to shoulder, Diana's group stares at the invaders from the top of the mound

Back and forth feinted the armies, first George charging and the opponents turning tail only to regroup, turn and charge in their turn. All that was missing were the bugles and the heraldic banners floating above them in the breeze. After three attacks, retreats and regroups the two armies met with a clash and then the world exploded into action. Mongooses went leaping every which way, springing into the air to avoid the snapping jaws of their opponents below; brown fur bundles wrestled with each other in tight embrace, teeth clamped in each other's neck-ruffs; I saw Rusty heading for the hills like a bullet, two little bundles of furry fury hard on his heels, the three of them disappearing from my range of vision, vanishing into the grass and bushes. George was standing, all four feet spread, head darting from one side to another in a little patch of open ground in the middle of the battle before, with a leap, he immersed himself in it again, grabbing one of the opponents who had bitten itself fast into Diana's neck-ruff by the skin of its back so that it whipped round and started to fight with him instead. The groups seemed evenly matched for size and individual fights were going on all around, unoccupied fighters just leaping and joining battling pairs when they themselves had managed to beat off their antagonists. I saw Diana and Scar trot back to the mound and go inside. Then, as if a truce had been called, the fighting stopped and the two armies retreated to their original positions, the opponents to a mound about twenty yards away where they started marking the marking post violently, especially with the cheek glands, scrubbing their faces over the wood and along the ground near it, completing this with intensive anal marking of the site, the little bodies leaping up and down as they tried to get their scent as high as possible on the post, toppling this way and that from their precarious handstand positions. Diana and Co. were doing exactly the same thing at their mound, Trifle.

Then the opposing army gathered again. Again the *tseee* call came from sharp-eyed Blackie who had been watching their doings carefully and gave the warning. George and his warriors clumped together shoulder to shoulder and, as the invading army approached, it was attacked again. Once more the strange 'battle order' could be seen, George first, the juveniles attacking hard on his heels, the subadults next and the older animals at the back. Again battle was joined and the brown bodies leapt hither and thither. I saw a dark juvenile from the opposing army charge through George's ranks in fast pursuit of Tatu who had turned tail and run when she saw him coming. It was only when he reached the other side of the home army that he realised what had happened. He had been cut off from his own troops by a wall of enemies! He gave a heroic leap to regain safety, right over the heads of the battle below, landed on a fallen tree-trunk and disappeared backwards, paws scrabbling, trying to get a hold on the smooth bark.

Right in the middle of the battlefront a shadow shot overhead. There was an explosive *tcheee* from somewhere behind the opposing army's lines and everyone dashed for cover. It was only a Bateleur swooping past, though, and once it was gone, the fight continued with unremittent fury. It looked as if George's group had won the day for, shortly afterwards, the opposing army retreated, followed by George and the remnants of his troops. They pushed the usurpers beyond the termite mound they had left their marks on and were finally in possession of it.

Diana came trotting up, I didn't know where from, sniffed the strange marks on the marking post carefully and then marked once. This was the signal. Like avenging furies the rest of the group leapt at the marking post and marked with a violence I had never seen before, testing carefully between their hops into handstand again whether all the smell of the intruders had been obliterated. Blackie had gone up on top of the mound to keep an eye on their enemies who seemed to be beating a disorderly retreat through the bush, straggling in ones and twos through the grass to regroup on a mound over fifty yards away. George and Co. made hesitant movements in that direction, heads flagging and fur bottlebrushed, but thought better of it and returned to their marking of the mound again.

Once they were sure that the others had left, Diana and Co. went into what I could only call a 'victory celebration'. Lots of grooming and marking each other and then they all, with the exception of Diana, started to play, even the rather staid warriors like Twin and Scar! They chased each other round and round, twittering the play call, rolled in mock fighting on the ground and went into paroxysms of 'Viennese Waltzing'. It was very hard not to be anthropo-morphic in such an obviously jubilant atmosphere. Only Tatu seemed not in the mood to join in. She was trotting up and down plaintively calling 'Where are you?' In a few minutes she was joined by M'Bili and the two little figures stared out into the grass. I made a quick head-count. Notch and Rusty were missing!

George didn't seem able to settle down and, with Blackie, Goldie and Fleck, Diana close behind, he kept leading forays into the bush in the direction in which the invaders had gone. Then I saw the group stiffen and stare at something on a log between them and the opposing army. As the little skirmish ran towards the two figures squatting there, the warning call was given and the two turned and ran, dashing back to the safety of their own lines. Of Rusty and Notch there was no sign. Tatu was still calling but there was no answer. George and Diana however seemed unperturbed and, once they had chased the Strangers' scouts back to where they had come from, returned to their family, and the play and general excitement went on. Finally the group laid itself to rest, some on top of the mound, which I had named 'Battle', and some inside it. Only little Tatu was still calling 'Where are you' to the empty bush. After about an hour's rest during which neither Notch nor Rusty rejoined the group, Diana finally stood up and led them down the side of Battle mound towards Castle, to which it looked as if she had been heading at the beginning. After a last look around and a plaintive little 'Where are you?', Tatu came scampering in her wake.

The little cavalcade moved slowly off at an angle from the mound, foraging as they went. They couldn't have gone more than twenty yards when I saw a little figure appear at Battle. My first thought was that this was Notch or Rusty, but when the figure was joined by a stream of others, I knew I had been mistaken. The invading army had waited their chance and, once Diana and Co.'s backs were turned, they had crept through the grass to retake the mound! A large female sniffed the marking post there, marked and then the whole thing was repeated in the same way as I had seen with Diana's family. The marking post received a third coating of scent substance from busily working anal glands. Battle mound was reconquered!

From the bushes to the east of the mound I heard a loud 'Where are you?' which was answered by two juveniles from the opposing army. A little grey figure trotted towards them and they trotted down the mound to meet it, the rest of the group still being busy with obliterating every trace of Diana and Co.'s scent. I trained my binoculars on the approaching figure and realised with horror that it was Notch! She was headed right into the teeth of the enemy! She trotted on oblivious of her fate. When she and the leading juvenile were only about five yards apart, though, she realised her mistake. This was a contact call she did not know! By this time it was too late, the juvenile had seen her and had broken into a gallop, several other animals running down the mound to join in. Notch gave a desperate leap and a twist in midair, jumping off the game trail into a thick patch of grass where she lay doggo as the charging party went by. They stopped, turned and headed back again but before they reached her position she was off, heading full tilt away from the mound as fast as she could go, her tail bottlebrushed and held out stiffly behind her. The attackers followed her for about fifteen yards then broke off the chase, returning to Battle mound again.

Luckily Notch had been heading in the right direction, for within a few minutes she had caught up with Diana. The group had reached Castle and were lying there, grooming and resting, when a rather dishevelled Notch, beeping the contact call loudly, came trotting up the game trail towards them. Tatu ran down to meet her, greeting almost ecstatically, and tapping Notch all over her head with one outstretched forepaw. George stood up, looked at her and then went back to grooming Diana again. Poor Notch just flopped down like a basking lizard on the nearest safe patch of ground and lay there, stretched out flat like a bathmat for several minutes before she finally got up and squatted with the others on the mound's top.

I thought the battle was over but I was mistaken. The Strangers seemed almost to be following on Diana and Co.'s trail for, about an hour before dusk fell, the *tseee* call came again, but this time from Whitethroat who was on guard at the moment. All heads craned and I saw that the invaders had moved down from Battle and were headed towards Castle. George's army formed its ranks once more and headed off at a gallop towards them, meeting them at a point half-way between Castle and Battle. Once again the surge of bodies back and forth and this time I was near enough to hear the growls and occasional spits that issued from angry throats as the combatants fought out their duel all around me. I was perched on the top of the car in the middle of a pandemonium of thirty or more furious little brown bundles of fur which were chasing each other this way and that, apparently oblivious of my presence. Maybe Diana's group had the advantage as they were not as wary of me as the Strangers were but, be it as it might, they forced the rival army backwards, round Battle mound and on beyond it into the bush. All I could hear was the rustle of grass and the occasional cracking of twigs as the battle raged unabated beyond my line of vision.

A little figure, rather dishevelled, with bite marks all over its flanks, appeared at the top of Battle. Peering through the gathering gloom, I could just make out that it was Fleck. Within a minute he was joined by the rest of the group and the serious business of removing the Strangers' smell from the marking post began anew. Once this had been completed to everyone's satisfaction, there was a brief grooming period on the mound's top and then, one after the other, the mongooses went inside. By this time it was nearly dark and my eyes were sore from straining through the dusk, trying to make out what was happening. I still hadn't seen Rusty.

The next morning I was back again before sun-up, eager to find out what was going to happen. The Strangers were not so far away and Diana and Co., although winning the battle for the mound last night, might not be able to hold their position there today if the Strangers attacked anew. I suppose I had expected them still to be excited about the happenings of the day before and show this in their behaviour the next morning, but this was not the case. It was just like any other morning, except that a sharp watch was kept in the direction from which they had come the night before. They had not forgotten that the Strangers were still around. All of them looked very bedraggled, bite marks in their neck-ruffs and along their flanks, but none of them seemed to have been badly injured. Diana kept rubbing her left eye with one forepaw and I saw that the lower lid had been split and had bled a little. Scar was worrying at his left forepaw and as he held it up to lick it, I noticed that one toe was bitten off. Apart from this, the family seemed to have got off lightly.

Diana led the group down the mound and further to the south. The day seemed to be going on like any other day. Rusty's absence didn't seem to be noticed and even Tatu now seemed to be quite happy since Notch had returned. The group meandered through the grass and bush and finally ended up on a mound about a hundred yards away for their siesta. Once they had gone down, I drove over to keep my vigil until they emerged again later in the afternoon.

Not long after I had settled down to my wait, I glanced back at Battle and saw a little figure perched on top of it. Although the shimmering air made it difficult to distinguish anything, the appearance of three other little figures in quick succession made me realise that this wasn't Rusty who had picked up Diana's trail but the Strangers again! They had waited until Diana and Co. had left Battle and claimed it once more. It was early days yet to be able to say what was going on, whether Battle was a mound at the edge of the home ground of two groups or whether the groups did not have home grounds in that sense of the word and just rivalised with one another for the mounds they slept in. When they woke up again in the late afternoon, Diana and Co. continued their wanderings south and made no attempt to return and reclaim Battle. I don't think they even saw that it had been retaken by the Strangers for they emerged after Diana and her group had already left their mound and were hidden in the grass, where their range of vision was very limited. There seemed to have been an exchange of hornbills between the two groups, however, for Diana's group now had two pairs of Yellow-bills and had lost one of the three pairs of Red-bills which usually accompanied them. Whether or not the birds had joined the Strangers I did not know, but it seemed very likely.

It was two days later that Vanessa, who was on guard at the top of the mound in which the group had held their siesta and from which they were just preparing to leave, gave the *tchrrr* warning and stared off into the grass. The group, some of whom were scattered in the grass around the mound in their never-ending search for insects, ran back up it and looked at what had caught her attention. Something was moving in the grass and I saw a small brown body. '*Tseee*', said M'Bili and the group closed ranks, flagging their heads up and down, trying to fixate what was rustling there and coming their way. Then a little brown body appeared on a game trail leading past the mound and the excitement twitter ran through the group like a wave. The little mongoose, for that was what it was, stopped and was about to turn and flee but then took a few hesitant steps forwards. George, with the juveniles behind him, rushed towards it. The little creature leapt to hide in the thick grass bordering the trail and I heard its protest screams as the four antagonists approached. Then George started threat-scratching and the three juveniles started running excitedly back and forth, greeting him and dashing towards the clump of grass in which the visitor, still screaming at the top of its voice, was hiding. The juveniles' greeting stopped George's attack dead. His bottlebrushed tail subsided and he went to investigate whoever it was that was keeping up the ear-piercing noise. As he approached the grass clump, a little brown body shot out and, with a paroxysm of greeting, literally grovelled at his feet. By this time the fuss and bother had attracted the other group members and they crowded around the little animal, still uncertain, bodies stretched and heads flagging. Then the new arrival managed to break away from George and the juveniles and came trotting towards Diana who was still sitting on the mound, ran right up to her and started to nibble her thoroughly on the neck-ruff, she reciprocating. It was Rusty! Somehow or other he had managed to trace the group through the tangle of bush and grass and had caught up with them two days later about half a mile away from Battle mound.

Rusty looked rather thin and very bedraggled. Patches of hair were missing from his neck and flanks. When I came to think of it later, I realised that this little animal must have had two days of hell behind him. Exactly what had happened to him I shall never know, but just the thought of him patiently trying to find his family again, braving the bush-world predators alone without even a hornbill to help him spot them at a distance, probably even being attacked again by the Strangers, for he must have come past them to find Diana and Co., made me realise what an ordeal he had gone through. The last I had seen of him was being chased away north by two of the Strangers. No wonder he looked so exhausted and battered.

I was especially curious about George's reception of the missing family member. It looked as if individual recognition worked only at close quarters, for the first time the group had spotted Rusty he was taken for an enemy, as the *tseee* call had told me. It was not until George had got near that Rusty was recognised. I began to have more evidence for my theory that the frequent anal marking that took place between the group members, especially before they attacked enemies, might be a means by which the smell of the other family members was put on all animals so that they would be recognised as 'belonging' if they happened to become separated from the group in the fray. The frantic anal marking before an attack must have *some* significance and, after seeing George's behaviour towards Rusty, I was coming to the conclusion that it was Rusty's smell, which George could perceive only at close quarters, that told him that Rusty belonged to the group. Even the strange 'Duel of the Marking Post' at Battle showed that for the mongooses, the familiar group smell was all-important.

As soon as he had greeted Diana, the next thing that Rusty did was trot over to the mound's marking post and mark there. He spent a good five minutes getting his smell well and truly established, leaping into handstand and controlling the post time and time again until it finally seemed to have been 'marked properly' according to him, and he rejoined the rest of the group at the top of the mound.

Although Diana and Co. occasionally encountered other groups in the bush, some larger than they, in which case they usually lost the fight, and some smaller, where they always won, the battles were conducted in very much the same way as the first one I'd seen. The bone of contention seemed to be a particular mound which both groups claimed as their own, at least for the night. I kept a record of these 'key mounds', which were frequently inhabited by Tawny Plated lizards and, with time, came to the conclusion that because of their distribution, the mongooses here had no 'territories' in the sense of a piece of land which they defended. It looked more as if they had regular routes which they took through the bush and, at certain points, these routes crossed those of other mongoose families, the crossing point being one of these 'key mounds'. It turned out that one of the key mounds happened to be Dragon and there I was to witness a battle which completely dwarfed all the ones I'd previously seen in its magnitude.

The battle took place early in the year when Diana's two new babies, Wart and Pickle, were only about eight weeks old. The day's foraging excursions had been much reduced once the little ones had joined the party and the group rarely went more than about five hundred yards a day. I had picked the group up at Cake mound and they slowly meandered towards Mountain, about twenty yards away, to hold their siesta. The day was slightly overcast and cooler than usual, a mere ninety-eight in the shade, said my thermometer, and they showed no sign of going down immediately to have their snooze. Wart and Pickle were playing next to the mound, watched like a hawk by Notch and Diana. Then a pennant of hornbills started to approach through the bush and, peering carefully, I could see a cluster of small brown shapes on a termite mound almost a hundred yards away. By this time, the sun had reached its zenith, the hornbills had left and it looked as if the two groups were going to take their siesta without even having seen each other.

Finally the hornbills gave the signal that the play was about to begin, flying from their sleeping trees to the trees above their groups' respective siesta mounds. One by one the gladiators of the rival teams emerged, still oblivious of one another. I saw a subadult from the invading group climb into a tree and look around, then he spotted the car and stared towards me. I saw his head flagging up and down as he fixated me and then he spotted Diana and Co. as well and almost at the same instant they spotted him. The two *tseee*s came almost simultaneously. Diana grabbed Wart by the scruff of the neck and Notch Pickle, and the two limp youngsters were dragged into the fastness of Mountain. The invaders headed over at a gallop and George and his troops, Diana in the rear, met them thirty yards from the mound. The invading army was huge. I counted twenty-nine animals before events became too confused for any count to be possible at all. George and his little band of thirteen were far outnumbered and were being driven closer and closer backwards towards me and Mountain. George's group fought desperately and George himself seemed to be a little thunderbolt, wreaking havoc right and left but to no avail. Inexorably he was battered backwards until only a few yards separated him and his battling companions from the mound.

I saw Diana break away and bound towards Mountain, only to vanish inside and, after her, Whitethroat. I was torn between watching her and watching the battle which was now taking place right in front of the car. Out of the corner of my eye I saw something move down the back of the mound, out of sight of the opposing armies. Diana and Whitethroat were leading the babies to safety! Wart and Pickle seemed to realise that something was wrong and stuck to the tails of their elders as if they were tied there, looking neither left nor right. The little group of four vanished into the grass behind Mountain. I caught a quick glimpse of them as they curved round, looking as if they were heading towards Monkey and Blacktip mounds.

In the meantime, the battle for Mountain reached a climax. George and his forces seemed to have become split in the process for I saw him, together with Moja and Tatu, Vanessa, Notch and Blackie and three others whose rumps were the only things I saw, fighting a rearguard action in the direction of

Blacktip. The Others had now conquered Mountain and were marking there furiously, and the remainder of the group were still fighting individual battles in the bush below the mound. One by one they ran up to join the rest of their family. I was feverishly counting. There were thirty-six of them that I could see. No wonder George and his army had had no chance. This was the largest group of mongooses I had seen in the Taru to date!

The Others went into the usual marking frenzy at the marking post, obliterating all traces of Diana and Co.'s scent. I thought it was all over but then, from the thick tangle of grass and bushes beyond the mound, two little voices raised their plaintive cry 'Where are you?' All heads on the mound turned to look. Two figures approached, going into high sit to peer above the grass stems. It was Twin and Goldie. The Others must have driven a wedge between them and the rest of their family and now they were on the other side, this huge army between them and the safety of their own group. Still approaching at a trot and stopping now and again to stand up and call, the two lost ones drew nearer and nearer to Mountain. Here bodies were flattened, necks stretched and flagging and all eyes riveted on the approaching figures. It wasn't until they were only about seven yards away that the two of them realised their mistake as the Storm-troops of the Others poured down the mound towards them. Goldie took to her heels, dashing in the wake of George and his group as fast as she could go, tail stuck out behind her and all her hair on end. Twin was less fortunate. Before he had a chance to join Goldie, the Others were upon him and he was chased far off in the opposite direction. Twice he approached Mountain and twice he was chased off, his 'Where are you?' giving him away each time.

Once Mountain had been marked, to my horror, the Others started to move off as a body towards Blacktip, the group moving in twos and threes in Indian file, one behind the other. I wondered what had happened to Diana and Co. I was debating whether to circle round and try to pick them up further along when a scampering object came dashing my way from the bushes that hid Blacktip from my sight. It was a large grey mongoose, bits of fur missing along its back, neck and haunches. It took me a while before I realised who it was. It was the Blacktip whose tail-tip Scar had amputated weeks before! It must have been in its mound when the army of the Others swarmed in and over it and had come out a very poor second in the attack from over thirty snapping jaws. It glanced up at me on my perch on top of the car and then trotted off to vanish along a game trail leading in the opposite direction from the one the Others had stormed along.

Twin was making another attempt to reach Mountain but this time he was

Once they had captured Dragon mound, the invaders went into a marking orgy ▶

successful for it was deserted. He sniffed the marking post, peered into the holes in the mound, all his hair on end, and then left in the wake of the departing armies. I decided to chance things and, starting the car, drove in a wide circle through the bush to end up near Dragon. Diana and Co. had reached Monkey but they were not safe there, for the Others were charging across the open space between the two mounds. Diana and her group fled to Dragon and I noticed with horror that Pickle and Wart were no longer with them. Once on Dragon, they turned and stared at the advancing army which, bypassing Monkey, only a few of the flank troops going up to sniff the marking post, were headed towards them again.

Again the two groups clashed. Diana and a few others didn't join in the fight but beat a hasty retreat to Big. George, the juveniles and the rest of the group were fighting a desperate rearguard action but the situation seemed hopeless. The Others outweighed them in sheer numbers and, one by one, they turned tail and fled to join the rest of the family on Big. By this time it was nearly dark and the Others, after having thoroughly marked the fallen log on Dragon, which was its marking post, headed inside for the night, only a few guards squatting on top of the mound in the gloom.

On Big, however, it looked as if there was no sign of Diana's group going to bed. They were all huddled on top of the mound, peering at the invaders on Dragon. Then Diana moved down towards it, the rest of them following one after the other so that the whole troop looked like a long grey snake in the gloom. Nose to tail they negotiated a path round Dragon that went right alongside the car. The contact calls were soft and almost inaudible. I couldn't help but get the impression of a band of guerrillas making a dusk foray.

They had no intention of challenging the Others for the possession of Dragon, though, but trotted on past it, a chain of grey bodies in the grey of the bush around them. Then I saw Diana and George, Whitethroat and Scar close behind, run up the side of Monkey. Diana stuck her head into one of the holes and I could see her jaws moving as she called to something inside. There was an explosion of action and two little bodies came shooting out of the mound, running from one family member to another, greeting, nibbling and being anally marked by the excited group. Diana must have left Pickle and Wart in Monkey when the Others swept by. They were still so small that a well directed bite from an adult could kill, or at least badly injure them, for strange mongooses will attack half-grown babies although very young ones are immune, as I have found out from my tame group. How Diana had managed to tell the two of them that they should remain hidden in the mound and not follow her, I had no idea. They had been there for at least two hours and, knowing how irrepressible baby mongooses were, it was a wonder that they hadn't come crawling out at some stage of the proceedings and been discovered by the Others, which could have ended fatally for them.

By this time it was almost dark and Diana and her family were just little dark blobs in the gloom. One by one they disappeared into the openings on Monkey until, finally, the mound was bare. I drove back to camp with all sorts of ideas running through my head. It was inevitable that the two groups would meet again the following day for the two mounds they were spending the night in were only about twenty yards apart. I thought I could anticipate what was going to happen, but what actually happened was more than I had bargained for.

I was back next morning before sunrise and positioned myself at an angle between Monkey and Dragon so that I could have a good view of what was going to take place. Slowly the light came in the east. A Striped hyena trotted through the bush, head low and back bowed, almost invisible amongst the network of twigs and grass. A herd of impala, their buck bringing up the rear, moved along in front of me. A second buck appeared behind him and the two stood parallel with one another, heads raised and eyeing one another. The herd buck walked stiffly over to a small shrub and urinated on it and then moved in the wake of his wives who were paying no attention at all to what was going on but were browsing slowly on their way. The challenger approached the shrub, sniffed it carefully and then urinated on it in turn, taking a few stiff steps towards the harem owner. The gauntlet had been thrown. As one man, the two bucks turned to face one another, heads tucked in so as to present their magnificent lyre-shaped horns to the antagonist, and then the fight was on. As if a switch had been thrown the two lowered their heads and charged to lock horns not fifteen yards from where I was sitting. I had a grandstand view of a harem take-over bid! Pushing with all their might, the muscles of their hindquarters and flanks bulging and rippling, the two bucks, horns still locked, moved this way and that, each attempting, with a twist of its head, to get the other off balance. I didn't know how the signals passed between them but heads would be raised and horns disengaged simultaneously and the subsequent charge to lock horns again also occurred as if they were one animal. Back and forth they struggled, clouds of red dust swirling up from their straining hooves. The ladies paid the whole thing no attention and wandered on their way.

Flanks heaving, the two broke off hostilities and, nostrils flaring, gasping for air, stood facing each other before the heads were lowered into the charge once more. The challenger seemed to be weakening, for the harem buck was now pushing him further and further backwards into the bush, away from the herd. Finally the challenger gave up the fight and with a quick jump backwards and a twist in midair, he was gone, bounding through the bush with the harem buck in pursuit. After a thirty-yard chase, the harem buck broke off and, head high, trotted past me in the wake of his ladies. He had been successful in keeping his position and I had been impressed by the tournament-like encounter. It was like two knights meeting one another at the lists for the favour of a fair lady, or rather, fair ladies – for the harem numbered at least twelve does! The fight was obviously conducted to a set of rules: no jabbing your partner in his flank; only horns should be engaged; no charging when your partner was not ready; short pauses should be laid down between bouts . . . it looked as if the idea of 'Nature red in tooth and claw' didn't hold for impalas at least.

It was getting lighter now and I was in a fever of anticipation for soon it would be time for the mongooses to emerge. The Others were awake first and their early guards took up their positions on top of Dragon; they stared at me but didn't seem to be too worried as no one warned. A few minutes later a figure appeared on Monkey. It was Whitethroat. He was soon joined by another whom I recognised as Twin. He had managed to rejoin his family after all, and probably under cover of darkness, for I had not seen him on Monkey the night before. Gradually the whole family gathered on the mound, marked the post, and went through their morning ablutions, the Others doing the same. I expected Diana to head off in the opposite direction, but to my horror she did no such thing. As a group the family trotted past the front of the car heading for Dragon. Of course they were spotted long before they got near it but Diana didn't seem to be heading for the mound itself but was leading her family along a game trail which went wide of it, heading in the direction of Big on the other side.

The Others did not let this go unchallenged. As Diana and Co. drew parallel with Dragon about fifteen yards away, they were down its slopes and into the attack before Diana knew what had happened. It looked as if she had been taken unawares. There was no time for George to group his army and the family was hit broadside on by the Others' spearhead attack and scattered every which way. I saw them dashing, one after the other, towards Big, but the Others were not going to leave it at that. In a tight group they headed after them. Fleck saw them coming and gave the alarm. After a quick look at the approaching army, Diana's family turned tail and vanished down the back of Big into the grass. I could see them moving along at a trot, Wart and Pickle like two little furled wings close to their mother's flanks. They seemed to be heading towards a mound far out in the grass that I had dubbed Spear but then the group, two Red-billed hornbills fluttering behind them, turned and headed south-west towards Log mound. Just as they had reached about the half-way point I noticed another pennant of birds approaching from the south. The Others had now taken possession of Big and were marking there. It looked as if Diana and Co. were going to be caught between Scylla and

Charybdis. Another mongoose group was heading their way and they were trapped between them and the Others!

The birds told me the moment at which Diana and the new group met. They exploded upwards and began zipping to and fro over a patch of grass and bushes. Then their direction changed and the whole flock came streaming towards me. Diana and her family were being chased in a straight line towards Big, right into the open arms of the Others who were standing there on tiptoe, watching what was going on!

The vanguard of Diana's group reached Big. A volley of *tcheees* broke the silence and the Others were down off the mound and after them before I knew what had happened. It was a completely hopeless task trying to pick individuals out of the total chaos that was now raging round Big and coming my way. There must have been at least seventy to eighty animals fighting madly in the grass, for the group that had pushed Diana's family back towards Big was also a large one. By coincidence the two groups of mongooses whose living areas lay to the south of Diana's must both have decided to cross 'her' borders at the same time.

I looked for Wart and Pickle in the mêlée but couldn't spot them. I had a glimpse of George, one ear half torn off, struggling with one of his opponents, two others joining in and poor George going down under a welter of bodies. The battle continued to rage unabated. Occasionally some animal would go shooting off into the bush with a couple of others hard on its heels to vanish into the distance. It was almost an hour later before the battle started to abate. The Newcomers had retreated to Log and the Others to Dragon, leaving Big deserted. Of Diana and Co. there was no sign. I scanned the bush on all sides but there was nothing. It looked as if they had been wiped off the face of the earth.

It was siesta time and the two armies vanished into their mounds. The sun beat down unmercifully and the air shimmered. I kept up my search of the mounds around for any sign of Diana but there was none. The hours dragged by. Only the little Grey flycatcher whose home tree was near Dragon showed any signs of activity, fluttering downwards every now and again to snap up some unwary insect. The hornbills had all disappeared.

After the waiting had got to the point of being almost interminable the hornbills came back again, some to Log and some to the trees above Dragon. It would not be long now and the next act of the drama would begin. Sure enough, within half an hour, the first mongooses started to emerge. After marking their respective posts, the two groups set off, the Newcomers heading south in the direction from which they had come, and the Others north. The battle of the Giants seemed to be over. Still there was no sign of Diana and her family. I thought they might be cowering in the depths of Big, waiting for the 'Superpowers' to leave before they dared to emerge, so I decided to wait. After two hours there was still no sign of them and I began to realise that I had been mistaken. They must have gone somewhere else. I climbed up on top of the car and scanned the mounds around. Just as I had finally about given up hope, I saw a little figure with two smaller ones pressed close to its sides squatting on top of Spear, looking into the bush around. I started the motor and drove over as slowly and carefully as I could, stopping the car about twenty yards away from the mound. Diana turned and looked at me and then turned away again. I had found *her* but where were the rest of her family? Wart and Pickle stuck close to her flanks and hardly moved, and Diana began the most plaintive aria of 'Where are you?'s I had ever heard.

The minutes dragged into hours, Diana sitting like a siren on her mound, calling hopelessly into the empty bush around. Wart and Pickle crept into the shadows thrown by one of the mound's buttresses and went to sleep, their little bodies curled tight against one another, neck over neck. Diana made no move to leave but kept up her dirge tirelessly. I was finally starting to think that she had been separated from her family for ever but then I heard an answer from the bush and grass to the east. Diana was on her hind-legs like a flash, calling 'Where are you?' as loud as she could go. A battered little squadron appeared, Notch leading a bunch of subadults, then Twin, Scar and Whitethroat bringing up the rear and, right at the back, Moja and Tatu. Tatu looked a mess and the others not much better. Lumps of fur were missing from all over their bodies and their ears were chewed, in some cases, to the point of little bloody lumps. Diana ran down the mound towards them, Wart and Pickle behind her. There was a flurry of greeting and anal sniffing but Diana still seemed frantic and then it dawned on me. George was not with them!

The family repaired to the mound and I took a head-count. M'Bili was not there either. Although the others kept making attempts to move off further to the west, Diana held her ground and kept up her lament, staring off into the bush. The rest of the group were lying about exhausted, licking their wounds, but Diana was perched above them all at the topmost point of the mound, still calling 'Where are you?', her voice almost cracking, and frequently all I could see were her jaws moving in the familiar pattern, but no sound emerging.

Dusk was falling but Diana did not give up. When it was almost dark and the rest of her family had crept into the mound to sleep, she was still sitting there. Her 'Where are you?'s were now few and far between. As the last of the sun's rays were swallowed by the thorntree branches and the world turned to shadows, a little figure came trotting towards the mound, limping badly. Diana stared at it and then dashed down to meet it. It was George! By the time she had finished with him he was even more bedraggled than before, for she nibbled his neck-ruff until it stood out in little wet spikes of fur and anal-marked him back and forth along his back and flanks until his hair stood on end. The nibbling and marking was reciprocated but with less fervour. Little heads poked out of Spear and some of the group, Moja and Tatu in the lead, came running down to join in the 'hero's welcome'. George was in a terrible state. One ear was bitten almost off, patches of fur were missing from all over his body and his right forepaw was so swollen he could hardly put it on the ground. I had no idea where he could have hidden himself all day but at least, now, he was back in the arms of his family. One by one they crept into Spear and within a few minutes, the mound was deserted. But M'Bili had not come home!

The next morning I was back at Spear again before sun-up, wondering what this day would bring in the way of surprises. One thing that had struck me the previous day was that although the rest of Diana's family had made it very obvious by their loud 'moving out' calls and concerted trotting down the mound and away from the danger that they wanted to leave, Diana had made no move to do so. It looked as if waiting for George was more important to her than bringing her family to safety. Things could have gone badly with Wart and Pickle if one of the other armies had decided to follow in the rest of the group's footsteps, for it was unlikely that they would have escaped. Maybe the loss of a life-long partner was more significant to her than the loss of this year's young.

The sun rose above the trees and flooded the bush with light. Only a solitary pair of von der Decken's hornbills flew over to sit in a bush next to Spear. It looked as if the rest of Diana's cortège of birds had split themselves between the two big armies for there was no sign of them. One by one the bedraggled crew crawled out of the holes on the mound and stood blinking in the sun's rays. Rusty and Victoria trotted down to the mound's base and started to do something I had never seen mongooses do before. Feet close together and fore- and hind-legs spread as far as possible, the two of them positioned themselves at right angles to the sun's rays, heads dropped, standing like little saw-bucks, soaking the warmth in through their bristling fur. None of the little party had escaped unscathed. All bore the scars of the battles of the previous two days, George worse than any of them. Diana's eye was still bothering her and she kept rubbing at it with her wrist. George's forefoot was still so painful that he could still not use it properly, but it did not seem to be as swollen as it had been the night before. Sundry bites and scratches were licked by concerned partners or the animals themselves. I saw George hobble over to Diana and carefully lick her injured eye, she holding her head upwards at an angle and letting him do so. One of Twin's ears looked like a cauliflower, a chewed remnant of its former self, and Vanessa was licking it carefully. Of the

After the battle, all the animals looked bedraggled and had bites on their necks and flanks

youngsters, Tatu looked as if she'd been run over with a steamroller. It seemed as if she had been in the thick of things. A big patch of fur was missing from her neck and shoulder, her tail was probably broken, for it had a very obvious kink that was certainly not there the day before, and her ears were just tattered lumps almost hidden in her fur. She squatted miserably in a hollow of the mound and Notch came over to lick her, washing her face like a mother cat licking its kitten, something I had never seen a mongoose do to another mongoose before. Tatu accepted this but soon broke away and went to sit next to Diana where the process was repeated, not only all over her head but across the wound on her shoulder as well. Tatu sat there, eyes half-closed, and let her mother groom her despite the constant interruption from Wart and Pickle who didn't seem to realise what it was all about, as they pounced on her and started playing. Finally Pickle pounced on her injured tail. Tatu gave a little protest squeak, whipped round, stared at her and then trotted into the mound's interior.

M'Bili had still not turned up and it looked as if Diana and her family were not going to move. The hornbills, after a few unsuccessful attempts to get the group to go foraging, vanished in the direction of Dragon. Only occasionally did small knots of animals disappear into the bleached grass around the mound and scrabble about there looking for insects, returning to the mound within a few minutes to rest and groom themselves and each other.

The morning came and went and the family retreated to the fastness of the mound's interior when the sun was high. There was still no sign of M'Bili and no one seemed to have noticed her absence. Not a single animal had called 'Where are you?' this morning and, when I compared it with Diana's frantic song the day before, the non-concernedness of the group seemed strange. Maybe it was because M'Bili was not such an important group member as George was that they seemed to accept her absence as 'one of those things'?

Midday came and went. The sun was sinking towards the west and the shadows were getting long before the first head appeared on Spear again. The group had held a much longer siesta than usual and, even now, showed little inclination to leave the mound. Finally the sun set and the group retired to sleep. They had not moved from Spear the whole day, not even to go foraging, and this was the first time in all the months I had followed them that this had happened.

The next day George's foot seemed better and, although he was still limping, he set off early with Wart and Pickle in tow to go foraging. The rest of the family seemed more active than they had been the day before, and about nine o'clock the group set off in the direction of Big, foraging slowly as they went. If a pair of drongos who lived in the area had not accompanied them, I would have had awful trouble trying to follow their meanderings through the high grass and bushes. It was almost a hundred yards to Big, across an area almost devoid of trees, and no guard was left at Spear. The group kept to the bushes as much as possible and finally, as the sun was starting to get baking hot, I saw the first figures arrive at Big, examine the marking post and start marking. Every time a cloud passed they would be up and marking but as soon as the sun was revealed again, they all retreated inside the mound. I drove over to station myself near them once I realised that they had gone down finally for their siesta and settled down for my usual midday wait.

Again they were late getting up. It was past four o'clock before the first ones appeared on Big and started marking the post there again. I was positioned between Big and Dragon and suddenly heard a little voice from the latter mound calling 'Where are you?'. I and all the mongooses turned to stare. Crouched in the leaves at the top of the mound was a little figure, practically invisible in the shadows. 'M'Bili!' I thought. The little creature started down the side of the mound towards the group at Big. As it trotted over an open patch of earth in front of the car I could finally get a good look at it. It *wasn't*

M'Bili after all, but another youngster about the same age as she was, but much darker in colour, almost black. The little animal trotted on until it was only a few yards from Big, then went into high sit and called 'Where are you?' again. A battery of heads stared down from the top of the mound at it and then, George limping in the lead, they were upon it. I saw George give the little one a bite and shake in the neck-ruff and then it was off, scampering as hard as it could back to Dragon again. The skirmish party followed it half-way to Dragon and then returned to the rest of their family at Big. It looked as if one of the two 'Superpowers' had lost a group mate.

Veronica, as I had named her, sat hidden in the leaves at the top of Dragon, watching the other mongooses grooming and marking at Big before setting off southwards towards Log, working their way along a row of toppled trees. She watched them go and then, to my surprise, trotted in their wake. She arrived at Big after Blackie, who had been on guard duty there, had left, Rusty having taken over his job at a fallen tree further along the group's foraging route. As soon as Veronica arrived, she ran to the marking post and sniffed it carefully up and down but did not mark herself. Then, hesitantly, she followed in the family's wake. All were busily grubbing out beetles from the grass clumps; the drongos, which had now been joined by a party of White-crowned bush shrikes, marked their route. Twice I saw Veronica go into high sit and call 'Where are you?' in the wake of the retreating group, only to be set upon by the animals nearest to her and chased back to Big again.

Diana and Co. had now reached Log and seemed to be settling in there for the night. Of M'Bili there was still no sign. Veronica made three attempts to get near them but was rebuffed with vicious attacks each time. Finally she retreated to Big and, as the sun set, I saw her squatting at the top of the mound, looking towards Log, giving a last plaintive 'Where are you?' before vanishing inside. Diana's family was not going to accept her.

In the weeks that followed, Veronica kept up her continual attempts to join the group but without success. She trailed them during the day and slept in a termite mound next to the one the group was using at night, but was never allowed in the same one that they had chosen. She had stopped calling 'Where are you?' as the days went past and had even got to the point of adding her mark to the marks of the group on the marking posts of mounds the family had left. Sometimes she was allowed to forage within a few yards of the family members but there was no sign of her being accepted by them yet. Every time she got too close, she was chased away, not as far and not as viciously as before, but chased away nevertheless.

It was therefore with surprise that one day, about three weeks after she had started trailing the group, I saw her dig in a grass clump in the group's wake and give a little feeding growl as she unearthed a large dungbeetle.

Whitethroat, who was nearest to her, lifted his head, looked towards her and started to trot in her direction. She made as if she were going to dash off but dropped the beetle. In two bounds Whitethroat was upon her, but instead of attacking her, he too saw the beetle she had found and turned to pin it with his forefoot. Veronica turned her head and shoulders away from him and gave a plaintive little protest scream but made no move to run. Whitethroat picked the beetle up in his teeth and chewed it, his jaws crunching on the hard carapace. Then, with a sidelong look at Veronica who was still frozen in her submissive stance, head turned away from him, he trotted back to the rest of the family. The first step had been taken! This was the first time that I had seen Veronica get so close to one of the group members without being attacked.

It took more than Whitethroat's single non-attack before Veronica was finally accepted by the group. Now that she could approach them nearer than before, she made full use of all the submissive gestures in her behavioural repertoire, turning away and freezing and giving a little protest squeal if one of the group members got too close, or greeting group members she happened to meet face to face before turning and disappearing into the grass again. To date she had not allowed any of them close enough to touch her and still seemed very nervous. Most of the animals she had contacted up until now were low-ranking members of the family, for Diana and George usually foraged ahead of their troop.

Things might have gone on like this for a long time if it had not been for a partial accident. The group was foraging along as usual, Veronica about ten yards behind the last straggler. They had just bypassed one mound and were heading over a space about fifty yards wide towards the next mound. There were few fallen trees here and only patches of sun-bleached grass and a few bushes. Suddenly the hornbills, which had rejoined the group during the last weeks (I didn't know, though, if they were the original ones or not), shot into trees and the group turned tail and ran back the way it had come. A goshawk came swooping over and landed in a tree in front of them. Veronica had seen the rearguard heading towards her and stood motionless for a moment before dashing to hide in a grass clump as the group rushed past her, heading for the safety of the mound. The first one there started the mobbing *tchrrr* call and, instead of staying hidden in the grass, Veronica galloped in the group's wake, rushing up the side of the mound to join them. A few of them gave her a quick glance but all eyes were riveted on their mutual enemy which was staring at them from the branches of a Commiphora tree. Veronica had finally joined the group, albeit under external duress, but now she was in the midst of them, mobbing as loudly as they were.

After a short wait, the goshawk flew off. George looked at Veronica and started to threat-scratch and Diana, her attention drawn to the newcomer, slunk towards her, body extended. 'This is it!' I thought, expecting Veronica to be made piecemeal of any second. As soon as she saw the older female's approach, Veronica dashed towards her, twittering the greeting call *fortissimo*, lying almost flat on the ground, tapping Diana all over her head with an outstretched forepaw and trying to lick her mouth. Diana was stopped in her tracks. She drew herself upwards, pulled her head into her chest as far as she could and weaved from side to side to try and avoid the persistently greeting youngster. Finally she turned tail and Veronica, still greeting her effusively as she trotted alongside her, followed. Head low, Diana trotted right round the top of the mound, followed closely by the still madly greeting Veronica, and finally vanished down one of its holes. The rest of the group just stood by impassively and didn't do a thing but stare.

A little while later Diana emerged again and went to sit next to George who, once Veronica had started her violent greeting, had stopped threat-scratching and gone to join the rest of them to watch the pantomime. Shortly afterwards, Veronica emerged as well, still a little hesitant, fur still on end, and looked about her. Diana glanced in her direction and set the whole thing off once more – an abjectly greeting Veronica literally chased her round the mound and back inside again. The process was repeated several times and it started to get ludicrous. Diana only had to glance in Veronica's direction to set the little animal off again.

Finally Diana, avoiding Veronica's eye, gave the 'moving out' call and the party trooped down the side of the mound to resume their foraging. Veronica stayed behind, still a little hesitant, and watched them leave. Then she trotted purposefully after them and I could hear her beeping contact call amidst those of the others. A few of the rearguards turned to look but then carried on their way. Slowly but surely, very busily grubbing in the grass clumps, Veronica worked her way in amongst them. It almost looked to me as if she was being *too* assiduous in her hunt for beetles and crickets, as she spent most of the time with her foreparts buried in grass clumps, but then I realised that maybe what she was doing was not so stupid after all. Even I had done the same thing at the beginning – avoided eye contact with the group members.

After about an hour or so's foraging, the group ended up on Mitre, the mound they had been heading for before the goshawk swooped. Veronica, by this time, had wormed her way forwards so that she was now foraging amongst the rearguard. I wondered what was going to happen. Was she going to be allowed to sleep with the group? From the top of the car I scanned the grass around the mound and finally spotted her still scrabbling in a grass clump at its base, sideways on to the family. She was still keeping to her policy of 'no eye contact' and remained there until the first of them went into the mound for the night. Then she hesitantly moved up the mound's sides, taking every excuse to drop her eyes and look as if she was busy with something else. She scratched in a little clump of grass here, dug in a little pile of dried zebra dung there, rustled around amongst some dead leaves . . . I had the impression that she was just trying to look busy for its own sake. Finally, she reached the top of the mound when all but Whitethroat and Fleck had gone inside. The two of them moved towards her and I heard a little protest squeal. She ran a few paces and then stopped, head bowed. Fleck trotted towards her and started sniffing her anal gland and was joined within a moment by Whitethroat. Veronica stood motionless, head still bowed, still giving little protest noises, and let them investigate her. She really looked a little strange, foreparts almost flat on the ground and hind-legs and tail as high as they could go while Fleck and Whitethroat sniffed beneath her tail. Finally they seemed satisfied and left her alone, vanishing one after the other into the mound's depths.

Veronica was now on her own. Very hesitantly she moved from one hole to another, peering inside, her tail still slightly bottlebrushed. Finally she selected a hole almost at the edge of the mound and vanished into it. I strained my ears to hear if things were going on inside the mound: protest screams, growls, spits . . . but all was quiet. Waiting another half-hour just in case, I sat still as a mouse, all senses strained to their utmost, but Mitre was shrouded in a deathlike silence. Veronica had managed it! After almost four weeks of trailing the group, she had finally got to the point where she was allowed to sleep in the same mound as they did.

Next day I was again out before sunrise, parking near Mitre so as to have a good view of what would transpire. Things seemed to be much as usual. Twin was the first one up this morning and he was soon followed by the rest of his family. I looked for a now familiar little black shape amongst them but did not see it. At first I thought they must have driven Veronica off during the night for there was no sign of her. When the group started their usual visit to the toilet and marking post, I became aware of a little black head poking out of one of the holes in the mound. It was Veronica. It looked as if she had spent the night in a different underground chamber from the rest of the group: I knew that within the termite mound not all these ventilation shafts connected.

Hesitantly, tail slightly bottlebrushed, she moved towards the group which was now busily marking a tree stump at the base of the mound. She was still very unsure of herself and ready to go into a wild greeting or dash back to safety if any of them made a move towards her. They glanced at her approaching and then returned to marking the post again. Veronica, body stretched, moved slowly but surely towards them. The next thing I knew, she was in amongst them, sniffing the post in her turn. Then I saw her spring upward and, with a twist, her anal gland connected with the marking post. She had made her first bid for full acceptance – her mark laid amongst the others!

When she descended, busy noses sniffed at the secretion she had deposited and at her as well. Noses bored into her anal gland and a few times her investigators were so rough in their investigation that her hind-legs were lifted from the ground. But still no attack. She turned and marked the post again. Again a great deal of sniffing from the rest of the group. Diana was still carefully avoiding her eye although I noticed that Veronica was well aware of her every movement, for every time Diana approached, Veronica would stiffen, waiting to see what would happen next. Nothing did.

The group trooped up the mound again and only Veronica and Goldie were left at the marking post. Veronica was still sniffing it when Diana gave the 'moving out' call that would signal the start of the day's foraging. This time there was no hesitation, Veronica turned and, trotting in Goldie's wake, joined the party.

It took some time, however, for Veronica to be fully accepted. She was mostly on the defensive and sat a little apart from the rest of the group. But little by little she was drawn more into the scheme of things, and her final acceptance came when Fleck, who was sitting next to her one day, nibbled her in the neck-ruff and was nibbled in return. It was several days after this before she dared to attempt to anally groom George like the other females in the group did but, once this hurdle had been sprung, she acted as if she had been part of the group all her life. Her friendship with Fleck, the first who had groomed her socially, remained, however, and I often saw the two of them sitting together and grooming each other. After almost six weeks of hope and fear, Veronica now belonged to Diana and Co.

Two things in the mongoose way of life had always been a puzzle to me. First, since they were so bitterly aggressive towards outsiders, how was it that fresh blood could be introduced into the group? Veronica had shown me how. Being accepted into the group, however, didn't automatically mean that she had the right to produce young of her own. This was Diana's privilege alone until her death. Maybe Veronica would have a chance to become 'queen' in her turn after this. Secondly, it always seemed strange to me that, of all the group members, it was the juveniles which were in the front ranks when two strange groups clashed, hard behind their father. The stronger and larger males, which one would have thought would be the most effective blocking troops, usually held a rearguard position while the relatively frail juveniles were the first to meet the foe. If anyone was likely to be scattered in the first clash, it was they. It suddenly dawned on me that this might be the strategy by which youngsters were brought on a chance basis to leave the group and join new ones. Veronica was a youngster and had succeeded. And then I remembered . . . M'Bili had never come back!

12 The Death of Tatu

After the terrible Battle of Dragon Mound, Tatu never really recovered. The wound on her neck and shoulder healed, leaving a patch of white hair, but it looked as if muscles and tendons had been damaged in addition to the skin for she only moved her shoulder with difficulty and sometimes had a hard time to keep up with the others, especially when they ran from some enemy. The worst effects of her injury could be seen in her food-hunting. She had all but lost the ability to dig around delicately in grass roots to unearth a hidden beetle. Although her right forepaw was as agile as before, all she could do with her left one was to scratch rather ineffectively and she would usually stand on her left foreleg and use her right paw continually. This meant that there was now a whole spectrum of possible prey that she could no longer catch . . . fast moving prey or prey that hid under bark or dug itself rapidly into the ground. For that she needed two active paws and she had only one.

In the weeks that went by, she started slowly to lose condition. Her body became so thin that I could see her hip-bones when she walked. The most dramatic change was in her face, however. She had already lost her short 'babyface' and had reached the stage at which mongoose faces usually become long in proportion to their breadth, a stage which lasts until their owners are about three years old, when the skull appears to broaden as the strong cheek and head muscles develop. On Tatu, however, the effect was skeletal. It looked as if her skull was covered simply with a thin layer of stretched skin and her eyes looked almost sunk in their sockets. Although she was now almost a year old, she looked very retarded in growth, but not baby-like. A miniature adult . . . almost like a wizened old lady. Her coat, instead of being smooth and glossy, had become sparse and staring and I could often see the white of the underlying skin shimmering through. The break in her tail had never healed straight and there was a noticeable kink at its end. I was tempted to try and give her extra food, meat I would bring from the camp, but decided against it. I was here to watch the mongooses as they really were and not to try and impose human restraints upon them by providing them with an easy meal and maybe thereby changing their natural behaviour.

I wondered if Tatu had been a weakling since birth, for I knew from my tame animals that birth weights amongst members of the same litter varied from about a quarter to half an ounce. Very often the weaklings would disappear overnight – I presumed eaten by their mother. It was a strange fact that, although most of the litters numbered about six at birth, never more than

Tatu was a sorry sight: her coat was no longer smooth and glossy and she lost weight rapidly

four reached the age at which they emerged from the nestbox – very likely a strategy to prevent overpopulation.

As the weeks grew into months it became obvious that Tatu was not going to survive much longer. She was always the last to reach the termite mound if the group had to run from some swooping goshawk and the only time she ever got there before or with the others was when they had to turn and run back in their tracks, as she always foraged behind them and seemed to have difficulty in keeping up sometimes. I wondered if, as she grew weaker, the group would just move on and abandon her, for this was the general rule in the Animal Kingdom. A troop can only move as fast as its weakest member and that could be a severe disadvantage. Usually, however, weaklings are weeded out by predators before they have a chance to act as a drag on the group as a whole. Predators have a predilection for the weak, and many of the larger ones such as lions and wolves have been observed to test groups of prey animals by walking amongst them, noting the responses of the individual group members as they fled. Should a weak one be amongst them – an old one, a sick one, a pregnant one or one with a youngster at foot – these would be the ones later singled out for the chase. I expected to see Tatu pounced on and carried away by a bird of prey at any moment.

Since she was unable to use her left forepaw properly, this resulted in her disablement getting worse and worse. I had not realised up until now what a delicate balance existed between the mongoose's body and its behaviour. Since a normal mongoose spends most of its time scratching and scrabbling in the earth, Nature has fitted it for this task as well as she could. Nails that are liable to be blunted should grow faster than those that do not have to face a sandpapering every day. Tatu's nails on her left foot started to grow but with a speed that was astonishing. Within a few weeks she had nails that a Chinese mandarin of old would have been proud of, long curving ones over an inch in length and totally useless for careful scratching. The worst thing of all was that she could no longer put her left forefoot on the ground normally. The long nails twisted her toes until they lay almost criss-cross at the end of her foot. This hampered her movements even more and she would now frequently lag behind the others when they were on the move, often limping along yards behind them when the group started to trot. Then began something which, as it progressed, I realised was unique in the Animal Kingdom. No animal takes care of its sick, with one notable exception . . . Man – and, as I was able to see with my own eyes, the Dwarf mongoose!

At first I thought it was coincidence and that individual animals simply changed their foraging direction on occasion and just happened to end up foraging with Tatu. As the days went by, though, I realised that these 'coincidental meetings' were just a bit too frequent to be true. George, who usually foraged at the head of the group with Diana, would for no reason at all, it seemed to me, suddenly turn round and trot backwards to forage next to Tatu. Then I noticed that Whitethroat and Scar, especially, would almost always forage near her, only a few feet away. Although it was difficult to tell exactly whether the group was waiting for her to catch them up or not, for the rate at which they foraged was very dependent on the number of insects and other creatures that they found in a particular area, I gained the impression that they were foraging more slowly in general. On a few occasions I saw that Twin or Whitethroat had caught a locust or a large cricket and, once it had been killed, Tatu would trot over to them if she was near and they would relinquish their prize. This didn't mean much, for being younger than they and a female, she was higher-ranking and had more or less a 'right' to take their food off them if she could. It wasn't until one day, when George was foraging near her, that I began to put another interpretation on what I had seen.

George was busily scrabbling about in the dead bark of a fallen tree. I saw him stiffen, suddenly dive forwards under the trunk and emerge with a gecko in his mouth. Tatu had seen his quick movement as well and came hobbling over. George didn't run off to eat his sumptuous meal in some quiet corner as was usual, but remained near the tree's roots and started to chew the lizard from the head down. Tatu was now only a few inches away from him and I expected any moment to see George dash at her and chase her away but he remained where he was. He was still giving the feeding growl which mongooses give whenever they have caught some large prey animal, and Tatu hesitantly limped nearer. George turned his back on her, still growling, but made no motion to dash off and leave her standing. Then, to my amazement, Tatu pushed her body next to his and started to feed on the gecko from the other end. And George let her! One of the mongoose Ten Commandments had been broken! This was the first time I had ever seen two mongooses feeding on the same prey without a fight ensuing or one just relinquishing its find to the other.

I kept a sharp watch in future and came to the conclusion that Tatu was getting almost half her food from the other group members, but it still did not seem to be enough. She got thinner and thinner and weaker and weaker. I realised then that it was not only a question of food. Tatu was dehydrating. Mongooses only drink rarely, lapping water drops from twigs if it has rained or licking dewdrops from the grass. Most of their water they get from their prey, breaking down the insect fat substances in their digestive systems and absorbing their water, which is one of the breakdown products. This water, which forms an essential part of their diet, had been drastically reduced in quantity for Tatu, once she was unable to feed efficiently. The little animal was not starving, she was dying of thirst!

Sometimes I had the impression that she could go no further, for she would climb with difficulty up the slopes of a termite mound in the group's wake and sit there, a huddled little figure, watching the rest of her family grubbing about in the grass and bushes. She rarely sat there alone for long, though. Sooner or later one of the family members would come and sit next to her, sometimes two or three of them together, cuddling her meagre body between them. Her hunched form, head dropped forward on her chest, became a familiar sight. She would sometimes spend up to an hour squatting on a termite mound, head lowered, tail curved to lie neatly across her forepaws, only a little hummock in the press of bodies surrounding her. Very frequently the group would swing round in their foraging sortie to end up on the mound on which she was sitting, but equally often they would hold their rest on a neighbouring mound and Tatu, together with the family members which had been sitting with her, would slowly make their way towards them.

Once the vicious circle of insufficient food and, as a result, insufficient water had started, Tatu went downhill rapidly. When she was on the mound with her family they all clustered round her, almost burying her in the crush of bodies. I noticed that she was getting too weak even to groom herself, something which is one of the prime activities of a mongoose, and she stopped grooming others. Then started one of the most touching episodes I had ever seen amongst animals. Since she could not perform her daily ablutions for herself, her family did it for her!

Although Whitethroat, Scar and Twin were most assiduous in cuddling up to her when she was crouched somewhere on a mound in the wake of the family's foraging path, Diana and George had shown little interest in remaining with her at first. Since the arrival of Wart and Pickle, Tatu's standing as 'Mother's darling' had ceased and the close body contact that had existed between them before came to an end. It was therefore with some surprise that I noticed Diana was starting to pay more attention to her sick youngster, as George did as well. Very often I would see the three of them, Tatu in the middle, cuddled together on a mound, the rest of the family surrounding them like satellites. Her littermate Moja was particularly active in trying to push his body as near to her as he could.

The little animal was groomed thoroughly by all her family, especially Moja and her parents. Sometimes the grooming sessions would get so intensive that afterwards Tatu looked wet and spiky, her fur matted from the nibbling of busy incisors. The less she looked for food, however, the more gaunt and weaker she became until, one morning, she struggled out of one of the holes near the base of the mound and, swaying from side to side, went down to visit the toilet as she usually did. She was so weak she could hardly stand and, after performing her morning task and tottering over to the marking post, she tried to mark. It was a terrible fiasco. She hardly managed to get her hind-legs off the ground, let alone spring swiftly into handstand, and fell with a scrabbling of paws onto her side. It was only with difficulty that she managed to right herself again.

She wobbled closer to the marking post and, turning round slowly, reversed towards it, lifting her tail and pressing her everted gland against its base. She was no longer able to mark properly like the other members of her family and had reverted to marking like a little baby. But this was to be her last 'signature' in the family 'album'. Once she had sniffed the mark she turned and attempted to climb up the mound but couldn't. Three times I saw her, claws scrabbling, inch herself up its slopes and three times she slid ignominiously backwards to the bottom again. The rest of her family watched this with interest but did nothing. Then Tatu seemed to give up and went to squat in a patch of sunlight at the mound's base. Within no time at all, and to my amazement, Diana and George, the rest of their family following hard on their heels, trotted down the mound and came to sit with her. Another of the mongoose Ten Commandments had been broken . . . when resting, rest as high as possible so that you can have the best view in case danger threatens. Only Vanessa stayed at the top of the mound, keeping a sharp lookout.

I expected the group to set off foraging as usual but, apart from a few quick sorties made by individuals or small bands into the grass around the mound, they did not leave. Tatu was sitting there, head bowed and eyes closed,

Everyone tried to get as near to Tatu as possible. She was groomed thoroughly by the whole family, particularly her parents

surrounded by her family. Then Diana started to do something I had never seen an adult mongoose do to another adult before – she started to lick Tatu thoroughly all over, George joining in. Tatu simply lay there, just moving sufficiently to expose parts of her body for the cleansing tongues to reach.

The group stayed on the mound all day, all going inside to spend their siesta but all, including Tatu, emerging again once the sun's power had slackened. Diana's licking of Tatu continued but she had got nothing to eat that day for she had not moved off the mound and no one had brought her any food. It looked as if food-bringing was simply not part of the mongooses' innate behaviour, even for invalids. Finally, as dusk fell, the group retreated into the mound, Tatu struggling to her feet to follow them. The last I saw of her was her kinked tail disappearing into one of the holes near its base.

Next morning I was back early as usual as I wanted to discover if the group would now move on. Whitethroat struggled out of a hole on the top of the mound and looked at me incuriously, for I was now such a part of their environment that I no longer warranted any interest. Then, one by one, the rest of the group emerged but not Diana and George. I waited and waited but they did not put in an appearance. Tatu was also nowhere to be seen and I guessed she had been too weak to clamber up the sloping tunnel of the ventilation shaft that led to outside. Mongooses kept disappearing into the mound and not appearing again. Only a few of them went down to the toilet and marking post, sniffed the latter or scrabbled about in the grass near the mound. As the hours went by, I realised that the group was not going to move. Tatu could not go so they were not going to go either.

Diana appeared briefly, went down to the toilet, sniffed the marking post but did not mark and then went inside again. Almost an hour later, George did the same. Neither of them showed any signs of leading their family on a food hunt although they had hardly eaten a thing the day before. By eleven o'clock the mound was deserted. All the group members had vanished inside. The same process was repeated in the late afternoon. The group were not going to leave Tatu to die alone!

The next day was a repetition of the day before except that most of the animals made short foraging excursions sometime during the day, but never strayed more than about twenty yards from the mound and never staying away long. I wondered if Tatu was dead already. She had been very weak indeed the last time I had seen her, two days before, and didn't look as if she would last out the night. I knew from experience, though, that mongooses are very tough little animals and her dying might drag on for days.

Day after day I kept my vigil and day after day the mongooses stayed at the mound. It wasn't until almost six days later that I saw Diana appear one morning, all one side of her body wet and sticky. George's haunches looked matted as well, as did various parts of the anatomy of other family members. This morning, however, Diana led the troop away from the mound, as if it were a normal day's foraging. As soon as she and the group were far enough away for me not to disturb them by getting out of the car, I went over to the mound and peered into the gloom of its depths. A smell of rotting meat assailed my nostrils and I knew then what the wetness was that I had seen on Diana and Co.'s sides. Tatu had been dead a long time.

I knew I could not attribute any human emotions like pity to the animals concerned, but their behaviour was still a puzzle. For a small semi-nomadic species dependent on insects for food, it would be very maladaptive to have a set of behaviour patterns that bound it to one spot should one member of the group be unable to go further. Not only would it mean that the food around the termite mound at which the group was held would be rapidly depleted but just their being there for several days brought danger with it. Predators are not stupid. If the group had once been spotted, it was very likely to be attacked frequently by some hungry animal on the lookout for an easy meal.

When mongooses have small babies, though, their range of movement is very much restricted as well. But babies can be carried from mound to mound should danger threaten, not so an almost adult animal. I thought that maybe all that was happening was that Tatu, by being helpless, was awakening maternal feelings in the rest of the group. But Tatu was the opposite of a baby. Babies cry continually, are always active and trying to establish contact with group members. Tatu had been the opposite. She had just sat there, not even giving her contact call any more, and even if she had wanted to, towards the end she was too weak to go to the rest of her family. They had to come to her. In addition, the animals that had taken most care of her in her illness were not those which usually took care of the babies.

I began to wonder what this behaviour could be good for. I knew there were close bonds between the members of the family but they were not close enough for the family to come looking for a lost group member. There must be something else behind this behaviour for it to have been selected for in evolution. The only thing I could think of was that it might be tied up with investment; a simple sum of investment and return. It takes mongooses a long time to mature and take their place in the society. They do not even become sexually mature until they are one and a half to two years old. Maybe it would be worth while taking care of a sick group member rather than abandoning it, for it would take a long time before a growing youngster would be able to fill the lost one's shoes, and the sick one might recover. These were all guesses, however, and I was still not sure how I should interpret this behaviour. I did not think that this careful protection of the invalid just came about because the sick animal happened to be Tatu, who had had a close bond with Diana earlier. This would not explain why Moja and his elder brothers had been so solicitous of her. Then there was the curious fact that they had stayed with her body long after she was dead. Maybe they had no concept, in the human sense of the word, of life and death. As long as the body was recognisable as Tatu, they stayed with it. Only when the corruption had set in to the point where the corpse had started to disintegrate did they finally leave it. There are many reports of mother animals, especially, staying by their dead young or even carrying them around with them for days like the chimpanzees do. But this still would not explain why the mongooses did not just leave and abandon Tatu to her fate.

One thing that made me reject the thought that the group had behaved the way it did just because the sick animal was Tatu and a special favourite of her mother's, was that I was later able to watch another case of invalid care where the sick animal, I knew, had practically no contact with his mother at all. The incident took place in my tame group. One of the lowest-ranking of the subadult males, which was just over five years old, had a severe kidney infection which, despite treatment, went into a chronic stage and it was obvious that the animal would soon die. When medical science could do no more for it, I decided to return it to its family instead of letting it die alone. What I had seen for Tatu repeated itself but the whole process dragged on over a period of almost a month. It was only in the last week, however, that the animal became immobile and could hardly drag itself to the sleeping boxes. Again the group came out and slept with it on the open floor just as they had slept with Tatu at the base of the termite mound. Again I saw the conscientious licking of the invalid's body, especially by his mother, although at his age, he could not have awakened any maternal feelings in her. Finally, when he died, I decided to leave his body with his family to see what they would do. My surmise in the case of Tatu had been correct. They cuddled up to it and warmed it as if it had been alive, licked it and nibbled it until the decomposition reached the stage of its hair falling out as soon as they touched it. I then decided to remove the corpse as it was beginning to smell.

So Tatu's case had not been an isolated one, and was not a function of age, sex or rank. As an ethologist I always ask myself when I see particular behaviour, 'What is it good for?' In this case, I could not be sure . . . or is there such a thing as pity amongst animals?

13   George gets a Rival

The rains were now long past and the hottest time of the year was upon the Taru. Leaves shrivelled on the twigs of the shrubs, turned brown and finally blew away in the hot midday wind. The once-green grass turned silvery and brittle and the desert drew in on itself, waiting for the next time the heavens would open. Many of the birds that had haunted the bushlands started to disappear. This was the time of the great spring migration when European visitors made the journey of thousands of miles to breeding grounds far to the north. I watched skeins of European storks, like little crosses high in the sky, their necks extended and their legs trailing behind them, pass overhead, hundreds of tiny dots which only resolved themselves into the familiar stork form through binoculars. The noisy, brilliantly coloured European rollers were leaving too. I watched their departure early one morning – a straggling flock approaching from the south-west, flying low over the tops of the trees, gathering azure-blue companions as it skimmed by, wings flashing metallic in the morning sunlight. The exodus continued for almost three hours, scores and scores of birds winging past, heading north-east as if with a purpose. This was a time of change in the dry bushlands, the animals which needed water to survive drifting off and new, hardier species taking their place.

The wave of Grasshopper buzzards and Pale Chanting goshawks, which had invaded the bush after the rains, drifted off north leaving only a few of their brethren at their posts in the Taru. Then the European visitors came through, the European kestrel and the Lesser kestrel. For a few days the birds seemed to be everywhere and then they vanished completely. In the wake of the European roller came the brilliantly coloured Lilac-breasted roller, one of the most beautiful birds I know, its dull wings flashing into metallic purple-blue as soon as they opened. I had never seen a roller forage with the mongooses before but a pair of Lilac-breasteds regularly did when the group moved through their territory. I watched the male dance his aerial dance above the tree-tops, a flight that would put most stunt pilots to shame. In circles he gained height, wings flashing as the sunlight hit them. When he was almost sixty feet up he peeled off the top of his turn and shot earthwards, wings waggling stiffly, until he was almost at tree-top level and then pulled out of the dive in a graceful loop-the-loop to land light as a feather in the top of a nearby thorntree. I didn't know whom this display was meant to impress, his mate or other rollers of the same species which might have been in the area and on the lookout for a territory . . . a roller 'Keep Off' sign written in the skies . . .

Wart and Pickle were now almost three months old and had just about stopped begging food from the rest of the family and were quite adept at catching insects for themselves and well capable of keeping up with the group on the day's march. Diana's daily forays were getting longer, for food was scarcer, but were usually restricted to just a few hours in the morning and again in the late afternoon. It was too hot at midday. It was during the time they were foraging one morning that I noticed something on a termite mound far to their rear, a large grey shape that was looking in their direction. At first I thought that it was a Blacktip mongoose but, as it stood up and trotted down the mound towards Diana and Co., I noticed that it was too short and squat to be a Blacktip and the species signature, the cockily turned-up black tassel to the tail, was also missing.

Within a few minutes the animal ran up a mound only about thirty yards away and went into high sit, peering at Diana and her family in the grass and Rusty, who was on guard on the mound near the car. Now I could get a better view of it I realised with surprise that it was another Dwarf mongoose, a large adult male. I searched the mounds around for signs of other members of his group or of the tell-tale string of birds that would be with them, but there was nothing. The stranger seemed to be alone. Rusty had spotted him long since and gave a mixture of excitement twitter and the 'attention' call. George and a few others ran up the mound Rusty was keeping watch from and stared towards where he was pointing with his head. When George saw the newcomer he started to threat-scratch, looking over towards him in between scratches and almost demolishing one of the twigs of the bush that crowned the mound in the process.

The stranger stayed where he was and just stared over to the madly threat-scratching George. By this time the rest of the group seemed to have got wind of the fact that something was wrong and had joined George and the others on the mound. I still couldn't believe that this single adult male could suddenly appear out of nowhere and was still searching for signs of his family, but there were none. George, fur bristling, Wart, Pickle, and some of the other youngsters trailing after him, headed towards the newcomer with a rush and the latter turned tail and ran down the back of the mound he had been perched on to disappear into the grass. As soon as he was lost from sight, George's attack petered out into thin air, he returned to the rest of his family and, as a body, they set out foraging once more.

I kept a sharp watch for the stranger but it was many minutes before I saw him again, this time on a mound flanking the foraging group and about fifty yards away. To have followed them he would have had to pass quite close to me and it appeared as if he was too nervous of the car and myself to attempt something as daring as that. His gaze kept flashing between me in the car and

Diana and Co. in the grass but he made no move to approach them closer. In this he was quite different from Veronica, who had attempted to join the family right from the first. She, however, had been a youngster and this animal, I called him Edward, was at least five years old judging from his size, headshape and the length of his canine teeth.

Edward continued his march parallel with Diana and her family but still about fifty yards away for the rest of the morning. When the group vanished into a termite mound for the midday siesta, Edward started to move through the grass towards them, obviously headed for a termite mound nearer to the one they were sleeping in. He still had made no real attempt to approach and I got the impression that he was mainly interested in keeping them in sight at this stage. He ran up the slopes of a mound not twenty yards away from where they were and stuck his head into one of the holes at its summit. From the way his tail started to bottlebrush, I realised that this mound was inhabited. I didn't know what by, but it was obviously no friend from the way Edward was behaving. He gave the *tseee* call but it suddenly dawned on me there was no one around for him to call, for he had no family with him. A battery of curious heads poked out of Diana and Co.'s siesta mound and stared around. They had obviously heard his call and were responding but they had not yet located where it came from. Edward was still with his foreparts in the hole at the top of the mound and practically hidden from Diana's group by one of the mound's buttresses. The little heads looked this way and that, found nothing that attracted their attention and, one by one, subsided again. Finally Edward emerged backwards from the hole and, after circling it a few times, still peering down into the mound's depths, he moved off and took up his station for the afternoon nap in a mound further on. To date he had not called 'Where are you?' once but had contented himself with just keeping Diana's group in view.

I found it particularly interesting that the group had responded to his 'Come quickly' call although his voice must have been strange to them. I had often wondered whether the group would respond to the voice of a stranger if it gave one of the important group-directed calls, like the 'Come quickly', or whether these calls were only effective within the family. As far as I could tell to date, the group had certainly reacted immediately they had heard Edward's voice but, being unable to locate him, had gone back to their nap again. Whether or not they would have come running over if they had spotted him, I would never know.

The afternoon's foraging proceeded very much like the morning's, Edward keeping a good distance between himself and Diana's group. Every now and again one of the guards would spot him and warn but each time he would slip off into the grass out of sight before an attack could be launched against him. I had the impression from his behaviour that Diana's group may not have been the first that he had tried to join, for he was very suspicious of them and as soon as they took the slightest notice of him, he was off. It almost looked as if he had had bad experiences with trying to join groups in the past. When dusk fell and the others had retreated to their mound, he crept up near them again but this time slept in a mound only about fifteen yards away.

I was there before sunrise the next morning, excited as to what would happen. Diana's group was up and around before there was any sign of a movement from Edward's sleeping mound. Then, to my surprise, he just climbed out of a hole half-way up it and sat in full view of the group, squatting on top of the mound grooming himself carefully. Now he was at close range, I could see that he had only half his left ear and that his neck-ruff was missing patches of hair. He had been in the wars – and recently too, by the looks of it! A cluster of little bodies were strained in his direction from Diana's mound, heads flagging up and down. George suddenly snaked forwards and dashed towards the still busily grooming figure, followed by a streamer of little brown bodies. The group was going to attack. Edward broke off his grooming, looked at them and turned tail to vanish into the mound in a twinkling. As far as I could tell at the moment, it looked as if he had made a bad mistake, for the group would catch him inside the mound and would make short work of him, but at this time I didn't know all the facts. He must have spent the night in an enclosed chamber that only had a single outlet and there he felt safe.

George and his warriors stormed up the mound, George going to the hole into which Edward had vanished, sticking his head inside and suddenly shooting backwards with a rush. Even I had heard Edward's furious spitting defence when George's head had blocked the hole's opening. The rest of George's companions were milling around, uncertain what to do. Some were sticking their heads into holes in the mound, tails bottlebrushed, or going hesitantly inside, bodies stretched to their utmost and ready to leap backwards at the slightest sign of danger. George was going through an orgy of threat-scratching right at the entrance of Edward's hole, every now and again dashing towards it and sticking his head down it only to be greeted every time with a fusillade of spitting. Sometimes, as he withdrew, I could see Edward's gaped jaws protruding from the tunnel entrance. He was effectively blocking any attempt at forcing an entrance with two rows of sharp white teeth! George looked as if he was in a quandary. He couldn't attack Edward for Edward had positioned himself so well that there was no way to approach him without getting bitten in the process, so he went back to what he usually did under the circumstances . . . threat-scratching.

George then started making darting attacks into the hole, braving the snapping jaws, and I heard violent protest screaming from the mound's depths. The rest of his family were now extremely excited and dashing in and out of the holes in the mound but even as a group, they could do nothing. From his position in the tunnel, Edward could hold them off all day if need be. It appeared only wide enough for one body to pass and that body was in there already . . . Edward!

After almost twenty minutes of futile threat-scratching and darting attacks, George gave up and rejoined Diana. The rest of the group then dashed towards the now vacated front-stage position, each of them poking their heads into the hole and being rebuffed with a volley of spits and protest screams. Finally Diana led them all off foraging again. I waited to see what Edward would do.

Hardly had the group moved out of sight in the grass when the stubborn newcomer popped out of his safe hole in the mound and sat there staring after them. His hair was still on end, especially his tail, but he did not give me the impression of being terrified and his subsequent behaviour proved he wasn't. He suddenly stood up and trotted in the group's wake. George's violent threats had not been enough to deter him from trying to join the family.

Edward continued to trail Diana and Co. for days, always keeping about thirty yards' distance between himself and the group. As soon as they disappeared into a mound to rest, he would trot up and vanish into a mound near them and wait for them to emerge again. Whereas Veronica had wormed her way submissively under their defences, Edward seemed almost to go out of his way to provoke attention. He would try and position himself in full view of the group when they awoke and either vanished into the grass when they approached him or retreated into a termite mound. I had still not heard him call 'Where are you?' but maybe this was because he always knew exactly where the group was and gauged to a nicety the distance between them and himself, always near enough for them to notice him but rarely to provoke them into an outright attack. George's threat-scratching when he spotted Edward was starting to get less and less violent and, with time, almost ceased altogether, although he was very aware of the newcomer's presence and would dart glances towards him, stiff-bodied and head low.

As the weeks went by I started to think that Edward's future role in life would be as a satellite to Diana and Co., never really accepted but still having some of the advantages of group life. He would dash for cover when the hornbills and other birds that accompanied the foragers gave the alarm and would move off with Diana and her family when they left on their daily hunt for insects. He started to visit the mounds they had abandoned, creeping in through the holes and exploring them from inside and marking at their marking post. There was still no sign, however, of his being accepted in any way, although his crouching figure on one of the nearby mounds in the morning had ceased to evoke the violent responses that it had done earlier. The system had started to reach a balance.

The situation continued in the same way for almost a month before Edward made his first bid for contact, but again, not openly like Veronica had done. He was sitting watching the group from a nearby mound and, once he noticed that George had gone off foraging in the early morning with the two youngsters and the majority of his family, leaving only Diana and Scar at the mound, he suddenly ran towards them, going into high sit every now and again to peer at them over the tops of the grass, maybe to make sure that George and the others had not yet returned. Then he trotted up the mound towards Diana and, body pressed close to the ground as he approached, started to groom her! I think that Diana must have been just as surprised as I was, for she just sat there, albeit rather stiffly, and let him do it. Scar rushed over to him, sniffed under his tail and then didn't seem to know exactly what to do. The conflicting stimuli of a stranger on the mound and the animal in question grooming his mother stopped him dead in his tracks. I heard him growl slightly but he went back to guard duty and left Edward still busily nibbling Diana's neck-ruff.

George and his little party had not foraged far, for this was one of the early morning excursions more for getting a quick breakfast than for moving from mound to mound. He appeared suddenly at the base of the mound, Wart and Pickle hard on his heels. He seemed not to notice that Edward was sitting next to his wife and being very friendly to her, for he went to sniff the marking post before heading up the mound quite unconcerned. Edward just sat there, watching his approach like a hawk. Then George noticed the interloper. Head down and tail bottlebrushed, he dashed towards him. Edward still didn't take to the hills but just turned his body away and gave the protest squeal. Diana looked as if she was going to get out of the way of the imminent clash, for she stood up and ran down the mound into the grass. George was now almost upon Edward and I expected to see an attack any moment but, at the last instant, Edward broke and ran, dashing full speed towards the mound he had come from. George followed him for a few yards but suddenly stopped. I could see him listening carefully, then he turned and galloped over towards his wife and seemed to be erasing the marks of the intruder, for he started nibbling her neck frantically, she reciprocating in the familiar neck-over-neck of the social grooming, something which she had not done in Edward's case.

From this point on, Edward made every attempt to approach Diana as soon as George and the rest of the group's backs were turned. I found it hard to understand why she allowed this and did not attack him and chase him off, but maybe his friendly intentions towards her blocked her aggression. The rest of the group eyed him with suspicion but made no attempt to attack him when he was close to their mother although, from the way they walked stiff-legged and heads thrust out, I could see that an attack would not be long in coming should he give them the excuse. The only group member from whom Edward still fled was George. I felt a bit sorry for the old man whose position seemed to be slowly undermined.

Edward started to do something else that I did not expect. Whenever he got an opportunity to do so, he would play with Wart and Pickle, who were almost always ready for a game at any time. He was very gentle with them and, although his first attempts at play were watched with great interest and almost trepidation by the rest of the group, the fact that Diana did not dash in and chase Edward off seemed to stay their hands. Soon Edward and the young-sters playing together became an almost everyday occurrence. It looked as if he was slowly being accepted.

However, George continued to resent his appearance, and the poor fellow was continually on the alert, hardly leaving his wife unattended and, when he did, dashing back to her at short intervals to displace his rival whose flight from the situation was getting less and less dramatic. On many occasions he would just slink down the mound and go into the grass at its base, George staring hard at his retreating figure from the mound's top. I was beginning to think that Edward was now fairly sure of his position and was starting to flaunt it in the patriarch's face, but it had still not come to an out-and-out confrontation between the two. Diana seemed oblivious of the tensions she was causing within the group and I think she must have enjoyed Edward's attentions, for she made no attempt to avoid them.

The inevitable finally happened. On one of George's returns to his flirting wife, instead of Edward dashing off, he only moved a few feet away and squatted on one of the neighbouring buttresses of the mound. George snaked towards him, neck outstretched, eyes riveted on his rival. Edward turned his head away but kept squatting where he was. When George was finally upon him, Edward did something I had not seen a mongoose do in such a situation before. He tucked his head between his forelegs, rolled his tail tight across the front of his body and curled himself into a ball . . . but a ball with a difference! Protruding from between his fore- and hind-feet were a pair of jaws gaped to show their formidable weapons and Edward's protest screams filled the air. George seemed to hesitate. This was the extreme defence posture of the mongoose and, on the few occasions I had seen it previously, could turn into violent attack if the enemy approached nearer. George prowled round Edward, head low and, as he reached the unprotected side of his body, the head whipped sideways underneath Edward's belly to present George with a mouthful of teeth on that side as well. After two circles around his antagonist, George went into his usual threat-scratching, Edward's screams still domi-nating the situation. None of the other group members made a move to join their father although, as a body, they would have easily been able to overwhelm Edward. Edward was still screaming protest when George finally finished his demonstration and went back to Diana to groom her neck.

Edward stayed curled in his ball for almost a minute afterwards, his screams decreasing in volume until they finally stopped altogether. Then he uncurled himself and looked about. George was busily anally grooming his wife and the rest of the animals were pottering about on the mound or around its base. Instead of leaving, Edward stayed where he was and started to put his fur in order. His ruse had worked. George had demonstrated his mastery over the situation and Edward had accepted his subordinate role . . . for the time being at least! He had finally managed to join the group, for that night he slept in the same mound as they did.

From this point on, Edward seemed to have been more or less accepted by all the group members although he still avoided George and the older males, spending most of his time with the younger animals, especially Wart and Pickle with whom he still frequently played. As far as he was concerned, though, the most important group member was and remained Diana and he continued to take every opportunity of sitting near her and grooming her when George was not looking. Most of the time, Diana did not reciprocate his attentions and only rarely gave him the return neck-nibble when he pushed himself under her chin to nibble her neck-ruff. I had not yet seen him anally groom her although he often attempted to get her anal scent on his body passively, creeping under her tail and rubbing his flanks across her anal gland. I only saw him trying to anally mark her once but it was an incomplete mark for Diana got up in the middle of it and walked away, Edward being left looking rather silly with one leg cocked in the air.

When George came to sit with Diana later I saw him boring his nose into her fur where Edward had marked her. Then he started to get very excited, boring his nose even deeper and licking the fur patch where the mark had been made. I saw his tail starting to bottlebrush, a sure sign that something was going to happen soon. Then he started to anally mark his wife with tremendous intensity. Usually she only got a quick leg-lift every now and again but this time George seemed to have decided to make a job of it! Diana was marked more than fifteen times, George controlling her back carefully with his nose after each mark, until he seemed to be satisfied that the rival's scent had vanished under a liberal coating of his own. He made no attempt to attack Edward, however, or even his wife. The only thing he seemed interested in was getting his signature put back on her again: 'She belongs to me!'

In the days that followed Edward remained persistent in his approaches towards Diana. Sometimes she would just get up and walk away from him, on other occasions she seemed to enjoy them and after several fruitless attempts to anally groom her, Edward finally succeeded. Diana sat, half-reclining, and let him lick her anal gland, the highest level of trust and acceptance that a mongoose could give. Edward did not leave things at this point. He seemed to be determined to challenge George for his position as Diana's consort and now he had been allowed so far, he attempted to take the final step to oust his rival.

George almost always took the youngsters out foraging in the early morning, leaving Diana on the mound where she would lie in the sun, groom herself and accept the attentions of those of her family who remained. There was usually a little knot of bodies surrounding her, either nibbling her neck-ruff or anally grooming her. Edward never went with George on these early-morning sorties and seemed to make full use of the latitude they afforded him with George's wife. Diana was slowly starting to respond to his advances and would often reciprocate the grooming and now rarely moved away when Edward's demands became too heavy. Then, one day, as Diana was getting up to move to another point on the mound, Edward saw his chance and rushed behind her, clasping her around the hips in the typical mongoose 'mount', his paws dug into her flanks. Diana's response was less than friendly. She stiffened, arched her back and flung her head backwards, mouth gaped to show her sharp teeth and gave an intense protest scream, snapping on both sides over her shoulder at her unwelcome suitor. Edward stayed clamped to her back, lifting his head high to keep it away from the snapping jaws, but made no effort to dismount. Diana then tried another tactic, whipping round left and right, trying to bite Edward in one of his hind-legs, but he shuffled them backwards so that her teeth connected on empty air. Diana's last resort was to bow her body downwards to try and grab his tail, bending almost double to do so, but again she could not reach. Edward remained stubbornly where he was and there seemed to be nothing that Diana could do to shift him. She was still screaming protest when George came trotting out of the grass, the youngsters after him, and headed towards the pair. Edward dismounted in a hurry and trotted off out of sight round the side of the mound. Diana moved over to George and, together, they climbed up the side of the mound where George gave her a thorough grooming. Edward kept well out of George's way for the next hours.

Although Diana had rebuffed him, Edward was not going to give up so easily. Sometimes his approaches would be hesitant, a forepaw lifted and laid along her back, and sometimes more violent, with him more or less springing on her from behind. Her response, though, was always the same, loud protest screams and a rigid body, back bowed and head and tail tucked in. George had still not really challenged Edward although he frequently returned to the

When Edward tried to usurp George's position, Diana responded aggressively to his advances, and snapped at her unwelcome suitor

mound when he heard Diana's screams. Edward would then just melt away unobtrusively and keep out of sight for a while. After this attempted cuckolding had been going on for six days, Edward became bolder and bolder in his assaults on Diana. He finally attempted to mount her right under George's nose!

I expected George to dash at him and a fight to ensue but all George did was stare hard and then approach, body stretched and chin close to the ground. When Edward saw this, he backed off and went to sit with his back turned towards the pair, head dropped. Diana was still standing there and George, still flattened, came up and started to investigate her anal gland. When he appeared to have finished his intense anal sniffing, she moved off as if nothing had happened. George only glanced at Edward, who was still sitting with his back to him, and then trotted off down the mound behind his wife.

Now that he had once mounted Diana in front of George and had got away with it unscathed, Edward's behaviour towards the leading male sometimes bordered on the downright cheeky. He would creep up and clasp Diana around her flanks whenever the mood seemed to take him, irrespective of whether George was in the vicinity or not. He even got to the point of coming up to Diana when George was lying near her and lying down next to her on the opposite side, despite glares from George. He shouldered the youngsters out of the way when the group went into a termite mound to sleep, following hard on George and Diana's heels. Although he had been in the group for only ten days now, he was acting as if he was equal in rank to George, and I knew that this state of affairs was not going to last long. George's breaking point was slowly being reached, for he was becoming more and more irritable and his tail was almost continually slightly bottlebrushed.

What started the fight I shall never know for it took place early one morning in the depths of the mound in which the group had spent the night. The sun had just risen and I was getting ready for the day's observations when, through the thick walls of the termite mound, I heard violent protest screams that went on and on. Then there was quiet. Then protest screams again and the faint sound of someone spitting in maximum defence. Then quiet again.

After almost five minutes of silence from the mound, during which I tried in vain to distinguish some flicker of movement in the darkness of the ventilation shaft holes, the ear-splitting screams suddenly started up once more. Something shot out of one of the holes in the top of the mound almost as if it had been fired from a gun. I had difficulty in recognising who it was at first, for it looked like a fur muff – all its hair on end, but when it turned to face me I realised that it was Edward – minus another half an ear! The long-awaited battle between him and George seemed finally to have taken place.

Edward, blood running down the side of his face, turned and peered down the hole from which he had emerged and started protest screaming again. There was no sign of George or any of the other group members. Edward kept circling the hole, peeping in every now and again and screaming anew. There must have been quite a battle for, apart from the torn ear, Edward also had two patches of hair missing from his neck-ruff and a cut on his nose. I had never seen him so abject and defensive before. Finally he moved away from the hole and went to sit on one of the mound buttresses in the sun, hunched in on himself and all his hair still on end. Whitethroat came out of the mound shortly afterwards and, after glancing at him, took up his station on the other side of the mound. Of George there was no sign.

Within the next ten minutes the rest of the family climbed out but Edward kept aloof and none of them came over to sit next to him. Then Diana came out and, after her, George. He was missing sundry patches of hair from his head and neck. Stiff-legged, he approached Edward. Edward did a half-turn, looked at him, gave a little protest cry, made as if to run down the mound but then suddenly whipped round to face George and, to my surprise, crawled over towards him, greeting loudly and tapping him all over his face with one outstretched forefoot. Edward had submitted and accepted George as rank-high to him. The final decision had been made.

George made no further attempt to impose himself on Edward during the following days and Edward kept out of his and Diana's way. He seemed to have lost all interest in wooing the matriarch and usually trotted in her wake with the rest of the family when they were on the move. He also started to take his turn regularly at guarding when the rest of the group was foraging, something he had done only on very few occasions before his downfall. Most of the group members were still friendly towards him and would come and sit next to him on occasion or groom him, but he rarely reciprocated to any great extent. Goldie and Notch seemed to be especially active in trying to awake his interest, cuddling up to him and grooming him both anally and around his neck, and he responded in kind.

It took some time, however, for the tension in the group to relax. This was the first time I had ever seen a real fight in which blood was drawn take place between two animals living in the same group. The mongooses, although very aggressive towards outsiders, seemed to keep to a policy of 'peace at home', for the little squabbles they had between themselves were usually blocked before they really broke out by someone running and greeting the antagonists violently, a procedure which seemed to stop future attack dead. Even the little fights that took place over food were never serious despite the ferocious growling, hipslamming and occasional open-mouthed darts and screams that often accompanied them. Protection against fights in the family was almost complete. It wasn't until I happened to observe something that occurred in my tame group that I realised how important these restraints on behaviour were for the mongooses. If the safety system failed, as it did in the case I saw, it usually meant death.

The victim in this case was a juvenile female, almost a year old. The group had had to be restricted to only a section of their usual run and this was starting to result in a great deal of friction between group members. I don't know what the female in question had done or why she was singled out for attack for the first thing I saw were her father and mother dashing towards her, hair on end. One of them grabbed her by the neck and the other by a back leg. She let out an intense protest scream and then the whole group descended upon her and she was buried in a welter of bodies. I dashed in with a broom and beat them off and tried to catch the little female but could not. I therefore decided to wait to see what would happen, if the group would attack her *en masse* again, but they completely ignored her after this episode. She retreated to a box in the corner of the room, huddled in on herself, head down and eyes closed, and just gave up. She never moved from her position for the next two days, coming down neither to eat nor drink. Her body was covered with bite wounds but none of them seemed fatal or even incapacitating. On the third day two of her brothers went up on the box and sat next to her, one on each side, cuddling her body between them and grooming her, but she did not respond. I resolved that, if her condition did not show any sign of improvement, I would remove her from the enclosure the next day and put her in a roomy cage where I could feed her titbits to try and get her appetite back. I was too late, however. The next morning she lay dead on top of the box on which she had squatted without moving for three days, a victim of the shock and stress of being attacked by her entire family at once.

It looked as though, from this observation, if the leaders decided to attack an animal, the rest of the group would join in, something that could be very useful if a predator or a strange group of mongooses had to be held off but that could have fatal results if they attacked a member of their own group. It was therefore necessary to have obvious and unmistakable threat postures and vocalisations so that the intention of the animals concerned could be clearly read and the appropriate measures taken. I had now seen on numerous occasions how effective the greeting could be in stopping attack; sometimes a threatening animal (usually George) would be surrounded by vigorously greeting group mates, usually juveniles and females, and his threat would just collapse like a bubble. The most common means of avoiding strife however was just that – avoidance. One of the animals would stop, freeze, turn slightly to one side and move away. In the days following George's fight with Edward, this was very typical behaviour for the group. Animals approaching one another would suddenly turn off, heads ducked, to the side and move out of

Edward had made his bid for princedom, and failed

each other's way. Edward kept well to the background and never tried to provoke an encounter with any of the group, especially not George, and after a few days the tension started to ebb away and the group's friendliness to each other emerged again.

Edward seemed to have learned his lesson well for he never made any further attempt to approach Diana and it wasn't until almost four weeks later that I saw him groom her for the first time, but that was all, a quick little friendly nibble in the neck-ruff. He seemed now to be established amongst the subordinate adult males but seemed to be low-ranking to all of them for even Whitethroat, who was the lowest-ranking of the three, could come and take a locust he had caught off him. By and large, however, he had settled into his role and took up his guard duties with the others and stood in the front rank when the group met a jackal or a snake. In his behaviour he was hardly distinguishable from Diana's older sons by this time except that he was still very attractive to the older subordinate females of the group, especially Notch. I wondered if this would be another bone of contention later in the year when the breeding season came round again, knowing George's attitude towards sexual relationships amongst the low-ranking group members. In time, Edward's ear healed but always retained the rip George had made in it, a scar he would carry to his death. He had made his bid for princedom, and failed.

14 Together we Stand
– Divided we Fall

It had taken me many years of patient observation, both in the Taru and other places in Kenya, as well as with my tame group in Europe, to begin to understand what life as a mongoose was all about. It was a hard life, in some respects, for death was hovering on dove-grey or dark-brown wings every day, not to mention trotting through the bush on four paws, but the Dwarf mongooses have managed to survive through developing one of the most complicated social systems known amongst mammals, a system that goes far beyond anything one could expect of the humble-looking little creatures. As their lives unfolded before me, I had come to know Diana's family so well that I almost felt a part of it. I knew each of the animal's little foibles: Vanessa's passion for Twin, George's bad-temperedness, Moja's friendship for his brother Rusty. I was more upset when Tatu died than I think Diana was, or at least showed she was, and when M'Bili disappeared after the Battle of Dragon, I almost felt like going to look for her. Now, however, the group had two new members, Veronica and Edward, and I was wondering how the group would rearrange itself to compensate for two missing members and the recruitment of two strangers.

After Tatu's death, Fleck's friendship with Blackie seemed to deepen and he spent most of his time with his littermate, when the two were not on guard or busy being 'nice' to other group members. As the weeks went by, however, I noticed him being especially 'nice' to Veronica. Goldie was about the same age as she was and, after the loss of her friend M'Bili, I expected other 'single' males in the group to make approaches towards her, but could detect nothing. Goldie seemed to spread her attentions almost equally over all the group members and I didn't even think, from what I could see, that she made much of a distinction between males and females. She, as well as the other members of the family, were so shattered after the Dragon mound battle that I didn't think they even realised that M'Bili was missing until several days later. Even then, Goldie made no attempt to search for or call her friend but huddled together with the rest of the group when they were resting, pushing herself amongst the crush of bodies. Even now, months afterwards, she had still not formed a friendship with any other member of the group and Veronica did not seem to be a substitute; in fact, the two females tended to avoid each other.

Fleck had been one of the first males to investigate Veronica when she arrived and had more or less 'broken the ban' on her by not attacking her immediately. This association, which had existed right from the first, was now becoming more prominent. I don't know whether Veronica felt 'grateful' to Fleck for being the first to accept her or whether she just found him attractive, as he very obviously did her, but whatever the basis behind their growing friendship, the two were now frequently seen together, almost a 'young love' version of Vanessa and Twin. Of course they were not blatant about their relationship and tried to keep it hidden as much as possible from George's prying eyes but their 'chance' encounters went well beyond the realms of chance!

Notch was still 'unattached' although her relationship to Scar still continued. Edward's arrival in the group must have sent a feminine flutter through her for she did just about everything a mongoose could do to catch his attention, but again it was all for nothing. As I watched Edward and his relationship with the other group members develop, I found that he was very much like Whitethroat in his behaviour. The only star in his heaven (or rather in the group) was Diana and all the other females, although he accepted their attentions, were more or less dust in the wind. This passion brought him into sharp conflict with Whitethroat on several occasions, two of which almost ended up in full-fledged fights but which were nipped in the bud by Wart, Pickle and Moja.

Whitethroat was sitting next to Diana nibbling her neck-ruff early one morning while George was down at the marking post. Almost casually, Edward came over to Diana's other side and started to nibble her as well. Diana was faced with a conflict. She was already nibbling Whitethroat but now this stimulus to nibble back was being given from the other side too. She stopped her grooming and just sat between the two males who also stopped and glared at each other over Diana's shoulder. I don't know if she could feel that trouble was brewing or not but she suddenly got up and trotted down towards George, leaving the two rivals face to face. They were still staring hard at each other and I could see the hair on Edward's tail starting to bristle although he made no movement or noise. Whitethroat kept up his aggressive stare and Edward should have turned away and left but he didn't. It had finally come to a showdown between the two. Before anything could happen, though, Pickle must have noticed what was going on for she dashed between them, greeting loudly and started to tap Whitethroat on the nose. Her twitters attracted Wart and, between the two of them, the situation was saved, the two males backing off from each other and the madly greeting youngsters. Even in the weeks that followed when such incidents looked as if they could turn ugly, the youngsters saved the day and the 'priority' of Diana's lovers was still not resolved.

I know of no other species of highly evolved mammal that has a group duty structure like the Dwarf mongooses. Evolution posed them with a problem that they had to solve somehow: how to live peaceably together in a group, ensure the maximal survival of every group member, and not increase in group size to the point where there would not be enough food for them. On top of all this, evolution also dictated that there be 'new blood' introduced into each group to prevent complete incest. The Dwarf mongooses have solved all these problems, and even gone further by developing real bonds of affection for group mates. They have come up with a solution that no other known mammal group can rival – except Man.

Over the long hours of watching them go about their daily lives I came to realise that what I was seeing here was a division of labour known in comparable form only from the social insects such as bees, wasps, ants and termites, and, amongst the mammals, Man. Every member of the group, despite its personal attachments, had a job to do if the group was going to run smoothly and survive at all. Diana was the group leader and it was also she who provided the group with new members, for she was the only one of them that appeared to be able or allowed to rear her young successfully. Notch's young had simply disappeared right after birth and I never knew what happened to them. George, on the other hand, apart from having the job of fertilising Diana, also had two other roles to play. He was the one that led the group into battle and who took care of group 'morals', and in general, he was one of the busiest of all the group members for he even got landed with feeding the babies when they were old enough to go with him! The youngsters, as well, were quickly drawn into different jobs. They were not only 'keepers of the peace' within the group but also followed close on George's heels when the group did battle with another one. They were, in fact, the 'cannon fodder'. The subordinate females, on the other hand, apart from being babysitters, also took their part in guarding the group when it was on the move and this was also the main role of the subadult males such as Blackie, Fleck and Rusty. When it came to facing real danger, however, situations in which an animal might get killed or badly wounded and where size and strength was of importance, then it was Twin, Scar, Whitethroat and, lately, Edward, who were in the fore. I remembered on how many occasions I had seen these males attacking snakes, jackals and Blacktip mongooses, always in the front ranks to face the enemy.

The system seemed to work perfectly but I still did not know how. Did the animals just take over these jobs when they reached a certain age or were they taught? I had one example of the former in the youngsters. Their food-begging had gradually turned into greeting as they grew older and no one 'showed' them how. They had just slipped into their role as 'peacemakers'

Guarding was the main job of the subadult males, and death hovered over them daily on outstretched wings or crept on four feet through the bush

with time. In the case of the young males, however, I knew that they were 'taught' how to guard by their older brothers. But who told Scar and Twin that they were to attack enemies first and the youngsters that they were to follow close behind George when he went into battle? These were all questions that I still did not have the answer to and it might take years before I would get it.

Although each of these 'roles' was primarily taken by one of the categories of animals, this did not make them exclusive by any means, for mongooses are jacks of all trades and any member of the group could spring in anywhere at a pinch. George never went into battle with the youngsters alone, the rest of the group followed behind, but it was significant that he and his youngest children were always in the front row. It was the same with attacking enemies. Although Scar, Twin and Whitethroat were the ones that stood in the front and bore the brunt of the attack, the rest of the group joined in almost immediately. Only George seemed to spend most of his time threat-scratching and Diana usually kept out of things and even kept her youngest children out of them too. Even the female babysitters usually had a male with them when they were taking care of the young, but he was functioning more like a guard than anything else and mostly sat on top of the mound while the babysitter stayed inside, at least for the first two weeks. It seemed that everyone could pinch-hit when the need arose but it still didn't explain why certain behaviour patterns fell into the sphere of action of certain group members and not that of others.

One of the questions that had plagued me right from the first when I started to study the Dwarf mongooses was 'How does new blood get introduced into the family?' I had seen how new individuals could join the group but it was a far cry from joining the group to becoming its leader and, as far as I could tell, this was essential if young were to be produced and raised. After seeing how Edward made his bid for Diana's affections and lost and how he and Whitethroat now played more or less the same role in the group, I wondered what would happen if, one day, George should have an accident and never return. What would Diana do? Who would she choose as a replacement for her husband, if she chose one at all? Would she automatically lose her position as group leader and have to abdicate in favour of one of the younger females who had a mate all ready and waiting? I did not know. Only patient waiting and watching would be able to solve the riddle. At least there were two males in the group just dying to step into George's shoes should something happen to him, but it all depended on whether Diana would accept one of them or whether Vanessa, who seemed to be next in line for the queen's position, would lay her claim first.

If she did, what would happen to Diana then? Would she be simply 'dropped' socially or would she even be forced to leave the group? I found it hard to envisage her as subordinate to one of the younger females, for hand in hand with her 'queenship' went a change in physical structure as well; she was almost twice as large as her daughters and I could not imagine her letting them push her around.

Although the practice of eating or killing the babies born to subordinate females seemed cruel, it was vitally necessary from two points of view if the group was going to continue as a functional unit. First, there was simply the problem of food. The mongooses lived in a superabundance of prey at some times of the year, but at others, during the dry season for example, food was more limited. It would be easy to visualise what would happen to a large group if the rains failed and there was no fresh greenstuff available to nourish the insect population on which they depended. This would mean death for at least some of the group members and a general weakening for all. Knowing how the youngsters had first priority when it came to food under normal conditions, I wondered how they would fare when the group was on a starvation diet, whether they would still be given food at the expense of the older group members or whether Nature would put a brake on the production of new youngsters by Diana simply not coming into oestrus. In many species of animals, when times are hard, this seems to disrupt the normal sexual cycle of the females and they simply do not conceive. This was another question for which I had no answer at present and that only further years of careful watching would be able to reveal.

Apart from the immediate necessity of food, there was also another problem that would rear its head should the subordinate females be allowed to raise their babies. It was simply this. The family would go to pieces, for their whole lives and, with this, their ability to survive at all, were based on division of labour within the group. The group as a whole could not afford to have a splinter group with another 'lead' female and male within its ranks. This would lead to tension, strife and ultimately group dissolution, and with group dissolution would probably come death from one of the many predators that haunted them unless the animals changed their habits completely and became solitary skulkers through the undergrowth. It seemed that millions of years of evolution had shaped them into perfect little tools to master their harsh environment and I could not imagine them changing completely in a short while. If they were going to remain a smoothly functioning group, there was no room for satellite 'kings' and 'queens' which would just disrupt things. Hard as it seemed, the babies must go.

As it was at present, Diana's little troop was geared perfectly for survival, but survival associated with true affection as well. Many times I had to stop myself from being too anthropomorphic and humanising them, giving them emotions that animals are not supposed to possess, but it was very hard not to. People often ask me, when they hear that I spend my life studying Dwarf mongooses, 'Why?' and I am stumped for an answer. It goes far further than just gaining knowledge about another species that shares life with us on this planet, for the mongooses, despite their non-kinship with the primates from which human beings have sprung, show so many human characteristics in

The mongooses' ability to live amicably as a group and to divide the group duties between them ensures their survival ▶

their behaviour that, someday, my discoveries might be of use to human beings and not just of interest to Science. They not only fascinate me as a scientist but they have enriched my life in a different way, just by letting me take a glimpse into theirs. I now find myself being able to analyse situations in which I find myself with my fellow-men by harking back to similar ones I have seen in the mongoose family. I have often found myself thinking 'What would Diana have done in such a situation?' or 'That fellow's acting just like George did that time!'

The mongooses have taught me something of value, how to objectivise things. Thanks to them I began to see my own life through new eyes and be more than content with my lot. Even if they had brought me nothing else, that by itself would have been worth while. Seeing their day-to-day struggle for survival despite hardships that I, as a human, could never conceive of, and how they lay personal enmities aside in order to master problems by helping each other in every possible situation, I sometimes wonder what human beings mean when they talk about 'the Brotherhood of Man'.

The time was drawing close for me to return to Europe for six months and I was going to have to say goodbye to Diana and Co. for a while. I spent my last free day with them before breaking up camp and heading with Danson and Sammy to Nairobi, where they would return to their families and I to Germany where my duties at the University were waiting.

It was a very normal day. They got up as usual, George was in a good mood, they marked, groomed each other and set off with the hornbills foraging. A Tawny eagle pinned them down for two hours and then they had their siesta, got up again, went foraging once more with their hornbill friends, and then went to bed for the night. I listened to their chatter: Diana's 'Come on, we're leaving'; George's 'Here I am, here I am' as he followed on her heels; Moja's 'Where are you?' when the group passed him as he was busily grubbing out a mouse and didn't notice that they were gone; the whole family's furious calls 'Look, look, an eagle' as they mobbed the bird sitting in the thorntree branches above them; Vanessa's growling 'Give me that!' and Twin's protesting 'Don't attack me – you can have it!' as they squabbled over an unearthed beetle. Although I could not see them, I knew just what was going on as they threaded their way through the maze of dried grass and bushes that formed their home, for they told me and I could now understand 'Mongoosese' almost as well as they could themselves. But how could I tell them in return that the huge metal monster which had been standing there with its human observer and accompanying them on their travels would not be there the next day or for months to come? Would they even notice that I was gone?

I sat there till the bitter end, until the last rays of sunlight, which tinged the little group's coats red, had gone and, one by one, they had slipped into the holes in the mound. Only Whitethroat remained on top and we looked at each other, eye to eye, I sadly, he incuriously. The last glimmer of light faded and, with it, Whitethroat turned and disappeared as well to join his family. I felt abandoned and very lonely. I had the sort of sinking feeling that one gets in the pit of one's stomach when one leaves old friends, some of whom, one knows, one may never see again. I would have no idea what was going to happen to the group in the months to come and how many of the familiar faces would be there when I returned. I would miss them all dreadfully. They had become *my* family.

Far off in the dusk a Pale Chanting goshawk chimed his call through the stirring bush and somewhere I could hear a jackal yelping. How do you say 'Goodbye' to mongooses? I did not know, for they have no sound in their language for this concept which is totally strange to them. Finally, I slowly set the car in motion and drove off into the gathering gloom – back to camp, Europe and Civilisation. I wondered, though, as I bumped along the familiar rutted road, what 'Civilisation' really meant. I was not sure of the answer.

Postscript: Five Years After

For the next five years I spent four months each winter with Diana and Co., watching their trials and tribulations in the harsh bush environment and sharing their little triumphs over adversity. Today only a few are left of the original group I met on Home mound. So much has happened in the meantime, part of which I was able to observe and part of which took place while I was away in Europe.

As I more or less expected, Notch left the main group in the following year, taking with her Scar – who was her mate and thus the new alpha male – and, to my surprise, Fleck joined them. She took up a small territory adjacent to Diana's and raised three young. I was very pleased with this observation since I believed, at that time, I had managed to observe the founding of a new dynasty with Notch and Scar as the progenitors of a new group. It took years of further data from this and other groups, however, to show how wrong I was. Notch's first litter met with tragedy. Only a week after the babies started to accompany the adults foraging, disaster struck on grey wings from the skies. With only three adult animals in the group and three babies to lead, Notch's little family found the going hard and frequently seemed to get their wires crossed. All three would start leading the babies to forage and no one remained on guard and, since the group was so small, hardly any hornbills went with them. They were thus terribly vulnerable, and the bush exploits vulnerability. Once more they set out one morning, each with a baby in tow and no one on guard, and the Chanting goshawks took advantage of their mistake. Within thirty seconds it was all over. Three pairs of wings folded in a stoop, three plummeting bodies with clawed feet extended and Notch's young had vanished. I watched one of the goshawks, which had landed in a tree near me, devour the mongoose baby in a few quick gulps. After their first panic was over, Notch's little group dashed about through the area peering into holes and termite mounds calling 'Where are you?' but getting no answer. After nearly half an hour of fruitless searching, the little group moved off, close-packed, at a trot.

In Diana's group all had remained more or less the same during my absence except that Pickle had vanished. I had no means of knowing what had become of her but, knowing her irrepressible ways and total disregard for danger, I was pretty sure that she had been snapped up by some hungry predator during my absence. Moja was now a fully-fledged guard and seemed to have formed a partnership with Rusty in this respect. Diana also produced two youngsters in this year, fat-bellied little bundles that were just starting to accompany the group on their daily foraging excursions when I saw them for the first time. For them, nemesis came creeping on scaled belly when they were just over two months old. I shall never know exactly what took place deep inside the termite mound that fateful morning. I could only record with horror what I saw.

Instead of the mongooses emerging for their usual 'happy hour' on the mound before taking off on their food-finding excursion, the head of a really huge Grey cobra slithered out of the mound and, following it, a two-yard long body with two ominous bulges about a third of the way down. The snake made off rather lethargically into the grass surrounding the mound and, following it, Twin, who staggered from side to side and finally collapsed on the apron, his lips writhed into a petrified snarl. A few scrabbling motions with his feet and then he lay rigid. The rest of the group charged the cobra, but keeping at a distance. I watched, horrified, as this reptilian monster alternately coiled and faced its tormentors, then crawled off at speed only to stand at bay again. Suddenly it gave a convulsive twist of its upper body and I saw it retreating backwards from some brown object half-hidden in the grass. It was not until snake and mongooses had moved off to a distance where my presence would not disturb them that I dared to dash out of the car to see what it was that the snake had left behind it. It was the body of one of the youngsters, wet and dripping with saliva, regurgitated by the reptile in its attempts to evade the irate family. The second baby still remained in the snake's belly. Twin still lay there, on the apron of the mound, a stiff little corpse, as I drove off to catch up with the family. He had obviously tried to defend the youngsters and been bitten for his pains. At least I knew now that the mongooses were not as immune to snake-bite as I had previously thought, but it seemed to be a terrible price that Diana's group had paid for this knowledge.

Tragedy struck again in the following year. When I arrived I found the bush almost empty of mongooses. In areas where large groups had lived, only a few survivors remained and these were thin and mottled with pale mange spots. In Diana's group Wart and Victoria were no longer there and Blackie and Whitethroat showed signs of the disease that had ravaged the population. Whitethroat looked like a skeleton with hair falling out in patches and Blackie's face was almost bald and his hip-bones stuck out. Others in the group showed similar symptoms but far less extreme. I watched, helpless, while over the next few weeks, the two males became weaker and weaker and, despite the attentions of their family, finally succumbed. A veterinary surgeon diagnosed the disease as probably being a form of *leishmaniasis*, a blood parasite brought in by infected herdsmen's dogs and transmitted by the sandflies which lived, like the mongooses, in the ventilation shafts of the termite mounds. It was not only the mongooses that suffered, though. The genets and civets almost disappeared, and with them the Bat-eared fox family that lived in the area. Its effect on the small carnivore population of the area was devastating. I searched for Notch and her group but there was no sign of them. Flourishing mongoose groups of twenty or more animals were reduced to five or less. Diana's family had got away lightly in comparison to many but even so, almost half of the family was gone and Diana, thin like the others, produced no young in this year.

The next year seemed a season of plenty. There were heavy rains and the grass stood tall. There was an abundance of food for everyone and animals I had never seen in the area before moved in to stay. The bush near Diana's territory now echoed to the harsh calls of Helmeted guineafowl, a flock of which had moved into the area round the waterhole, and many small birds that I had never seen before hopped and fluttered amongst the bushes. Diana's family looked sleek and fat and three youngsters were with them. This abundance attracted another member of the mongoose family, an enormous African Grey mongoose which now took up its abode in the area around the waterhole and which gave me another insight into the enemies of my mongoose family. It was not long before I was to realise how disastrous the presence of this animal was for Diana and Co.

I lost an old friend this year, Rusty, whom I had known since he was a youngster. By this time, however, he had grown into a stately broad-headed male with a rust-red ruff, and still he seemed to be one of the most assiduous guards when the group went foraging. It was his death that showed me how dangerous guarding could be. One morning, as Diana was leading the family off at a relatively fast pace through the bush, he was on rearguard as usual, scanning the surrounding trees and the sky for marauding birds of prey. The group was almost sixty yards away before Moja took over the next guarding post and Rusty galloped off to catch them up. His fate overtook him in the form of a Brown Snake eagle that descended from high in the sky like a stone, with a noise like ripping canvas. Brown wings beat the air and Moja's warning call came too late. Rusty, dangling from the eagle's talons, was carried off out of sight above the tree-tops. The group had dashed to the nearest mound and stood there, warning uselessly at a now empty sky.

It was almost two weeks later that tragedy struck again, this time in the form of the immigrant African Grey mongoose or Ichneumon. The family were foraging when the ground predator warning came from Goldie on guard and this biggest of the African mongooses, more than three times the length of the Dwarfs, came trotting purposefully towards Diana's group. I was not sure, in the clouds of dust that were thrown up, exactly what happened next. The Ichneumon made a bound right into the middle of the group, which seemed to be almost paralysed since they hadn't made their usual dash for cover. I saw

Brown wings beat the air . . .

. . . and Moja's warning came too late.
Rusty was killed by a Brown Snake eagle

two of the babies shooting away, one to hide under a log near me and one into a small hole. The rest of the group were attacking the Ichneumon like mad things, spitting and throwing themselves at him while he chewed on something he was holding between his front paws. The family's attacks seemed to be futile for the giant didn't even bother to raise his head until he had finished what he was eating and, as he raised the last bit of it in his mouth, I realised, with horror, that it was one of the babies. A gruesome episode then followed. Ignoring the furiously attacking family, the Ichneumon cast around until he discovered the second baby hiding under the log near me. The spits and screams of Diana's little group reached a crescendo as the Ichneumon, with a quick pounce and snap, grabbed this youngster as well and made off with it in his jaws into the bushes, the group hard on his heels, biting his tail and hind-legs, but to no avail.

I was stunned by what had happened. This was the first time that I had ever heard of species belonging to the same family actively preying upon one another. Usually the competition between species is more subtle and based on different food preferences or breeding requirements, not the active killing of one another – but I had seen this happen with my own eyes. I knew that the cats will kill the young of other cat species or even of their own if they find them, but these dead young are not regarded as prey. There was no doubt, however, that the Ichneumon considered the Dwarf mongoose youngsters as food and little else for he did not kill them and leave them lying but ate them before my eyes and the eyes of their parents. The whole episode had a genocidal flavour!

Diana's family rushed back and then followed an interlude that really tore my heart-strings. In a closed bunch they rushed from one mound to another in the area, peering inside and calling 'Where are you?' over and over again, but without result. For half an hour or more they crossed and recrossed the area where the tragedy had occurred, still bunched together, still moving at a fast trot. I began to think that something must have happened to the third youngster as it had still not emerged from its hole. Finally, when I was beginning to get worried that the group would take off and leave the baby behind, still cowering in its hiding-place, Diana must have heard something for she made a beeline for the hole, poked her nose into it and called, on which the surviving youngster shot out like a cork from a bottle and was greeted effusively by the rest of the group and thoroughly marked by George. The baby, whom I called Sindbad, made off with the group, sticking like glue to his mother's side. Diana continued her search for the missing young, almost as if she could not believe that they were gone for good. In all, she spent almost an hour hunting for them before she finally gave up and led her depleted family away from the scene of the massacre.

The Chanting goshawk was the worst predator of both mongooses and hornbills

When I returned the following year, Diana's group had been joined by two yearling males who looked so much alike that I called them the Twins. From their even, red-brown colour pattern, I surmised that they had come from Red group, a family whose territory lay just over half a mile away from Diana's borders. My supposition proved correct, for when I visited Red group, two of the three youngsters which I had seen with them the previous year were missing. When, and under which circumstances they had joined Diana's family, I did not know, but they appeared to be completely integrated there by the time I arrived. Sindbad had also survived his first year intact and again Diana had three young with her. This was again a year in which the callousness of bush life was to leave its indelible impression on her little band. Within a week of my arrival, one of the youngsters was grabbed by a juvenile Pale Chanting goshawk but the effectiveness of the mongooses' method of attacking predators as a group paid off this time. The young goshawk was too late in taking off and was met by a furious George, backed up by Edward and Goldie, who literally threw himself at the bird, just off the ground and holding on to the baby. With flailing wings, the bird took off, leaving its prize behind. As the youngster dashed back to the mound I could see its tail bent almost at a right-angle dragging behind it. The tail grew from that day onwards with a sharp kink in it, witness to the narrow escape its owner had had, and the youngster was promptly christened 'Tail' to distinguish it from its littermates.

The smallest of the three was not so lucky. Only two days after Tail's escape from death, Little One, as I had called her, lagged behind at the termite mound and, although Vanessa, on guard, gave the warning call, all help came too late and she was snapped up by a Grasshopper buzzard that swooped in over the tree-tops. Vanessa darted down the mound towards the bird but it took off before she reached it, Little One hanging limp in its claws. The rest of the group dashed back to join Vanessa but to no avail – Little One had gone for good. The third one of the group I called Blackie II, because he reminded me so much of his dead brother, the original Blackie. He had the same dark face and the same cheeky habits and, up until the time I left, he and Tail were still thriving, the most dangerous period of their lives, the first three months, behind them.

In contrast to the previous year, when food had been in abundance, this year was the complete opposite. The land was stricken by drought, for the short rains in October and November had failed and trees and bushes were barren of leaves. The elephant herds rampaged through the area, breaking down the fragile Commiphora and Boswellia trees to eat the juicy branches and digging up the Grewia bushes to reach the roots. Grass was sparse and the area almost desolate and littered with broken branches which caused me a lot of trouble in the way of puncture repairs. Diana's little family struck me as being especially exposed as they trod the now, to me, well-known paths through their territory and used the well-known lookout posts which, over the years, had become as familiar to me as to them.

I thought that I knew Diana's 'territory' now almost as well as she did herself but, yet again, she was to show me differently. Without warning, one day she set out eastward of her normal territorial boundary and into what was, for her, uncharted land. I followed her over the next fifteen days as she covered an area almost equal in size to her original territory but east of it. The north and south boundaries of this new hunting zone remained extensions of those of the original territory. Her hunting area had just become twice as broad but remained the same in length. I expected her to take twice as long to cover an area twice as large as her original one, but again she showed me differently. She still took between twenty-six and twenty-eight days to make a circuit of her extended living area, leading her family on forced marches of up to and above half a mile per day. It was then that the penny dropped for me and the connection between this relatively rigid time-keeping and my laboratory studies on marking behaviour was made. I had shown that the mongooses' anal marking secretion had an effective life of about twenty-five days. At the time of discovery, this was just an interesting fact but now I could see the reason for Diana's long route-marches. She had to return to 'her' termite mounds before her scent and that of her family had dissipated from them to reclaim them, through fresh marks, as her own. Again she posed me the question 'Is this instinct or intelligence?' At the very least, it was a marvel of animal time-sense.

It was towards the end of my stay with the group for this year that one of the biggest catastrophies of all, at least from my point of view – and, I took it, Diana's too – occurred. A pair of Wahlberg's eagles had moved into the area earlier in the season and I frequently saw them cruising at height above Diana's territory. The mongooses warned violently each time they appeared and I knew from previous observations on other groups that these birds were serious predators on Dwarf mongooses. Over the years, though, none of Diana's group had fallen prey to them but this was to be changed by one stoop, and a frantically milling, warning group of mongooses. I suppose, ultimately, it was Vanessa's fault, staying behind in a clump of bare bushes with Moja, intent on a little subversive mounting. George, as usual, dashed back towards them as soon as he noticed they were missing and it was during this solitary gallop that the Wahlberg's eagle stooped. Edward, on guard, was facing in the opposite direction when the bird came down like an express-train and although he and the rest of the group galloped towards it, it took off, George dangling beneath it, and headed towards the distant hills. Diana was distraught, dashing from mound to mound, calling 'Where are you?', the rest of the group hard on her heels. I had not seen them do this when Rusty was caught two years previously but George had been Diana's constant companion and mate for over five years now and the bonds here probably went deeper. According to my reckoning both of them were at least ten years old (the oldest recorded age for a Dwarf mongoose is eighteen).

As in the case of the lost babies, Diana searched for her missing mate for over an hour, finally giving up and retreating with the rest of the group to a nearby termite mound, all of them going inside at about five in the afternoon and not emerging for the rest of the day. I was appalled at how quickly it had all happened and wondered what Diana would do now that her mate was gone. Would she be deposed by Vanessa, Veronica or Goldie, the only other adult females in the group, or would she take another mate?

The next day Diana remained near the same mound, only leading the group on short trips to look for insects in its immediate vicinity. She kept herself apart, sitting mostly high on the mound and occasionally calling 'Where are you?' just as on the last occasion that George had gone missing, after the group had got caught between the two great armies and Diana had fled to Spear mound with the youngsters, five years before. She stayed at the mound for two days, only then leading the group off on its usual long-distance foraging excursions. During this time she maintained social contact only with the two youngsters, Blackie II and Tail. All attempts at grooming or cuddling-up from other group members resulted in her simply getting up and changing her position.

The long rains of March and April started early this year and, with them, the desiccated bushland burst into life. Buds on trees and bushes burst into delicate green and grass sprouted from what had been bare red earth. It was in this period that Edward made his move. Slowly but surely he took his place next to Diana and groomed her, she usually getting up and walking away and only rarely reciprocating his advances. He was not to be shaken off so easily, though, and stuck with her until she succumbed to his friendly nibbling and returned it with nibble-grooming of her own. It was when he tried to mark her, though, that she would jump up under his raised leg and dash down the mound, the rest of the group behind her and Edward galloping to catch up. For five days she resisted him staunchly, never letting him 'put his mark on her', but then I was to see something that I had not seen in the last five years – Diana came into oestrus in summer! Still she did not seem ready to accept Edward and would gallop off, with him in hot pursuit, the rest of the group trailing behind them, when his attentions became too disturbing. Finally, Edward did something I had never seen George do and that was to grasp Diana by the scruff of the neck and almost forcibly mate with her. After this, Diana's total resistance collapsed and, while Edward still mated with her, she tended only to half-resist him by dashing off while he mounted, he following her as if tied to her by a string, or trying to snap at his feet when he finally got her cornered, often at a mound at some distance from the rest of the group, things she had never done with George.

Once Diana's oestrus was over, Edward seemed to slip naturally into the role of alpha male, as he *was* the oldest male in the group. His behaviour towards his subordinates, though, seemed much more aggressive than George's had ever been and I was often to witness prolonged bouts of threat-scratching outside holes in the mound into which one of the group members had fled, protesting, while Edward demonstrated his authority amongst clouds of red dust outside. Diana showed absolutely no interest in these proceedings and would almost pointedly wander off with the rest of the group in tow, leaving Edward and his victim behind to catch up. In the weeks that followed, Diana accepted Edward's attentions little by little and, by the time I had to leave, he was firmly ensconced as her new mate. It had taken him five years of patient waiting to reach the top, but he had finally made it, despite Diana's initial reluctance.

During the five years I spent with the mongooses, I was to see Notch's story and its consequences – a fruitless attempt of a small nucleus to separate from the main group and try to found a group of their own – repeated again and again in other groups and with the same result, annihilation. Not one of the small 'splinter groups', as I called them, managed to raise any young of their own and they themselves were wiped out within a year or so. The critical number seemed to be five adults. When more than five were there to take over the various jobs such as babysitting, guarding and defending the group against predators, the mongooses were able to survive. With less than five, though, they seemed doomed to extinction. It was by patiently recording such instances over the years that I realised the group members, who I erroneously thought were sacrificing their lives and the chances of having young of their own for the welfare of their brothers and sisters, were actually doing nothing of the sort. They were really, indirectly, reproducing their genetic potential in the most effective way. By helping to raise their full brothers and sisters, they were actually helping to raise young of half their own genetic potential. Every two of their parent's young that they helped to raise was, genetically, equivalent to one of their own. At the same time, they were protecting themselves by remaining in a group large enough to defend itself against the majority of the bush predators against which small groups had only little chance.

This pseudo-altruistic behaviour I could understand on the part of George and Diana's own children, but it long seemed to me meaningless when applied to Veronica, Edward and the Twins since they were not related to the group they had joined although they enjoyed its protection. No reproductive advantage accrued to them in raising Diana's babies. It was Edward's rise to the top that showed me that, although protracted, a reproductive advantage *was* there for those that wait. There was always the chance that the alpha position would become vacant and then the years of helping would pay off. Now Edward could produce young of his own in a group large enough to ensure their survival.

When I left Diana and Co. this year I realised that my rather naïve concepts of mongoose family life had undergone a radical change over the years. The bonds and the obvious affection between the members of the group were clearly evident, but I wondered if they were proximate or ultimate effects: things that caused the evolution of such close group life or things that had to develop because of it, otherwise the group could not remain stable. I had my proof now that Dwarf mongooses live in families as a means of defence against predators, but I was still faced with the problem 'Which came first: the chicken or the egg?' Maybe the primitive ancestors of my mongooses once developed the tendency for young to remain with their parents until past maturity and such groups were able to keep more young alive by helping than groups that did not have this trait. In this way, a behaviour change could be rapidly transmitted through a population, culminating in the highly social behaviour I had been able to observe all these years, for those animals that did not show tendencies to remain social would be eradicated fairly rapidly from the population. This could explain why single mongooses try so desperately to join groups, even though they are rebuffed and it might take weeks of patient trailing before they are accepted. When I left my bush home this season I realised more deeply than ever that, for the mongooses, there is only one motto, and one that means life or death for them: 'Together we stand – divided we fall!'